MW00380768

ON THE LAM

"Certainly there is no hunting like the hunting of man and those who have hunted armed men long enough and liked it, never really care for anything else thereafter."

— Ernest Hemingway[1]

"It is very uncomfortable to be wanted, if you can imagine."

— Mark Giuliano, FBI deputy director, 2013–2016[2]

ON THE LAM

A HISTORY OF HUNTING
FUGITIVES IN AMERICA

Jerry Clark and Ed Palattella

ROWMAN & LITTLEFIELD
Lanham • Boulder • New York • London

Published by Rowman & Littlefield
A wholly owned subsidiary of The Rowman & Littlefield Publishing Group, Inc.
4501 Forbes Boulevard, Suite 200, Lanham, Maryland 20706
www.rowman.com

6 Tinworth Street, London SE11 5AL

Copyright © 2019 by The Rowman & Littlefield Publishing Group, Inc.

All rights reserved. No part of this book may be reproduced in any form or by any
electronic or mechanical means, including information storage and retrieval systems,
without written permission from the publisher, except by a reviewer who may quote
passages in a review.

British Library Cataloguing in Publication Information Available

Library of Congress Cataloging-in-Publication Data

ISBN 978-1-4422-6258-4 (cloth : alk. paper)
ISBN 978-1-4422-6259-1 (electronic)

♾™ The paper used in this publication meets the minimum requirements of
American National Standard for Information Sciences—Permanence of Paper
for Printed Library Materials, ANSI/NISO Z39.48-1992.

To our families

CONTENTS

PART III: THE CHASE GOES ON

ACKNOWLEDGMENTS

Writing about fugitives in America meant exploring a wide range of American history, including accounts of the Constitutional Convention to tales of how the movies and television have portrayed criminals and those on the run. As always, we are grateful for the support and expertise of librarians and other research specialists who showed great interest in our project and great patience with us. They include Russ Hall and Jane Ingold, reference and instructional librarians at the John M. Lilley Library at Penn State Behrend in Erie, Pennsylvania, where Matthew Ciszek is the head librarian. We also appreciate the assistance of the staff at the Nash Library at Gannon University, also in Erie, who tracked down books and other resources for us. John Fox, the historian for the Federal Bureau of Investigation, continues to be a trusted resource, though all views expressed in this book are the authors' alone. Thanks as well to our editor at Rowman & Littlefield, Kathryn Knigge, and our literary agent, John Talbot. We value our relationships with both of them.

Jerry Clark: Researching this book brought back many memories of my law enforcement career and my time spent in the FBI Cincinnati Division, Dayton Resident Agency. I immediately recalled the dedication and persistence of the outstanding agents, officers, and prosecutors whom I worked with during my time on the Dayton-Montgomery County Violent Crimes Fugitive Task Force. I especially want to thank my good friend and task force commander, Dayton Police Department Lieutenant Chuck Gift, who taught me so much about the art of policing. I also wish to express my sincere gratitude to Dayton Police Detective Tim Bilinski, Montgomery County Deputy Sheriff Bill Fahrig, U.S. Deputy Marshal Bill Taylor, and every law enforcement officer who spent time on the task force. The time shared with these extremely talented individuals was both educational and enjoyable and has provided a bond that will last a lifetime. We were a highly productive and efficient force for good that accomplished amazing things in our six years together. The task force members taught me the professional skills and personal values I have used throughout my career and my life. Lastly, I would like to thank my wife, Danielle, and our children, Michael and Isabelle, for their unconditional and unwavering love, support, and patience.

Ed Palattella: As a newspaper reporter for twenty-nine years, with all but a year spent at the *Erie Times-News* in Pennsylvania, I have witnessed every day how hard reporters and editors work to find important stories and to get things right. Our research for this book sent me into the archives—both on microfilm and online—of any number of newspapers and magazines in the United States from the earliest days of the republic to the present. Without the work of all the editors and reporters at those publications, much of American history would be a blank, and certainly this book would be nonexistent. I continue to be grateful to work in journalism, a profession that, while it is undergoing rapid and often unsettling change, continues to prove itself a critical part of American life. At the *Erie Times-News*, I appreciate the support of executive editor Doug Oathout as well as my fellow reporters and editors, including Kevin Flowers, Tim Hahn, Pat Howard, Jim Martin, Matt Martin, Madeleine O'Neill, and Lisa Thompson. And thanks as always to my wife, Chris, and our children, Henry and Nina, who have lived through five book projects and still put up with me.

INTRODUCTION

The hole in the floor was the giveaway in the end, though the deputy U.S. marshals, the police officers, and the agents with the Federal Bureau of Investigation needed time to find it. The officers, agents, and deputy marshals, all members of a fugitive task force, had descended on a house near Dayton, Ohio, in 1999, looking for a man wanted for murder and drug crimes in Detroit. The Detroit office of the U.S. Customs Service had called the task force for help in finding the fugitive, and the task force went on its way. Its members sat in vehicles outside the house where the fugitive was thought to be hiding. As often is the case in stakeouts, nothing happened for hours, until something suddenly did. Eventually, amid all the buzz of activity, someone discovered the hole in the floor.

The task force members a short time earlier had watched the owner of the house pull into the driveway, get out, and go inside the front door. The officers, agents, and deputies surrounded the house while one of them knocked on the door. The owner walked outside and shut the door behind him. He denied that he was harboring a fugitive, but he invited the members of the task force to come inside and look for themselves. Getting in was not easy. The owner had inadvertently locked himself out of the house. The only way in was to take apart a window whose frame was screwed into the house from the outside. Once the window was off, the members of the task force faced another problem: two Doberman pinschers were barking at them from the inside of the house. The owner called the dogs to the window and pulled them out. At last, an officer with the task force climbed in and opened the front door. The other members swept through the place and . . . found nothing.

The task force members were trying to get into the attic when they were called back downstairs. A deputy marshal had heard the floor creak in the first-floor bathroom, and he got suspicious. He pulled back a rug, and there it was—a hole in the floor, in the form of a trapdoor that opened into a crawl space underneath the bathroom. The police officers, FBI agents, and deputy marshals pried open the door with a crowbar.

A police lieutenant shouted down the hole.

No response.

The lieutenant shouted down the hole again.

"Fuck you," came the reply. "I'm not coming out."

The lieutenant told the fugitive to get ready—a flashbang stun grenade would soon come tumbling down the hole.

"Don't do it," the voice said. "I'm coming out."

The fugitive, with help from the task force members, made his way out of the hole and was handcuffed on the bathroom floor. On the way to the county jail, the fugitive mused about how things might have been different, how, if he could not have gotten away, he at least would have died trying. He said he was watching from a window when he saw the task force members arrive, and he said he was prepared for a shootout. He changed his mind when he saw the number of task force members and realized that each was armed. The fugitive figured hiding was better. He turned away from the window, walked past the two Doberman pinschers, opened the trapdoor in the bathroom, and climbed down the hole. And he might have escaped—had the bathroom floor not creaked.[1]

Tens of thousands of fugitives from justice roam the United States each year. Some of them stay on the lam, getting help from friends or relatives or getting by through such tricks as trapdoors in bathroom floors. Many more are captured. In fiscal year 2017, which ended September 30, 2017, the U.S. Marshals Service—the primary federal agency for finding criminals on the run—arrested a total of 84,048 fugitives, including 57,658 wanted on the state or local levels and another 26,390 wanted on the federal level.[2] The immensity of the numbers shows how the pursuit and arrest of fugitives represent an integral component of the American justice system—and why the long arm of the law really does need a powerful reach and a tight grip.

Fugitives are also as old as the justice system itself. As long as laws have been codified, people have been willing to run from them. And though fugitives are by no means limited to the United States, the fugitive has taken on an outsized, even iconic, role in American culture. The United States, founded in a rebellion, often seems more apt to embrace the fugitive, who has been a consistent character in literature and in the movies and on television and in popular music, where country-and-western stars often warble about the loneliness of life on the lam. "We have been a nation of fugitives from the start. Some colonists literally fled England's religious persecution or poor laws, but even the most law-abiding were fugitives in a larger sense," as one astute writer of the fugitive phenomenon has observed. "But America's greatest fascination is reserved for another kind of fugitive: the outlaw, the man on the run from the law."[3]

With outlaws plentiful in the cultural landscape, *on the lam* became a phrase of American coinage. The term *lam* for more than a hundred years has been American slang for "a hurried flight from the law," though the origin of the word is somewhat elusive. *Lam* is believed to be derived from the Old Norse *lemja*, meaning "to thrash," a word that developed, by the sixteenth century, into *lam*, meaning "to beat soundly,"[4] so that to escape a beating, or a lamming, "one lams."[5]

Another theory is that *lam* comes from the word *lammas*, a variant spelling of *nammou*, used on the streets of London in the mid-1800s to mean, as one lexicographer has written, "to depart, esp. furtively."[6] Whatever its roots, *lam* by the late nineteenth and early twentieth centuries had come to mean, in America, a flight from the law, and by the 1900s, *lamster* or *lamister* had entered the American lexicon as street jargon for a fugitive.[7] As a reporter for the *New York Times* wrote in 1936, explaining the limited legal options for a prostitute who was arrested while working in the underworld vice ring of legendary mobster Lucky Luciano, "If the case was 'straight,' making conviction likely, she would be advised to become a 'lamster,' forfeiting the bail that usually ran from $200 to $500."[8]

The fugitive from justice in American history—the one-and-only American lamster—is the subject of this book, which focuses on pursuits within the United States and includes a look at how those on the lam have become mythologized, similar to how bank robbers have stolen into the nation's imagination. Just as bank robbers can be considered noble outlaws because they take from what some consider corrupt banks, so fugitives can be seen as heroes or anti-heroes, real-life examples of men and women who dared to fight the law, even if the battle was all but certain to end with capture and conviction. In a slim number of instances, a fugitive truly is innocent. That was true of the slaves who fled the South before the Civil War, despite two iterations of the Fugitive Slave Act. The innocent fugitive is also the conceit of the 1993 blockbuster film *The Fugitive* and the equally popular 1960s television series of the same name. And during its time, the popular 1932 memoir *I Am a Fugitive from a Georgia Chain Gang!* and the film it inspired also contributed to the public's understanding that fugitives could be justified in their flight. But in most cases, a fugitive is on the run in a futile attempt to outrace his or her deserved legal fate. In the past several decades, reality-based television shows like *America's Most Wanted* have emphasized that point seemingly beyond all others.

To fully understand fugitives also requires a close look at the system from which the fugitives are trying to escape. The system dates back thousands of years, to medieval England and continental Europe, where family-centered societies developed the concept of bail, first as a form of recompense and then as a way to guard against accused individuals from running away and never facing the consequences of their crimes. With the creation of bail as we know it today also came the creation of the bail jumper, one of the three kinds of fugitives considered here. The others are fugitives who are fleeing from arrest warrants and inmates who have broken out of prison. Members of each category, no matter what their circumstances, are alike because they are all on the run.

These fugitives are often all on the run from the same people. They include FBI agents, police officers, U.S. marshals and their deputies, county sheriffs and their deputies, members of other law enforcement agencies, and bounty hunters, who occupy a profession that is just outside law enforcement. These pursuers, like the fugitives they track, also have been mythologized or at least have come to occupy a central place in the story of the American justice system. The FBI has relied on fugitives to bolster its image and its standing. Under its indomitable director, J. Edgar Hoover, the FBI first presented itself as a force of good against gangsters and other "public enemies," such as John Dillinger, who populated public enemies lists that were commonplace in American cities in the 1930s. Hoover publicly disavowed ever having the FBI create its own list of public enemies, but the concept undeniably contributed to the FBI introducing its Ten Most Wanted Fugitives list in 1950. For nearly seventy years, the FBI's official list—a fixture in post offices and other public places across the United States and now on the internet—has reminded citizens that fugitives are constantly out there, maybe even in your hometown, but that constantly behind them and continually chasing them are men and women with badges and guns and handcuffs.

One of those pursuers was Jerry Clark, a retired FBI special agent and coauthor of this book. In his twenty-seven years in law enforcement, which spanned jobs in several agencies from 1984 to 2011, Clark tracked any number of fugitives. And from 1995 to 2001, early in his sixteen-year career with the FBI, Clark coordinated a multi-agency task force, based in Dayton, Ohio, that specialized in investigating violent crimes, such as bank robberies and kidnappings, and in finding violent criminals who were on the run—such as the murder suspect pulled out of the hole under the bathroom floor in 1999. This book draws on Clark's experiences and expertise in tracking techniques, and it relies on the observations and experiences of many others, on both sides of the law. Of particular interest is how technology has advanced to assist the fugitive and the pursuer. The smartphone is just one tool that FBI agents and others use to locate their human targets in the digital age.

The psychology of the fugitive is another focus of this book. While the reason someone is on the run—to avoid getting caught—might seem obvious, the mind of a fugitive is constantly racing. Where can I go next? Whom can I trust? Will I ever be able to stop worrying about getting caught? And does getting caught, and ending a life on the run, with all its uncertainty and danger and anxiety and continual need for disguise, come with any sense of relief?

The mental burden of being on the lam nearly paralyzed serial bank robber and fugitive Willie Sutton, who was caught, for the final time, in New York City in 1952, five years and one month after he broke out of prison. "I found it strange to change identity every time someone seemed to be catching up with me, and when a man changes his identity, he begins to think more deeply," said Sutton, who spent much of his life trying to outrun the authorities. "It's hard to be somebody different, over and over again. You're never sure of who's around you."[9] The goal of the fugitive—to create a story without an ending—is difficult to achieve. Someone is almost always looking for you: driving up to your house, asking to get inside, listening for the creaks, prying open the trapdoor.

Jerry Clark
Ed Palattella
Erie, Pennsylvania
November 2018

PART I
A HISTORY OF FLIGHT

1

PRICE OF FREEDOM

The Consequences of Bail

This was a special manhunt. On the Saturday afternoon of April 27, 1901, in the seaside town of Asbury Park, New Jersey, a group of fox hunters turned their horses and hounds away from their four-legged quarry and pursued a different target: an accused jewelry thief. He had jumped bail of $3,500, an amount that would equal more than $97,000 in 2018.

The fugitive was named George O'Brien. He had gone on the lam as he was awaiting prosecution on a larceny charge in Brooklyn, New York, where he was charged with stealing $1,000 worth of jewelry from a woman's home while she was at church in February 1901. O'Brien sat in prison for a week. His aunt got him out by posting a bond of $3,500, with an assurance that her nephew would show up for his next court date. O'Brien failed to appear. The chase was on. O'Brien, also known as Jack Sloan, was worth pursuing. Authorities believed he was a serial burglar who had broken into residences throughout New York City.[1]

The chase brought two detectives from Brooklyn to Asbury Park, where O'Brien was discovered working as a plasterer on new buildings near the town. Upon spotting the detectives on April 27, 1901, O'Brien jumped from a second-story window and fled. The two detectives and a local police officer fired revolvers at O'Brien. He was unharmed and kept running. The chase slowed when one of the detectives fell in a swamp and got stuck.

O'Brien could not outdistance the fox hunters. In their pursuit, the police officers came across a group of three hunters from the local hunt club. The officers stopped the hunters, explained the predicament of trying to find O'Brien, and asked for help. "The horsemen," as the *New York Times* reported, "abandoned the fox chase for a more exciting man hunt. They pursued O'Brien across fields

CHAPTER 1

and over fences until they finally ran him down, holding him until the officers came up."[2] O'Brien was arraigned and returned to Brooklyn, where he was a fugitive no more.[3]

Of the three types of fugitives—those who escape from prison, those wanted for arrest, and those who jump bail—George O'Brien falls into the category that is perhaps the most colorful: the bail jumper, or the bail skipper, the criminal who, while awaiting prosecution, makes a last-ditch effort to stay free, disappears, and fails to show up in court. Bail jumpers carry with them a certain public fascination, almost a romantic quality, that makes reports of their exploits more intriguing than the tales of most ordinary criminals. Most everyone likes a good chase, which is why O'Brien's story was notable in a city of more than 3.4 million people in 1901. He was a man on the run, a person trying to evade legal responsibility. But he was by no means an aberration. His flight through swamps and amid barking hounds in February 1901 made him the latest character to be linked to an element of the legal system invented thousands of years earlier. As long as systems of justice have existed, so has the fugitive, and so has the concept of bail—a concept enshrined in the Bill of Rights.

"Bail" is derived from the Old French *ballier*, which means, among other things, to bear, to handle, to control, to take away, or to give.[4] The concept of bail developed and flourished most prominently in Anglo-Saxon culture in medieval England. It was created out of the need for the justice system to guarantee that the accused or the guilty were going to appear for their trial or punishment or otherwise fulfill a promise to provide recompense for their criminal wrongdoing or civil error. The development of bail also recognizes that, "since time immemorial," an accused has been allowed pre-trial liberty except in rare circumstances, such as when the crime is murder.[5] Bail recognizes that the accused is innocent until proven guilty, and that, unless convicted and except in rare instances, the accused is entitled to be free.

The origin of bail can be traced to ancient Rome, where authorities held that a person convicted of a crime could not be detained or incarcerated until after sentencing. In one notable case, however, a Roman prosecutor argued that a defendant could not be released before sentencing because he was a flight risk. The Senate determined that the defendant could be freed with the condition that he promise to return and pay a sum of money if he failed to appear. The Senate set the amount.[6]

Bail's creation during ancient times proves that fugitives have been seen as a danger to the justice system since the system's earliest forms took hold. A defendant on the lam threatens the authority of the justice system and prohibits society from closing a criminal case through conviction and punishment or an acquittal. Fugitives are able to commit more crimes while on the run, further damaging society. Any fugitive, as Thomas J. Miles, a law professor who has studied fugitives, has found, "imposes a social cost by frustrating the traditional purposes of criminal punishment."[7] As John W. Marshall, a director of the U.S. Marshals Service, once said at a Senate subcommittee hearing on fugitives, held on June 22, 2000, "The security problems that fugitives pose for every citizen of this county are numerous, costly, and most importantly, life-threatening. By definition and nature, fugitives are mobile and opportunistic, preying on innocent citizens by committing crimes against persons and property everywhere."[8] Marshall continued, commenting on other ways fugitives can put society at risk: "Fugitives threaten the very fabric of our criminal justice system. By definition, they have been charged with violation of law. They may have been charged but not yet arrested, released on bail and fled to avoid prosecution, escaped from jail or prison, or absconded or otherwise violated the terms of their probation or parole. These actions constitute an affront to our criminal justice system. When fugitives flee from their charges, our legal system is severely threatened. Prosecutors cannot try cases, society is deprived of justice and order, and crime victims are denied their rights. They may, in fact, live in fear and isolation while the criminals who have victimized them remain at large."[9]

Bail, from its earliest formation, was a tool for preventing fugitives from undermining society. Bail guarantees a pledge; as indicated by the meaning of *ballier*, bail was a method by which one person and, eventually the state, was authorized to take control of another person if a pledge was unfulfilled. "The beginning of bail," as one prominent historian on the subject has written, "can be traced to tribal customs on the continent of Europe."[10] In England, where the bail system of today's American jurisprudence took root, the concept of bail evolved as the justice system became less bloody and more humane. Before the Norman Conquest, in 1066, Anglo-Saxon tribes initially used vengeance to settle disputes, leading to "blood feuds," in which the victims could punish the offenders themselves, which fueled a never-ending cycle of bloodshed that jeopardized the community's well-being.[11]

As this eye-for-an-eye arrangement was phased out, the Anglo-Saxons used, for compensation in cases of murder, the payment of what was called *wergild*— Old English for "man payment," akin to blood money. The Saxons brought the use of the wergild with them from Europe. The wergild was based in ancient Germanic law, which the Romans influenced; "Instead of meeting death with death, a system gradually developed whereby the family of the slain man was compensated by the slayer through the payment of wergild."[12] The payment of the wergild ended the blood feud and provided a guarantee that the perpetrator would not be executed. The promise of payment, and then the payment itself, bought a measure of peace.

The wergild-based system functioned to ensure justice during an era of weak central authority and before the creation of a police force and a court system in which punishment, whether capital or corporal, was imposed upon lawbreakers. The wergild, for instance, existed alongside the hue and cry as a legal practice in early England. It required that someone who witnessed a crime had to raise a *hue* and *cry* (Anglo-Norman French for *outcry* and *cry*), often by shouting or blowing a horn, to alert his or her neighbors. Failure to do so would make the group of neighbors liable to the victim. Those who raised the hue and cry were allowed to pursue the accused and administer summary justice if the accused fled or was found with evidence of guilt. Otherwise the accused was prosecuted and had to abide by the payment of the wergild.[13]

The Anglo-Saxons created fines similar to the wergild, such as the *bot* and the *wite*. The bot was payable to the victim's family for nonfatal injuries and the wite was payable to the king as a kind of atonement. Like the wergild, the wite and the bot institutionalized the requirement that the convicted criminal repay society, and the victim's family, to compensate for a crime and to settle wrongs and injuries.[14] The amount of the wergild and bot corresponded to the nature of the crime, and to the standing of the victim. The amount was the highest for the death of a king, and Anglo-Saxon law included "long tables fixing the amount to be paid for the loss of various limbs and bodily faculties."[15] For example, 50 shillings "was payable for a severed foot, but 10s for a big toe, piercing of the nose was 9s, mutilation of an ear 6s, striking out an eye, a hefty 50s."[16]

Another theory holds that bail in Anglo-Saxon England also was related to the Germanic system of what was called *frankpledge*, which was also part of the culture of medieval England. Frankpledge required that all adult males in the community be bound together to ensure the common good. An association of ten households, or a tithing, took a pledge that they would guarantee the appearance in court of any of their members who violated the law. Before the creation of justices of the peace and constables in the 1400s, frankpledge acted as the primary tool to keep and restore order in medieval England. Like the hue and cry, the frankpledge put the responsibility for social order directly in the hands (and voices) of the community, such as those in a tithing. The frankpledge also took the process of suretyship to a new level.[17] "The process was such that an association of ten men formed a perpetual collective surety for the appearance in court of any one of their number who might infringe on the law. It was, in fact, a Norman substitute for the modern police."[18]

The system based on the frankpledge or the wergild or bot, however, worked only if the victim had some type of assurance that the accused would show up for trial and, if convicted, pay the bot. A fugitive could wreck the administration of justice.

Incarceration was not a solution. Prisons of the era were "costly and trouble-some," and only those accused of the most heinous crimes, such as murder, were incarcerated while awaiting prosecution.[19] To keep control of the majority of accused criminals who were out of a prison, a trust-based system developed. The accused was required to find another person to act as a surety: If the accused fled and was never prosecuted, the surety, standing in as a trustee, had to make amends to the accuser and his or her family. Initially, according to some historians, the surety had to present him- or herself to the accuser if the accused fled, an arrangement similar to a hostage situation; the surety acted as a kind of human bail, to be seized in case of the accused's flight.[20] This system eventually advanced to an apparatus based on money. The surety, rather than pledging him- or herself, promised to satisfy the wergild or bot if the accuser fled. Bail was the instrument of satisfaction. "The amount or substantive worth of that pledge, called 'bail' (akin to a modern money bail bond), was identical to the amount or substantive worth of the penalty."[21] The bail had to be equal to the bot.

Even as payment of bail satisfied the victim, it did nothing to exonerate the fugitive. The accused who went on the lam was made an "outlaw" and subject to summary execution if caught.[22] Terms were also harsh for the accused who chose not to flee and was convicted but was too poor to pay the bot. In those cases, the victim was entitled to execute or enslave the accused. But corporal punishment was rare. As long as the bot was paid, whether directly or through bail, justice was served. As one study of bail has noted, "This early system of bail killed two birds with one stone: It simultaneously provided strong incentives to sureties to ensure their charges appeared in court, and guaranteed payment to victims if they fled."[23]

The system of bail became more refined in England after the Norman Conquest of 1066. The invaders established a justice system based more on the authority of the state rather than on private arrangements to settle disputes and punish criminals. The grand jury process came to England, as did the use of sworn statements, circuit-riding judges, and other tools central to the operation of the modern justice system. Capital punishment replaced the wergild as the form of compensation for murder, and corporal punishment replaced the payment of the bot for other crimes. But fugitives remained a concern; the increase of the use of corporal punishment was among the reasons behind an offender's unwillingness to go to trial.[24] Bail, instead of being a surety to guarantee the payment of a wergild or a bot, became a surety to guarantee the appearance of the accused. Though it originated as a tool to help preserve the collective good, bail came to be associated with the more singular purpose of preventing those charged with crimes from turning into fugitives.

Following the Norman Conquest, the introduction of circuit-court judges who traveled from shire to shire—the equivalent of a county—left the responsibility for setting bail to the shire's reeve, or the sheriff. Long periods of time elapsed between when the accused was charged and when the magistrate arrived to hear the case, so bail was necessary in many instances. Sheriffs had wide discretion in both setting the amount of bail and determining which offenses were bailable, with a few exceptions. Those accused of murder could not get out on bail, nor could those accused of what were known as "forest offenses," such as poaching in the royal forests.[25] The reliance on sheriffs for setting bail varied from shire to shire, and the practice was open to abuse and corruption. One sheriff might set bail at one amount and allow a crime to be bailable, while another sheriff might not—except for a price. Other defendants were "unjustly arrested, probably for the express purpose of demanding payment to be released to pledges."[26]

Parliament stepped in to curb the corruption. It defined nonbailable and bailable offenses in the first Statute of Westminster, passed in 1275, which codified many laws that were already included in the Magna Carta, the first version of which was enacted fifty years earlier. The Magna Carta set forth the fundamental right to pretrial liberty: "No free man shall be arrested or imprisoned . . . or victimized in any other way . . . except by the lawful judgment of his peers or by the law of the land."[27] The Statute of Westminster tightened the rules sheriffs had to follow in granting bail; the statute established bail law in England for the next five hundred years. The statute prohibited sheriffs from releasing on bail prisoners who were accused of such crimes as homicide, forest offenses, "house burning feloniously done," and "treason touching the King himself."[28] Bailable offenders included "those arrested for petty larceny that amounteth not to twelve pence, if they were not guilty of some larceny aforetime," and "those guilty of some other trespass of which one ought not to lose life nor member."[29]

As in all previous iterations of Anglo-Saxon law, the Statute of Westminster looked unfavorably on the fugitive, who was considered just as much an outlaw as he or she had always been. Among those prohibited bail absolutely were "such prisoners as before were outlawed, or have abjured the realm" and those prisoners who have "broken the King's prison."[30]

The Statute of Westminster, in a more radical change, gave sheriffs new criteria to use to decide whether a prisoner, if accused of a bailable offense, should get bail. No longer did the sheriff only have to consider the seriousness of the offense. The Statute of Westminster also required the sheriff to consider the strength of the evidence against the defendant. Those accused of more serious but bailable crimes could be released if the evidence was slight, while those accused of lesser crimes could be held without bail if the evidence was strong, such as based on a confession.[31] In the words of one historian of bail laws, the bail system, under the Statute of Westminster, "was ultimately concerned with the same issues to be decided at trial and sentence. Although the danger of flight was a concern, the system used the severity of the penalty and the likelihood of conviction to define the danger."[32] This balancing of interests applied also to those accused of nonbailable offenses. Though the Statute of Westminster prohibited sheriffs from releasing these prisoners, they could win bail from the higher courts.[33]

Incremental reforms of the bail laws in England occurred to address new abuses. By the fourteenth century, the authority to determine bail moved from the sheriff to the justices of the peace. Parliament in 1486 then required two justices instead of one to review an accused case and determine bail. Nine years later, Parliament required that judicial decisions on bail occur in open court, with two justices holding a hearing on the evidence. Out of these bail reforms grew the "notion of a preliminary hearing," now a standard feature of Anglo-American jurisprudence.[34]

The justice system's need to protect the rights of the accused, while guarding against fugitives, made bail law the arena for other major developments in English law; the changes represented refinements of the Magna Carta and the Statute of Westminster. With the Habeas Corpus Act of 1679, Parliament prohibited the delays that had kept the accused in prison for long periods of time as they awaited a bail hearing, even when they were charged with bailable offenses. Despite the reforms to make court proceedings speedier, corrupt justices still were able to keep the accused in prison for bailable offenses by setting the bail so high that release could never occur. The English Bill of Rights of 1689 set out to fix the abuse by stating that "excessive bail ought not to be required." The language survives as a cornerstone of American law in the Eighth Amendment, the shortest of the amendments in the American Bill of Rights: "Excessive bail shall not be required, nor excessive fines imposed, nor cruel and unusual punishments inflicted."

The Eighth Amendment, however, does not provide an absolute right to bail in all cases in the United States. Clarification on that issue came with the Judiciary Act of 1789, which Congress passed the same year as the ratification of the Constitution. The act established what crimes were bailable. The act also provided a statutory right to bail, which the Eighth Amendment requires must be of a reasonable amount if granted. "Upon all arrests in criminal cases," according to the Judiciary Act of 1789, "bail shall be admitted, except where punishment may be death, in which cases it shall not be admitted but by the supreme or a circuit court, or by a justice of the supreme court, or a judge of a district court, who shall exercise their discretion therein."[35]

The Judiciary Act of 1789 set forth bail requirements in federal cases. Following American independence, the states approved constitutions that detailed the rights regarding bail for crimes committed within each of their borders. With a few exceptions, the state constitutions, like the Judiciary Act of 1789, made the granting of bail more liberal than it had been under English law, particularly the Statute of Westminster. Above all, newly formed American law eliminated lists of bailable and nonbailable offenses, and made bail generally available, with judicial review, except for those accused of capital crimes. A primary reason for the more expansive view of bail under American law—a view that originated in the colonies and became codified in federal and state law after American independence—was the relative calm of the New World compared with life in England. "Crime was never as serious a problem in the colonies as it had been in England," one commentator has written. "Because crime was a less serious problem, the colonies used pretrial detention less frequently, even while under the terms of the Statute of Westminster. Once the colonies began to liberalize criminal penalties, the liberalization of bail followed."[36]

In the end, the United States and England still saw fugitives as a threat to the operation of the justice system, but they calibrated their bail laws to address that threat in different ways—ways that reflected each nation's culture and concerns over crime. Even today, as will be explored more fully elsewhere, the United States continues to grapple with efforts to change its bail laws to address concerns that the current laws still unfairly punish poor defendants, many of them members of racial minorities, who are unable to post bail of almost any amount. The result is fewer fugitives but a large number of inmates awaiting trial who, though presumed innocent, remain incarcerated for months or years before a jury has issued a verdict.

The federal courts have refined bail law in the United States periodically, with the focus often on what constitutes an "excessive" amount under the

Eighth Amendment. The Supreme Court is generally believed to have issued its first views on bail in 1951, in the case of *Stack v. Boyle*. The justices found that a federal judge in setting bail had to provide reasons for the amount and that the granting of bail should come only after a thorough review of each defendant's case. But in the *Stack* case and later cases, the Supreme Court reaffirmed that release on bail, while allowed under the law, is not an absolute right, even under the Eighth Amendment. "The right to release before trial is conditioned upon the accused's giving adequate assurance that he will stand trial and submit to sentence if found guilty," according to the majority opinion in *Stack v. Boyle*.[37] Federal and state courts were empowered to determine when bail was appropriate—except when the crime was punishable by death, in which bail was prohibited in most cases—and those courts were empowered to set the amount of the bail, as long as the figure was not excessive. And the main reason for bail was to guarantee a defendant's appearance in court and prevent him or her from turning into a fugitive. The probability that the defendant would show up, based on his or her background, was the main criterion for setting bail under *Stack v. Boyle* and a related Supreme Court case, *Carlson v. Landon*, decided in 1952.[38]

As was the case even in thirteenth- and fourteenth-century England, corruption and disparate treatment of pretrial defendants fueled bail reforms in the United States in the 1950s and 1960s. Several high-profile studies showed that those defendants held in prison before trial were most likely unable to make bail because they were poor. "The studies also revealed that bail was often used to 'punish' defendants prior to a determination of guilt or to 'protect' society from anticipated conduct, neither of which is a permissible purpose of bail."[39] The bail system, designed since ancient times to guard against fugitives, had devolved into a system in which high bail amounts were used to detain pretrial defendants for extended periods of time largely because of their limited financial means or because prosecutors and judges considered them too dangerous to be released.

The Federal Bail Reform Act of 1966 sought to rectify the inequities. Rivaling the Judiciary Act of 1789 in importance as related to bail, the Federal Bail Reform Act of 1966 established a standard that federal judges should favor releasing defendants in non-capital cases on their own recognizance, or with no money bail set. The act allowed for money bail in cases where the defendant was deemed a flight risk, but also let judges release defendants after they deposited 10 percent of the full bail amount with the court. The defendant had to pay the full amount if he or she absconded and was later caught, but the 10-percent refundable option eliminated the need for bail bonds and made bail more affordable for many defendants. Following the lead of Congress, most states passed similar legislation that authorized the release of defendants on their own recognizance or after posting percentage bonds, with electronic monitoring and similar options available to keep track of defendants out on bond. The main criterion for any evaluation of bond continued to be whether the defendant was a flight risk. The safety of the community was a factor only in capital cases or for those offenders who sought to be released on bail after they were convicted.

Fears of crime eventually shifted the nature of the debate over bail. The Bail Reform Act of 1966 had come under criticism for creating the potential for dangerous non-capital defendants to be released on their own recognizance or on a percentage bond. The criticism resonated with the administration of President Richard Nixon and his law-and-order emphasis. Congress in 1970 amended the Bail Reform Act of 1966 to allow federal judges in the District of Columbia to consider, when setting bail in non-capital cases, not only the risk of flight but also the potential danger the defendant posed to the community. Never before had the dangerousness of a defendant been part of the calculus in determining bail. The change expanded to the entire federal court system in 1984, under the administration of Ronald Reagan, another law-and-order president. Congress passed the Bail Reform Act of 1984, "which amended the 1966 act to include consideration of danger in order to address the 'alarming problem of crimes committed be persons upon release.'"[40] States later changed their bail laws to adopt the same expanded standard.

The Supreme Court accepted the changes. It ruled the Bail Reform Act of 1984 constitutional in 1987 in the case of *United States v. Salerno*, "one of its most important criminal law decisions in years."[41] In a 6–3 decision, the court expanded the scope and understanding of the Bail Clause of the Eighth Amendment in a way that seemed unlikely for hundreds of years, given the clause's legal lineage, dating to the Magna Carta and the Statute of Westminster and the English Bill of Rights, all of which held that the risk of flight was the sole consideration for determining bail when the law had already deemed the offenses bailable. If lack of crime in the nascent United States made American bail law initially more liberal than its English counterpart, the Supreme Court in the *Salerno* case found the Congress was justified in making American bail law less liberal—because of the threat, or potential threat, of crime.

The Supreme Court in the *Salerno* case overturned a 2–1 decision from the Second United States Circuit Court of Appeals, which agreed that pretrial detention—or the refusal to release a defendant on bail—was appropriate in non-capital cases if the defendant was a flight risk or posed a threat to witnesses or to the operation of the trial process. But the Second Circuit concluded "that the Government could not, consistent with due process, detain persons who had not been accused of any crime merely because they were thought to present a danger to the community."[42] Writing for the majority, Chief Justice William H. Rehnquist ruled that the Bail Reform Act of 1984 violated neither the Due Process Clause of the Fifth Amendment nor the Bail Clause of the Eighth Amendment, as long as judges followed the legal standards for determining the dangerousness of a defendant. Rehnquist wrote,

> Nothing in the text of the Bail Clause limits permissible Government considerations solely to questions of flight. The only arguable substantive limitation of the Bail Clause is that the Government's proposed conditions of release or detention not be "excessive" in light of the perceived evil. Of course, to determine whether the Government's response is excessive, we must compare that response against the interest the Government seeks to protect by means of that response. Thus, when the Government has admitted that its only interest is in preventing flight, bail must be set by a court at a sum designed to ensure that goal, and no more. We believe that when Congress has mandated detention on the basis of a compelling interest other than prevention of flight, as it has here, the Eighth Amendment does not require release on bail.
>
> In our society liberty is the norm, and detention prior to trial or without trial is the carefully limited exception. We hold that the provisions for pretrial detention in the Bail Reform Act of 1984 fall within that carefully limited exception. The Act authorizes the detention prior to trial of arrestees charged with serious felonies who are found after an adversary hearing to pose a threat to the safety of individuals or to the community which no condition of release can dispel. The numerous procedural safeguards detailed above must attend this adversary hearing. We are unwilling to say that this congressional determination, based as it is upon that primary concern of every government—a concern for the safety and indeed the lives of its citizens—on its face violates either the Due Process Clause of the Fifth Amendment or the Excessive Bail Clause of the Eighth Amendment.[43]

Justice Thurgood Marshall, in a dissenting opinion, highlighted what he saw as the Eighth Amendment's role in guaranteeing liberty—specifically, pretrial liberty. Expanding federal bail law beyond fugitive-related concerns, he wrote, was, in all but a few circumstances, a threat to liberty for all. He also found that the expansion endangered the core concept of innocent until proven guilty. Marshall wrote,

> Honoring the presumption of innocence is often difficult; sometimes we must pay substantial social costs as a result of our commitment to the values we espouse. But at the end of the day the presumption of innocence protects the innocent; the shortcuts we take with those whom we believe to be guilty injure only those wrongfully accused and, ultimately, ourselves.

Throughout the world today there are men, women, and children interned indefinitely, awaiting trials which may never come or which may be a mockery of the word, because their governments believe them to be "dangerous." Our Constitution, whose construction began two centuries ago, can shelter us forever from the evils of such unchecked power. Over 200 years it has slowly, through our efforts, grown more durable, more expansive, and more just. But it cannot protect us if we lack the courage, and the self-restraint, to protect ourselves. Today a majority of the Court applies itself to an ominous exercise in demolition. Theirs is truly a decision which will go forth without authority, and come back without respect.[44]

Three decades after the *Salerno* decision, bail law in the United States continues to allow for a defendant to be held without bail if he or she is deemed too great risk to the community. American bail law, despite its roots in Anglo-Saxon law, is now concerned with both the fugitive and criminal kind.

American bail law differs from the English system in another major way—the American's system's allowance for the use of bail bonds. The endurance of the bail-bond industry in the United States has given the American fugitive a legal doppelganger: the bail bondsman and, by extension, the bounty hunter empowered to bring the fugitive in. For those fugitives who jump bail, the bounty hunter is yet another person, along with police officers, Federal Bureau of Investigation agents or U.S. marshals, who is on the fugitive's trail.

Though most jurisdictions in the United States allow percentage bonds or recognizance bonds to avoid pretrial detention, the overall system of bail in the United States is still based on money bail, in which some type of financial surety can be required for a defendant to get out of prison while awaiting trial. The system, as shall be seen in the final chapter of this book, is coming under scrutiny throughout the United States as reformers point to how many defendants are held before trial only because they are poor and they cannot afford bail, no matter how small the amount. California has gone so far as to ban the use of money bail altogether, opting instead for a system in which only those defendants deemed highly dangerous are held in prison before trial. Other states have passed similar measures, and, under the administration of President Barack Obama, the use of money bail in the federal courts drew closer analysis.

But the use of cash bail is still prevalent throughout the United States, and integral to the operation of that system in the United States is the for-profit bail industry, built around the use of bail bonds. Only the United States and the Philippines still allow the for-profit bail industry, in which a defendant's family or other representative pays a bail-bond company a nonrefundable amount, typically 10 percent of the total bond, to get the defendant released before trial. Other countries have outlawed the practice, instead using such methods as the percentage bond that a defendant deposits with the court—and which the defendant gets back automatically if the defendant appears at all his or her court hearings.

Such a practice, an outgrowth of the Bail Reform Act of 1966, is widespread throughout the United States, but so is the continued use of bail bonds, despite the international condemnation of the for-profit system: "In England, Canada and other countries, agreeing to pay a defendant's bond in exchange for money is a crime akin to witness tampering or bribing a juror—a form of obstruction of justice."[45] As long as the for-profit money bail system has existed in the United States, so has another American original—the bounty hunter, or bond-enforcement agent, whose job is to find the fugitive and save the bail-bond company from forfeiting its bond and losing money.

The forging of the bail-bond apparatus out of the bail system originated in the American West, where the nation's "open frontier and entrepreneurial spirit injected an innovation into the process: by the early 1800s, private businesses were allowed to post bail in exchange for payments from the defendants and the promise that they would hunt down the defendants and return them if they failed to appear."[46] The Supreme Court in an 1872 case, *Taylor v. Taintor*, referred to the authority of a bail bondsman to pursue a fugitive, though in an *ober dicta* passage that contained no precedential value:

> When bail is given, the principal is regarded as delivered to the custody of his sureties. Their dominion is a continuance of the original imprisonment. Whenever they choose to do so, they may seize him and deliver him up in their discharge; and if that cannot be done at once, they may imprison him until it can be done. They may exercise their rights in person or by agent. They may pursue him into another State; may arrest him on the Sabbath; and, if necessary, may break and enter his house for that purpose. The seizure is not made by virtue of new process. None is needed. It is likened to the rearrest by the sheriff of an escaping prisoner.[47]

Though the *Taintor* decision involved bail of $8,000 and bond sureties who guaranteed that amount, the first true commercial for-profit bail bondsman business in the United States is believed to have started in San Francisco in 1898, in the firm of McDonough Brothers Bail Bond Brokers, which was "established as a saloon [but] found its niche by underwriting bonds for defendants who faced charges in the nearby Hall of Justice, or police court."[48] The McDonough brothers, Peter and Thomas, learned the practice from their father, who made free loans for bail bonds for lawyers' clients as a favor to the lawyers who drank in the saloon. The brothers monetized the custom by charging a fee to underwrite the bonds. They created, in McDonough Brothers, one of the most influential and underhanded institutions in the history of San Francisco, which, in its early days, was a fast-growing city where laws were often loosely enforced.

The McDonoughs cornered the bail-bond market in San Francisco by getting information on would-be defendants through bribes: "Policemen of all ranks could be seen visiting the McDonough office every day. Booking sergeants reportedly provided daily lists of who had been arrested, the charges, and the bail set."[49] Using their networks and peerless street-level intelligence, the McDonoughs expanded their bail-bond business into a protection racket, in which the brothers, for a fee, were able to bribe the authorities to shield underworld figures, gamblers, and others from arrest, allowing vice to go unchecked throughout San Francisco. "Prostitutes," for example, "contributed 10 percent of their income to the McDonoughs and 'as long as they paid they had immunity from arrest.'"[50]

The business model, which made a millionaire out of Pete McDonough, who ran the bail-bond business, could not last. In 1935, as the old political order in San Francisco was changing, the district attorney hired a former agent with the FBI, Edwin N. Atherton, to investigate the San Francisco Police Department. His probe undid the stranglehold that the McDonoughs had on the city. He wrote in his report, "McDonough Brothers was found to be a fountainhead of corruption willing to interest itself in almost any matter designed to defeat or circumvent the law."[51] The residents of San Francisco, struggling to survive the Great Depression, read the results of the Atherton investigation in the newspapers: "Figures such as $1 million a year in police graft and $4–$5 million a year in vice payments shocked people who were individually facing economic oblivion."[52]

Pete McDonough was done. The California insurance commissioner stripped him of his bail-bond license in 1937. He never got it back before he died ten years later. His invention—the bail-bond business—has survived him.

That the first known bail-bond business in the United States operated outside the law is perhaps no coincidence. Fugitives, as the Anglo-Saxon justice system first recognized, are outlaws. At the same time, perhaps it is no coincidence that the most recent challenges to legality of the bail system have originated in California, with one of the most significant cases involving a defendant from San Francisco. The issue, as will be explained in more detail later in this book, is not whether bail is constitutional, but whether money bail is an effective and fair way to keep defendants incarcerated before they have been tried. When is bail set so high that its lack of affordability violates the law, especially for poor defendants? That has become the lasting issue for a number of state legislatures and some members of Congress.

In San Francisco, robbery defendant Kenneth Humphrey, charged in 2017, argued that his $350,000 bail was excessive and unfair, mainly because he lacked the means to pay it. By raising his objections, he also challenged the money bail system in California, where, as in many other states, judicial officers set bail at fixed amounts, regardless of the defendant's ability to pay. California's First District Court of Appeal ruled for Humphrey on January 25, 2018. In a decision that upended the cash bail system in California, the court found that setting bail in unaffordable amounts is legal only if the defendant is such a danger that his or her release on bail would have the potential to harm the community. Humphrey's did not represent such a case, the court ruled. A judge initially set his bail at $600,000, and it was lowered to $350,000. Humphrey, sixty-four years old in mid-2018, still was unable to make bond and remained incarcerated.[53] "A determination of ability to pay is critical in the bail context to guard against improper detention based only on financial resources," Presiding Justice J. Anthony Kline wrote in the opinion for the three-judge panel. Judges in California, he wrote, have responsibility to ensure "that a defendant not be held in custody solely because he or she lacks financial resources."[54] The determination of the amount of a defendant's bail, Kline also wrote, must be based on individualized criteria, including an analysis of whether the defendant is a threat to the community and whether any other means are available to monitor the defendant while not keeping him or her in prison before trial. "[A] defendant," Kline wrote, "may not be imprisoned solely due to poverty."[55] For precedent, Kline cited state and federal law, including the *Salerno* ruling.[56]

As a result of the decision in the Humphrey case, prosecutors in San Francisco changed how they handled bail. They asked judges to set no bail only when a defendant posed a danger to the community; otherwise the judges were to release defendants under pretrial monitoring systems. In effect, the prosecutors had eliminated the reliance on money bail.[57] A judge on May 9, 2018, released Humphrey under the requirement that he wear an ankle monitor, among other restrictions.[58] But his case is not over. He awaits prosecution, and the California Supreme Court on May 23, 2018, agreed to review the Court of Appeal ruling on what had been his excessive bail of $350,000. The state Supreme Court acted on a request from San Francisco District Attorney George Gascón. He is a proponent of eliminating money bail but said he wants the state Supreme Court to clarify the Court of Appeal's decision in such areas as when a defendant can be deemed too dangerous or too great a flight risk to be released before trial.[59]

In its ruling, the Court of Appeal stated how it believes the dispute over cash bail should be remedied: in the California legislature. As will be seen, state lawmakers did take up the issue with a bill that was pending when the Court of Appeal ruled in Humphrey's request regarding his $350,000 bail. "We hope sensible reform is enacted, but if so it will not be in time to help resolve this case," Justice Kline wrote.[60] He and the other justices also expressed a fundamental concern over the operation of the bail system in the United States—concerns that had been around since shortly after independence and concerns that, Kline wrote, had led "close observers" to conclude that the American bail system was nothing less than "a blight on the system."[61]

One of those close observers, Kline wrote, was Alexis de Tocqueville, author of the influential *Democracy in America*, published in 1835 and 1840. Tocqueville's comments, from 1835, reveal the early tensions in America over the need both to keep society safe and potential fugitives in check and the recognition that those accused of crimes, but not convicted, are innocent under bedrock American jurisprudence. That tension, particularly over whether the bail system discriminates against poor defendants, has never gone away. The tension persists despite, Tocqueville's finding that a bail system for Americans that favors the rich over the poor was "repugnant to the general tenor of their legislation and the mass of their ideas."[62] Tocqueville, in remarks Kline also quoted, additionally found that the American bail system "is hostile to the poor, and favorable only to the rich. The poor man has not always a security to produce . . . and if he is obliged to wait for justice in prison, he is speedily reduced to distress. A wealthy person, on the contrary, always escapes imprisonment. . . . Nothing can be more aristocratic than this system of legislation."[63] Putting the problem in contemporary legal terms, Kline wrote in his opinion in the Humphrey case, "[T]here now exists a significant disconnect between the stringent legal protections state and federal appellate courts have required for proceedings that may result in a deprivation of liberty and what actually happens in bail proceedings in our criminal courts."[64]

Perhaps most notable about Tocqueville's commentary on bail is the reason that he highlighted that particular aspect of the American justice system. Tocqueville referred to bail to illustrate how, in his experience, Americans had adopted practices that contradicted the nation's emphasis on freedom and liberty. "Laws and customs are frequently to be met with in the United States which contrast strongly with all that surrounds them," Tocqueville wrote. "These laws seem to be drawn up in a spirit contrary to the prevailing tenor of American legislation; and these customs are no less opposed to the general tone of society."[65]

He continued by writing "I shall quote a single example to illustrate my meaning" and went on to criticize the American bail system as favoring the rich.

At the same time, Tocqueville summarized what remains to this day, as evident in the Humphrey decision, a lack of a middle ground in the American bail system. The criminal procedure in the newly created United States, Tocqueville wrote, "has only two means of action—committal or bail."[66] Either the accused is held in prison or, if he or she has the means, is released on bail. Implicit in Tocqueville's analysis is the existence of another possibility in the American bail system. Tocqueville wrote in full that a wealthy person, "if he has committed a crime, he may readily elude punishment by breaking his bail."[67] In other words, by becoming a fugitive.

2

LONG ARMS OF THE LAW

The U.S. Marshals Service and the Federal Bureau of Investigation

Timothy Pickering, the third secretary of state for the United States, sent the letter on February 11, 1797, when George Washington was president. The subject was urgent. Pickering wrote to the U.S. marshal for Virginia, David Meade Randolph. He asked him to head to Norfolk to intercept a French frigate called the *Medusa*. On board, Pickering wrote, were five men—two Americans and three Spaniards—wanted for the murder of Captain Andrew Peyton, of the ship the *James*, whose home port was Philadelphia. Pickering believed that Peyton had been killed for the $7,000 he had on board the *James* and that Peyton was supposed to bring to Gibraltar.[1] In any case, the five murder suspects had been placed on the *Medusa* in Cape Francois, the city known today as Cap-Haitien, on the north shore of Haiti. The *Medusa* had sailed to Norfolk. Pickering asked Randolph to take custody of the five in Norfolk so they could appear for an examination before Cyrus Griffin, the U.S. district judge for Virginia, who was to set a trial date. Pickering's orders were coming from the top. "This I do," Pickering wrote to Randolph, "by the direction of the President of the United States."[2] Pickering was afraid the men, who were fugitives from justice, would get away.

His fears became reality. Randolph went after the men as soon as he received Pickering's letter, but his search came up short; the men had "made their escape,"[3] Pickering wrote on March 7, 1797, to U.S. Attorney General Charles Lee. Pickering asked Lee what else should be done, including whether the government should consider "advertizing [*sic*] the murderers," presumably by publishing information about them in the newspapers.[4] But Pickering was not optimistic. Also on March 7, 1797, he wrote to the owners of the *James*,

Thomas and Peter Mackie, of Philadelphia, that the capture of the fugitives was unlikely. "I conclude now," Pickering wrote, "that the blood of your Captain Peyton, shed by those murderers, will remain unavenged."[5] And five months later, Pickering had all but given up on anyone finding the fugitives. On August 17, 1797, Pickering wrote to Judge Griffin to ask for the return of legal papers in the case, "there being no hope of obtaining the murderers of Capt. Peyton."[6] Despite the quick efforts of a U.S. marshal, one of the early cases of a search for fugitives in the United States yielded disappointment.

From its inception, what is now called the U.S. Marshals Service had the authority to track fugitives, though it handled a wide variety of other duties early in its development. The U.S. Marshals Service and the FBI today represent the two main federal law enforcement agencies responsible for pursuing fugitives in federal cases, though they often assist local and state police departments through task forces and other arrangements. Due to portrayals in movies and on television, the federal marshal is often seen as the nemesis of the fugitive. But not until 1979 did the federal government specifically give the modern U.S. Marshals Service jurisdiction over federal fugitives—an area that the FBI had exclusively handled for decades. The two agencies continue to have roles in the chasing fugitives on the federal level. As set forth in the 1979 agreement, the marshals are responsible for finding escaped federal prisoners, federal bail jumpers, and federal offenders who violated probation and parole. The FBI still has jurisdiction over finding fugitives in certain high-profile cases. FBI special agents search for fugitives whom state and local authorities have accused of "crimes of violence, high property loss, and illicit narcotics traffic" as well as escaped convicts accused of committing crimes.[7] Highlighting their joint roles,[8] the U.S. Marshals Service and the FBI continue to post separate lists of most wanted fugitives. The marshals call theirs the Fifteen Most Wanted. FBI special agents ask for the public's help in finding those on the bureau's Ten Most Wanted Fugitives list.

The oldest of the agencies, by far, is the U.S. Marshals Service, which is the oldest law federal enforcement agency in the nation. Congress created the service in the Judiciary Act of 1789—the same seminal piece of legislation that created the federal judiciary, established the statutory right to bail in federal cases, and identified bailable offenses under federal law. The act simultaneously instituted two mechanisms to guard against fugitives: bail and the U.S. Marshals Service, then called the offices of the U.S. marshal, with the president appointing a marshal for each of what were then the thirteen judicial districts among the eleven states that had ratified the Constitution. The eleven states each had one judicial district, except for Virginia and Massachusetts, which each had two. Virginia's second district encompassed the part of the state that later became Kentucky, and Massachusetts' second district encompassed the part of the state that later became Maine. Each marshal had authority only in his judicial district.

The Judiciary Act of 1789 gave marshals and their deputies broad responsibilities to serve the federal courts, including delivering writs and transferring prisoners. The act did not mention fugitives, though their pursuit—as Secretary of State Pickering made clear years later—could reasonably considered to be within the realm of a marshal's duties. Section 27 of the Act states "[t]hat a marshal shall be appointed in and for each district for the term of four years, but shall be removable from office at pleasure, whose duty it shall be to attend the district and circuit courts when sitting therein, and also the Supreme Court in the District in which that court shall sit. And to execute throughout the district, all lawful precepts directed to him, and issued under the authority of the United States, and he shall have power to command all necessary assistance in the execution of his duty, and to appoint as there shall be occasion, one or more deputies."[9]

Just as the United States imported the use of bail from the English judicial system, so it borrowed the marshal system from the other side of the Atlantic as well. Marshals handled administrative duties in the vice-admiralty courts that the British established in 1697 to hear maritime cases involving the American colonies. By the time of American independence, the vice-admiralty courts represented the closest the colonies had to a national court system; modeling the functions of the new federal court system after those of the vice-admiralty courts made sense. Marshals in the vice-admiralty courts served subpoenas, writs, and other court process, seized condemned ships, and transferred prisoners, among other duties. Federal marshals performed many of the same jobs for the courts following the passage of the Judiciary Act of 1789.[10] The marshals were initially under the jurisdiction of the State Department, where they took orders from the likes of Secretary Pickering and other top officials.

Though the Constitution and federal laws did not specifically state that marshals were to catch fugitives, the Constitution made the pursuit of fugitives in the United States a less complicated affair than in other nations, such as those in Europe, where fugitives could make extradition—the return of fugitives to their original jurisdiction—more complex by fleeing from one country to another. In the United States, as one historian has written, "[t]he U.S. Constitution effectively created one of the largest extradition zones in the world, binding all of the states with the pledge to return fugitives to each other."[11] The Extradition

Clause of the Constitution—Article IV, Section II—authorized such a system by providing that "[a] Person charged in any State with Treason, Felony, or other Crime, who shall flee from Justice, and be found in another State, shall on demand of the executive Authority of the State from which he fled, be delivered up, to be removed to the State having Jurisdiction of the Crime."[12] Once a marshal caught a fugitive, the path to extradition was straightforward and meant to be swift.

The marshals and their deputies handled both law enforcement and administrative functions for the federal court system, often for little pay. The nation's first Congress and presidential administration quickly discovered that the federal government "had no provision for a regional administrative structure stretching throughout the country."[13] The marshals and their deputies, as the only appointees charged with what could be considered general administrative responsibilities, were called upon to handle money for the courts, assemble jurors, rent and clean the federal courtrooms, and even administer the census every ten years—all while also chasing fugitives, arresting offenders and taking them to prison, and performing other functions required of what was, for an extended period of time, the nation's only federal police force. The marshals were the equivalent of federal "handymen."[14] Pursuing fugitives was only one of many of those functions, and certainly not one that the marshals designated as a primary duty. "These diversified duties precluded the marshals from developing any particular specialty. They were not only law enforcers but administrators."[15]

The marshals and their deputies got some relief in 1880, when Congress created the Bureau of the Census and the marshals were relieved of the requirement that they take the count. But well before then, the marshals' duties became more expanded, and politically charged, as they were made responsible for capturing fugitive slaves in the era of the Civil War. For the North, these fugitives were not offenders on the lam who deserved to be caught and brought to justice. They were unfairly enslaved people who should be allowed to flee to freedom. The South saw the fugitives as runaways who were breaking their service to their slaveholders and who had to be caught and punished. The marshals were squeezed in between as they sought to enforce the Fugitive Slave Act of 1850.

The law's predecessor, the first Fugitive Slave Act, which Congress passed in 1793, supplemented the Extradition Clause in the Constitution and triggered the clause that follows it in Article IV, Section 2: "No Person held to Service or Labour in one State, under the Laws thereof, escaping into another, shall, in Consequence of any Law or Regulation therein, be discharged from such Service or Labour, but shall be delivered up on Claim of the Party to whom such Service or Labour may be due."[16] The clause held that government officials in the North, including marshals, had to return runaway slaves to slaveholders in the South, even if a slave had escaped to a free state. Federal judges and state magistrates were empowered to decide on their own, and without a jury trial, the status of a fugitive slave and whether a return to his or her slaveholder was warranted. The Fugitive Slave Act of 1793 became less effective in 1842, in the case of *Prigg v. Pennsylvania*. The Supreme Court ruled that state officials had no duty to assist in the capture of runaway slaves if the particular state prohibited such assistance. The ruling allowed states to pass their own laws to weaken the Fugitive Slave Act of 1793. But the law also left intact the federal government's authority; marshals and other federal officials still had the undisputed responsibility to enforce the Fugitive Slave Act of 1793.[17]

That responsibility became even clearer for the marshals with the passage of the Fugitive Slave Act of 1850, which amended the act of 1793 to address the various state laws meant to circumvent it. These personal-liberty laws allowed for jury trials for escaped slaves and, in some cases, banned state authorities in the North from cooperating with the federal authorities to capture and return escaped slaves.[18] To offset the states' efforts, the Fugitive Slave Act of 1850 banned jury trials for fugitive slaves and increased the legal pressure on federal marshals and their deputies to pursue and capture them, even if the slaves had escaped to a free state. Dereliction of duty meant heavy fines. According to the act, "Should any marshal or deputy marshal refuse to serve such a warrant [for a fugitive slave], or other process, when tendered, or to use all proper means diligently to execute the same, he shall, on conviction thereof, be fined in the sum of one thousand dollars."[19] The law also punished marshals and their deputies if a fugitive slave escaped, "whether with or without the assent of such marshal or his deputy." In such a case, the marshal could be prosecuted and held liable "for the full value of the service or labor of said fugitive."[20]

The Fugitive Slave Act of 1850 enraged the North, moved the United States closer to civil war, and spurred a more efficient Underground Railroad to shuttle slaves to freedom and elude the federal marshals. The 1850 law revealed a nation increasingly divided over slavery and wrestling with the question of whether an unjust law had to be obeyed. As one historian has observed, "Although many Northern whites sympathized with the slaveholders or viewed it as their legal and constitutional duty to enforce the law, even those who cared little about slavery were often repulsed by the specter of slave catchers swarming into their communities and enforcing Southern law in Northern states."[21] Under the law, the marshals and their deputies had little choice but to execute their duties and pursue and find the escaped slaves. But they were following a heinous law that prolonged the existence of an abominable institution. The marshals were not pursuing accused criminals or prison escapees who had been convicted in court. They were pursuing people who deserved to be free. In the North, marshals who went after fugitive slaves suffered ignominy: "They became strangers in their homeland, hated by their neighbors because they enforced a hated law."[22] In one case, in Oberlin, Ohio, in the summer of 1858, a mob cornered two deputy marshals and other "slave catchers" in the attic of a tavern to try to prevent them from capturing a runaway slave. A federal grand jury indicted those who interfered with the pursuit of the slave, and a county grand jury indicted the deputy marshals and others on kidnapping charges.[23] A compromise led to the release of all the accused, but the opposing prosecutions illustrated the divisiveness of the Fugitive Slave Act and how federal marshals had come to be seen as enemies of freedom. The fugitive slaves' only offense was breaking a morally indefensible law. They were fugitives whom marshals should have never pursued.

The Civil War eliminated the Fugitive Slave Law, as the federal marshals—who only existed in the Union—no longer were required to return slaves to the South. Before the war, however, President Abraham Lincoln required that the marshals continue to capture fugitive slaves, signaling how even the same president who would go on to abolish slavery also believed in following the law as Congress determined it at the time.[24] The federal marshals' slave-catching responsibilities permanently disappeared from American justice system with the end of the Civil War, in May 1865, and with the ratification, in December 1865, of the Thirteenth Amendment, which abolished slavery. The amendment also repealed Article IV, Section 2 of the Constitution, which had mandated the return of escaped slaves to slaveholders—the same article that the Fugitive Slave Law sought to enforce. As if to emphasize the changing times after the Civil War, President Rutherford B. Hayes in 1877 appointed the abolitionist Frederick Douglass the U.S. marshal for the District of Columbia. He was the first African American to be named a U.S. marshal.[25]

Federal marshals and their deputies still went after regular fugitives after the Civil War, even as the government curtailed or eliminated their duties in other areas. The creation of the Secret Service in July 1865 introduced a new federal agency dedicated to pursuing and charging counterfeiters, whose assault on the currency had been under the purview of marshals and their deputies. Also after the Civil War, the government clarified oversight of the marshals, whose management initially fell under the executive branch and specifically the secretary of state. The Interior Department later adopted a degree of supervision over the marshals until the attorney general became their supervising authority in 1861. Nine years later, with the creation of the Department of Justice, the marshals and their deputies found "a permanent home."[26]

Following the Civil War, the marshals and their deputies achieved a high level of national recognition by patrolling the vast and mostly lawless territories of the Old West during the late 1800s. The marshals enforced the laws and acted as the federal government's representative in places such as the booming Dodge City, Kansas, where the exploits of fictional U.S. Marshal Matt Dillon played out on *Gunsmoke*, a hit on both radio (1952–1961) and television (1955–1975). Marshals during the late 1800s also deputized local authorities to act as special deputy marshals, partly because the terms of regular marshals were limited to four years. The use of special deputy marshals provided continuity in the Western locales and provided reinforcements for the regular marshals in their enforcement of the laws and the pursuit of fugitives. The use of special deputy marshals preceded the westward expansion, but "from this concept developed the role of the posse in the Old West, and later non-agency personnel in modern-day task forces. It also allowed for hybrid service—a cross-deputation in certain cases. For example, Lincoln County Sheriff Patrick Garrett, the famed pursuer of the outlaw Billy the Kid in Territorial New Mexico, was cross-deputized as a special deputy U.S. marshal."[27] The marshals during this time also continued to enjoy broad law enforcement powers, including hunting fugitives, in each individual judicial district. Using deputies and special deputies, the marshals could "command all necessary assistance to form posses within their districts." The posses were made up of bystanders and citizens, but also members of the armed services, "whether militia of the State, or Federal troops," though the government in the late 1800s eliminated marshals' power to direct the military to help them carry out their duties.[28]

Many U.S. marshals and their deputies became household names as they patrolled the Old West during the late 1800s. Among them were Wyatt Earp, Bat Masterson, and the "Three Guardsmen": Deputy U.S. Marshals Chris Madsen, Henry "Heck" Thomas, and Bill Tilghman, who hunted down the members of the Doolin Gang, who robbed banks and otherwise terrorized the Indian Territory, which today is Oklahoma, in the 1880s and 1890s. The Indian Territory's size made it hard to police, and so did the law-breaking antics of a large part of its populace, including crooks, thieves, and other scoundrels who fled there looking for refuge and a new way to make a living after the Civil War. Between 1884 and 1889, fifty deputy marshals were killed in the Indian Territory,[29] which fell under the jurisdiction of the Western District of Arkansas. In July

1893, the district got a new U.S. marshal—E. D. Nix, whom President Grover Cleveland appointed to capture the members of the Doolin Gang. As fugitives, the gang members had become increasingly harder to find because they enjoyed the sympathy and cooperation of many law-abiding citizens in the Indian Territory. Nix had as many as 150 deputies working to find the Doolins, and he broke off his three best men from that group to form the Three Guardsmen.[30]

Nix and the trio focused on Ingalls, about ten miles east of Stillwater, Oklahoma, in the Indian Territory. The Doolin Gang made Ingalls their homestead when Bill Doolin and Bill Dalton and the other gang members, some of whom also made up the erstwhile Wild Bunch, were not hiding out in a secret lair called Dalton Cave. On September 1, 1893, Ingalls witnessed one of the Old West's bloodiest shootouts. The Three Guardsmen and other deputy marshals traded gunfire with Bill Doolin, Bill Dalton, and other gang members who were holed up in a saloon. Three deputies and an innocent bystander were killed, and all but one of the Doolin men escaped. Three years later, Heck Thomas, one of the Three Guardsmen, caught up with Doolin on a road that was near Doolin's father-in-law's house outside of Stillwater. Doolin a year earlier had robbed a bank, and six months after that he had broken out of prison. On August 25, 1896, Heck and his seven-member posse gave Doolin the chance to surrender. He refused, shot back, and was riddled with buckshot and suffered more than twenty wounds. Heck got a $1,500 reward for capturing and killing Doolin; Heck shared the money with his posse.[31]

Doolin was the last holdout of the Doolin Gang, whose members deputy marshals had killed over the previous two years. Doolin lost his trusted friend in crime when Bill Dalton was killed on June 8, 1894. Dalton after the gunfight at Ingalls had formed his own Dalton Gang, which robbed banks. A deputy U.S. marshal, Loss Hart, tracked Dalton by intercepting a package of liquor that was on its way to his cabin. Hart and his posse sought to arrest Dalton for the deaths at the Ingalls shootout a year earlier. When Dalton jumped from the window, Hart shot him dead before his body hit the ground.[32] And two months before Dalton's demise, a number of the Dalton Gang members were killed in a shootout in Perry, Oklahoma, where deputy U.S. marshals finally caught up with them "after trying to effect their capture for some time."[33] The deputies involved included Tighlman and Heck, two of the Three Guardsmen, and they were heralded in the newspapers for their efforts: "They have a reputation all over the Western States and Territories for bravery and skill in sharpshooting. It had been expected for some time that a fight would take place, and the desperate character of the extinct band of outlaws, combined with the determination of the officers of the law to hunt them to their death, gave assurance of a determined battle."[34]

The members of the Dalton and Doolin gangs could have never expected to live once their time on the lam ran out. Marshal E. D. Nix had made that clear to the Three Guardsmen and the other deputy marshals who hunted Doolin, Dalton, and others for years. Nix's order, which he gave in 1894, was "Bring them in dead or alive."[35] The phrase was known throughout the Old West. It sometimes appeared on a new form of communication—the most-wanted poster, which would go on to become one of the government's most integral tools in finding fugitives. The posters distributed throughout the Old West named and described the fugitive as well as the reward offered for the person's capture; the bounty for Billy the Kid, for instance, was $5,000. A drawing of the fugitive also appeared on the posters, whose general design has not changed since. They are placards meant for direct and immediate conveyance of a message. "In a time where mass media didn't exist, issuing a most wanted poster served as a means to distribute information," author Martin J. Kidston has observed. "They were primarily used on the local level for neighboring cities and towns, given that an alleged criminal couldn't hop in a car and drive hundreds of miles in a matter of hours. There was no radio, television, or internet—no social media or twenty-four-hour news channel. Issuing a poster was one's best bet for the public's attention and alerting nearby law enforcement."[36]

The dominant element on some of the posters—that the fugitive was wanted "dead or alive"—was not an idle threat. It carried importance in the tradition of Anglo-American jurisprudence. Just as the law in Anglo-Saxon England allowed for the summary execution of the fugitive who had been declared an outlaw, vigilante groups and ordinary American citizens in the Old West often acted on their own to capture and sometimes kill fugitives without turning them over for prosecution. The lawlessness was so great that fighting crime in such a summary fashion became an accepted way of the West until the territories became more organized and were eventually made states. When vigilantes took up arms, "most were actions taken without legal precedent or proper lawful credentials," said David S. Turk, the historian for the U.S. Marshals Service. "There were fewer lawmen to be found in the expanse of the territories (no state police), not to mention a greater number of dangers to face."[37]

The West, especially after the Civil War, became a place of refuge for Union and Confederate soldiers who were seeking new lives but lacked the means of skills for success. They often turned to crime—bank robberies, train robberies, cattle rustling—to survive, opening battles between them and the rest of the populace. Many of the settlers were law-abiding transplants from the East who lived in big cities where organized law enforcement was a given. The clash of cultures became inevitable. And so did vigilantism and frontier justice: the hardworking settler versus the outlaw. As one writer found, "Honest men were more liable to be beaten, knifed, shot, and have all their worldly goods stolen. As a result, pioneers and settlers found that they were individually responsible for their own protection and that of their families, and defense of their property from crime. Each man had to defend himself and protect his own rights, if necessary, by force. . . . Under these conditions, taking a human life was not viewed the same as it was in the more thickly populated areas of the country."[38]

Nonetheless, few of the most-wanted posters declared a fugitive was wanted "dead or alive," and those posters that did were not products of the U.S. marshals and other government agencies, Turk said. Private companies, such as railroads and banks, both of which were targets for robbers, were more inclined to post rewards for fugitives sought "dead or alive." U.S. marshals, their field deputies, and other lawmen typically put up signs seeking a fugitive's arrest—while alive. The U.S. marshals and their field deputies "would need warrants to pursue the outlaws they sought, unless associated with those in the perpetration of a crime," Turk said. "The preference was 'alive,' as the field deputies would get more money that way. Posters were expensive, so they were not always used unless for cause. Incidentally, very few actually said 'dead or alive' on them, but might give monetary amounts as incentive for an informant."[39]

However they were caught, the outlaws made names for themselves and the marshals who pursued them. Nix, Tighlman, and other marshals and deputies added to their fame by appearing in movies and writing books in the early 1900s. They satisfied the public's desire for real-life stories about outlaws and fugitives and the upright lawmen who brought them down after long searches. But, as one historian has commented, movies, books, and other forms of popular culture failed to shield the U.S. marshals and their deputies from a loss of stature. Though marshals and their deputies had operated as members of the country's only national police force since 1789, that distinction vanished in the early and mid-1900s with the creation of a police agency specifically designated to enforce federal laws: the agency that would become the Federal Bureau of Investigation. The FBI's ascendency, with iconic director J. Edgar Hoover guiding it, meant the new agency got more responsibility for catching fugitives while marshals and their deputies slid more into the background. In some respects, their roles were reduced to that of bailiffs, in charge mainly of keeping order in federal courtrooms.[40]

The FBI's development was a product of the New Deal, though the land-mark series of federal programs is mainly remembered for its legacy of economic and social relief. President Franklin D. Roosevelt's creation of the Works Prog-ress Administration, the Federal Deposit Insurance Corporation, the Social Security Administration, and other now-familiar agencies rescued the nation from the Great Depression and further economic collapse. But the New Deal also included policies that focused on crime, particularly crimes such as bank robbery, which exploded during the Great Depression and gave rise to such infamous yet celebrated criminals as John Dillinger, Pretty Boy Floyd, George "Baby Face" Nelson, Machine Gun Kelly, and Ma Barker and her gang of sons, thugs, and thieves. In 1933 and 1934 the nation experienced what the federal government considered its greatest crime wave ever.[41] Financial desperation led more crooks to rob banks. The end of Prohibition, in December 1933, left bootleggers and rum runners looking for new lines of work, primarily as gang-sters and racketeers.

The federal government looked to the agency that became the FBI to help keep the peace on a national scale at a time when robbers were said to be holding up banks at the rate of two a day.[42] In 1934, Roosevelt's new attorney general, Homer S. Cummings, thundered about the need to expand federal law enforcement powers as bank robbery and other crimes became more interstate in nature with the advent of the automobile. Cummings spoke not of U.S. mar-shals and their deputies; he spoke of expanding what was called then called the Justice Department's Bureau of Investigation. "We are no longer a nation whose problems are local and isolated," Cummings said. "The growing density of our population and the development of high-speed methods of transportation have resulted not only in a large increase of our crime rate, but, also, have given way to many crimes of an interstate character."[43] Cummings and Roosevelt wanted the creation of "an elite federal police force,"[44] or a "super police force"[45] that could take down the army of criminals.

The Bureau of Investigation by then had been around in various iterations since Congress created the Department of Justice in 1871. Congress appro-priated the department $50,000 for the detection and prosecution of federal crimes, but the department had no investigative arm of its own. It cobbled together a detective unit first by hiring private investigators and then, when Congress outlawed that practice, by borrowing investigators from other federal agencies, such as the Secret Service. These investigators were called "special agents" because they were brought in from outside the Department of Justice to investigate "special cases"—a designation that lives on today in the use of the title of "special agents" for officers of the FBI.[46] By 1908, the Department of

Justice had established a unit of thirty-four special agents, and by 1909, the unit had a name: the Bureau of Investigation.

Within ten years, in 1919, the Bureau of Investigation had taken on the responsibility of helping to find fugitives, though the agency at the time still lacked the broad type of law-enforcement powers that Congress would grant in the 1930s. The Bureau of Investigation in December 1919 created what it called the identification order, or IO, a precursor to the most-wanted fugitive program that the FBI would launch much later. The IO was born out of a request from the Army's military intelligence division. It asked the Bureau of Investigation for help in finding William N. Bishop, a twenty-three-year-old soldier who had left the stockade at what is today Fort Belvoir in northern Virginia on December 2, 1919.[47] An assistant director at the Bureau of Investigation, Frank Burke, offered assistance and sent a letter to "All Special Agents, Special Employees and Local Officers" in which he asked them to "make every effort" to catch Bishop. The letter was a landmark. As the FBI states in its official history, "little did anyone know at the time, but that letter set in motion a chain of events that would forever change how the FBI and its partners fight crime."[48]

Burke included in the letter detailed information about Bishop, such as his physical description (including a "smooth scar ¾ [inches] long on left thumb" and a "pigmented mole near his armpit"), as well as the names and addresses of people whom Bishop "may communicate with," including a sister in New York City.[49] Burke included in the letter "a photostat copy" of a recent photograph of Bishop. Burke urged anyone with information on Bishop to contact the Bureau of Investigation, the military intelligence division of the Army, the War Department, and the military police at the Army base that Bishop had fled. Burke called the letter "Identification Order No. 1." "In essence," according to the FBI, "it was the Bureau's first wanted poster, and it put the organization squarely in the fugitive-catching business."[50] Bishop was caught on April 6, 1920.

The Bureau of Investigation soon distributed IOs of other fugitives throughout the United States and Canada. The format evolved from a letter to a piece of paper with a standard size of eight inches by eight inches, replete with information about the fugitive's criminal history as well as, eventually, his or her fingerprints, drawn from what would become the FBI's vast archives of fingerprints and other identifying information of criminals and fugitives. By the 1930s, the FBI was sending IO flyers to police departments nationwide.[51]

But when the Bureau of Investigation first developed the IOs, it did so as a way to create a network among law enforcement and government agencies. The bureau at that time was more of a facilitator of law and order rather than an enforcer. Federal criminal laws remained limited for more than two decades after the creation of the Bureau of Investigation. The Department of Justice faced opposition in establishing a national police force, which President Herbert Hoover feared would impinge on states' rights. In 1930, in a speech in which he attacked racketeering, public corruption, and gangsters, Hoover declared that the authority for eradicating the menace of crime rested with the states and their police agencies and not with the Department of Justice in Washington, D.C. "Every single State has ample laws that cover such criminality," Hoover said. "What is needed is the enforcement of these laws, and not more laws. Any suggestion of increasing the Federal criminal laws in general is a reflection on the sovereignty of State government."[52]

Then came the Great Depression, the great crime wave, and the plan of President Roosevelt and Homer Cummings to fight crime nationwide. With Roosevelt's backing, Cummings in 1934 introduced a package of twelve anticrime bills to Congress, including the Federal Bank Robbery Act, which made bank robbery a federal crime—not because banks were federally insured but because bank robbery, according to the Roosevelt administration, had become an inherently interstate crime. The proposed law allowed what was still known as the Bureau of Investigation to investigate bank robberies and cooperate with local police forces only when it became clear that those local forces "cannot cope with the criminals."[53]

Any Hoover-era reluctance to expand what would become the FBI's powers at the expense of states' rights largely evaporated with an embarrassing victory for a notorious group of fugitives in the spring of 1934. John Dillinger and his crew of bank robbers escaped the Bureau of Investigation and local police who had descended on Dillinger's hideout in the summer resort town of Little Bohemia, in northern Wisconsin, on April 23, 1934. Baby Face Nelson shot and killed a special agent with the Bureau of Investigation, W. Carter Baum, and another agent and a local constable were wounded. Dillinger and his gang ran free once more, and Roosevelt cited Dillinger's rampage as the latest reason Congress had to pass his anticrime bills, called the Twelve Point Program, which led to the Crime Control Laws, as soon as possible. Cummings, as a historian of the FBI, Richard Gid Powers, has written, saw his anti-crime measures as complementary to Roosevelt's New Deal message that the most effective form of government was "government in action."[54] Cummings saw that changes to law enforcement, like changes to government programs, could foster the type of unity that was necessary to bind the nation together to survive the Great Depression and defeat the likes of John Dillinger, whom the FBI would eventually capture in memorable fashion.[55] "The Roosevelt administration was astute enough to understand the connection between social solidarity and law enforcement," Powers has written, "and in the war on crime that began in 1933 the New Deal exploited this relationship with spectacular political results."[56]

The political results materialized when Congress acted swiftly in May and June of 1934. The House and Senate approved six of the twelve anti-crime bills, also known as the Crime Control Laws, in Roosevelt's plan, and the president signed them. The new laws, in addition to making bank robbery a federal crime, outlawed on the federal level such crimes as killing or assaulting a federal officer, the transportation of kidnapping victims across state lines, and inciting a riot at a federal prison. One of the laws, the Fugitive Felon Act, passed May 18, 1934, made a class of fugitives into federal offenders—those who fled from state to state to avoid prosecution for certain felonies, such as murder, kidnapping, and robbery.[57] The agency—first known as the Bureau of Investigation (1909–1933) and then the Division of Investigation (1933–1935)—got more power to enforce the new laws, including those against fugitives. On June 6, 1934, Roosevelt signed an act that allowed federal authorities to offer rewards of up to $25,000 to help in the capture of anyone accused of breaking federal laws—a financial tool that would benefit the authorities in their pursuit of fugitives for years to come. Less than a week later, on June 18, 1934, Roosevelt signed a law that authorized special agents in the Division of Investigation to carry firearms and make arrests. And on June 26, 1934, he signed the first piece of national gun legislation, the National Firearms Act. It allowed the federal government to tax the making and sale of machine guns—the gangsters' weapon of choice—and other firearms and to regulate the interstate transfer of them.

The work of Roosevelt, Homer Cummings, and others in Washington, D.C., had created a new enemy for fugitives—the "G-men," or government agents, of what would become the Federal Bureau of Investigation. J. Edgar Hoover, the director who more than anyone was responsible for the public-relations tactics that created the mystique around his special agents, renamed the Division of Investigation the Federal Bureau of Investigation by July 1, 1935.[58] The United States now had a federal police force that the government said equaled the best in the world, such as the criminal investigation division of the British police. "Just as England has its C. I. D.," the Associated Press reported, "the United States will have its F.B.I., which stands for the Federal Bureau of Investigation."[59] By July 29, 1935, the FBI had started its first school for local and state police officers, who traveled to Washington, D.C., for a twelve-week course in which they learned the crime-fighting techniques of the FBI, including firearms training and scientific methods of investigating cases.[60] Their teachers were FBI special agents, who now were stationed in thirty-seven cities throughout the United States.[61] Fugitives had more people looking for them.

Around this same time, in the late 1930s, states also became more aggressive in their efforts to catch fugitives, particularly those who could race across state lines in automobiles. In 1937, Kansas became the first state to pass a "fresh pursuit" law, which allows police to cross state lines in pursuit of a fugitive as long as the chase is ongoing, or "fresh," and the suspected crime is a felony.[62] "Fresh pursuit laws," according to one analysis, "are numerous and differ substantially in language and effect throughout states, tribes, and the world. However, their overarching goal is to extend the authority of an officer when necessary in order to achieve safety and avoid lawlessness."[63] Soon other states would also cede some of their sovereignty in exchange for the national interest by passing the Uniform Act on Fresh Pursuit. It reads, in part, that any member of a police agency from one state who is chasing a fugitive in fresh pursuit into another state "shall have the same authority to arrest and hold such person in custody" as a member of a police agency in the state into which the suspect fled.[64] Fresh-pursuit laws also came to allow police officers to cross municipal borders while chasing fugitives, which helped to extend the reach of the law on a local level. In such cases, according to the laws, the officer had to be in "hot pursuit" of the suspect.[65]

On a national scale, the reach of the FBI grew the most in the 1930s. J. Edgar Hoover's genius for public relations helped fuel the FBI's standing among the American people during the decade of the Depression and the gangster, but so did the FBI's rigid internal structure. The government had a U.S. marshal in each judicial district, and each, due to the presidential appointment, was largely autonomous; each marshal could even design his own badge for the district.[66] Not so with the FBI. It was a top-down organization, with Hoover at the top dictating standards for each agent—federal officers who, in turn, inculcated local police officers who visited their "crime school" with the FBI's values and techniques. The marshals, by their organization's design, lacked a cohesive structure and a unified image, particularly compared with those of the FBI.[67]

The FBI special agents further eclipsed the marshals and their deputies in the 1930s and beyond because the government gave the FBI the authority to search for fugitives. As they patrolled the Indian Territory and other areas of the Old West, little did the marshals know that the era would represent, for a long time, the apogee of their agency in terms of finding those on the lam. Marshals have always been authorized to execute arrest warrants in their judicial districts, and that responsibility often requires searching for the would-be arrestees. But, with the creation of the FBI, the marshals had to share the responsibility of catching fugitives with another federal agency. The loss of that primary responsibility, for an extended period of time, was not the fault of the marshals. From the start, they had belonged to a hybrid agency—one that worked for the courts as well as the Department of Justice. The marshals had so many different duties that sharing one of them with the FBI was reasonable. The advent of so many other federal agencies with law enforcement powers, such as the Bureau of Narcotics (established in 1930) and its eventual successor, the Drug Enforcement Administration (1973), and the Internal Revenue Service (1918), further eroded the law-enforcement responsibilities of the marshals.[68]

But the marshals got other duties. Over the years, they were put in charge of the federal Witness Security Program, commonly referred to as the witness protection program, in which the government legalizes a person's disappearance. The marshals also continued their "hooking and hauling" duties of transferring inmates between federal prisons and to federal court, where the marshals still oversaw courtroom security.[69] The marshals also worked in a more centralized fashion. They got a national badge in 1941, which introduced more order to the ranks,[70] and the marshals got a headquarters in 1956 in Washington, D.C.

In 1969, more standardization arrived when the U.S. attorney general created the U.S. Marshals Service as a bureau in the Department of Justice. The president, with Senate confirmation, still appoints ninety-four marshals—one for each federal judicial district, except for the Virgin Islands, whose marshal the attorney general names.[71] But, since the creation of the U.S. Marshals Service, the attorney general has supervised the marshals through the director of the Marshals Service, who is an appointee of the attorney general. Deputy marshals are career civil service workers hired through the federal government's employment process.[72] As of 2017, the U.S. Marshals Service had a budget of $1.23 billion, with 5,238 total employees, including 3,709 deputy marshals and criminal investigators and 1,435 administrative employees and detention officers.[73] The FBI employs approximately 35,000 people and had a 2018 fiscal year budget of $8.7 billion.[74]

One of the biggest shifts for the U.S. Marshals Service and its relationship with the FBI came in 1979 in a memorandum of understanding between the two agencies. The attorney general's office signed off on the deal, which moved many of the FBI's responsibilities for fugitive apprehension to the marshals. "Not since the closing of the Old West," one historian has written of the arrangement, "had the U.S. [m]arshals handled a wide-ranging fugitive warrant program."[75] And as a 1986 report from the U.S. General Accounting Office, now the Government Accountability Office, stated in an analysis of the arrangement, "Although the Marshals Service has always had statutory responsibility to execute federal arrest warrants, prior to 1979 it did not have department authority to investigate fugitive cases. As a result, its fugitive efforts were limited, involving only those cases referred specifically to the Service by the courts or undertaken as thought appropriate by individual U.S. Marshals."[76] The deal made the U.S. Marshals Service principally responsible for capturing federal prison escapees, federal bond jumpers, and those who had violated federal probation or parole.

The FBI still retained extensive fugitive responsibilities under the deal. The FBI kept the authority to find offenders wanted as part of its investigations, as well as offenders who violated laws regarding unlawful flight to avoid prosecution, even if those fugitives were fleeing from state rather than federal charges. But the transfer of what had been many of the FBI's other fugitive-capturing duties to the U.S. Marshals Service was a boon to that agency's often muddled image. "The fugitive treaty with the FBI offered the marshals the avenue to escape their complete dependence on the courts and to prove their professionalism as law enforcement officers," one historian of the U.S. Marshals Service has written. "Now they could mount investigations, pursue the fugitives, and make the arrests."[77]

The shifting of duties, which was effective on October 1, 1979, was necessary because the FBI lacked the resources and the attention to focus on federal fugitives, which had come to number fifteen thousand by 1979. Budget cuts had limited the amount of money the FBI could devote to finding fugitives while it addressed mandates to investigate more cases of white-collar crime and organized crime, which Attorney General William H. Webster had designated as priorities. The move to shift more responsibilities to the U.S. Marshals Service, the FBI said in a statement at the time, meant the bureau's special agents could concentrate on "more complex investigations, such as white-collar crime, corruption of public officials, organized crime and foreign counterintelligence."[78] The budget cuts, the FBI also said, had left it with "less money to do more work."[79] The U.S. Marshals Service got the call.

The roundups started quickly. During the first year in which the U.S. Marshals Service led federal fugitive operations, marshals closed out 9,500 of the 15,000 outstanding fugitive warrants.[80] And to execute its newfound responsibilities further, the U.S. Marshals Service soon launched the kind of joint fugitive operations that remain a hallmark of the agency's work. The marshals in 1981 started the first Fugitive Investigation Strike Team, known as F.I.S.T., which operated in Miami, Florida.[81] The marshals worked with state and local police departments, whose officers were familiar with the area, to catch the most dangerous and violent fugitives. After the success of what was called F.I.S.T. I—seventy-six fugitives caught in Miami—the U.S. Marshals Service undertook a number of other F.I.S.T. operations in cities throughout the United States, including in the New York City area in late 1984. That effort lasted eight weeks, and marshals and police officers captured 3,309 fugitives wanted in eight states. "The largest and most successful fugitive manhunt in law-enforcement history," was how Attorney General William French Smith described the operation.[82]

In 1988, after the U.S. Marshals Service had worked on fugitive task forces for years, Congress further defined the service's fugitive-catching powers in the law that sets forth the powers and responsibilities of the service. Marshals and their deputies, according to the law, are empowered "to investigate such fugitive matters, both within and outside the United States, as directed by the Attorney General."[83] The FBI came to interpret the section as authorizing "the Attorney General to 'direct' the USMS to investigate fugitive matters to the fullest extent permitted by the Constitution in the exercise of [the Attorney General's] discretion"—even if the offense is not a federal crime, such as when marshals and their deputies are working on task forces with state and local police.[84]

The joint fugitive task forces became more formalized in 2000, when Congress in December of that year passed the Presidential Threat Protection Act, meant "to provide clearer coverage over threats against former Presidents and members of their families, and for other purposes."[85] The act, which became law on December 19, 2000, allocated federal funds for the U.S. Marshals Service to establish and coordinate, with federal, state, and local law-enforcement agencies, the operation of what became seven permanent Regional Fugitive Task Forces. They are designed to capture what the agencies consider their most dangerous fugitives, such as career offenders and those wanted for violent crimes, weapons offenses, felony drug offenses, and failure to register as a sex offender.[86] The Regional Fugitive Task Forces cover New York/New Jersey, based in New York City; Capital Area, in Washington, D.C.; Pacific Southwest, in Los Angeles; Great Lakes, in Chicago; Southeast, in Atlanta; Gulf Coast, in Birmingham, Alabama; and Florida/Caribbean, in Orlando, Florida.

Building on the regional concept, the U.S. Marshals Service also created local fugitive task forces, which now number sixty. Federal, state, and local police officers and agents also serve on those task forces, which focus on the capture of violent criminals and which act as clearinghouses for all the members to share information on fugitives. The non-federal officers who are members of the task forces are special deputy marshals, just as their predecessors in the Old West and elsewhere were special deputy marshals. The deputation allows the state and local police officers to cross state lines and exercise the authority of a U.S. marshal.[87]

For the FBI, the legal authority for its agents to get involved in the pursuit of fugitives, even if those fugitives have not crossed state lines or have not been accused of federal crimes, continues to be derived from the Fugitive Felon Act, or the Unlawful Flight to Avoid Prosecution law, known as UFAP. The date that Congress passed the law—May 18, 1934, as part of Roosevelt's New Deal crime package—was significant. The fatal shootout between the fugitive Dillinger gang and the federal Bureau of Investigation and the local police in Little Bohemia, Wisconsin, on April 23, 1934, proved to the federal government that a "twilight zone" of jurisdictional confusion was hindering the apprehension of fugitives during the great crime wave.[88] Local and state police were unsure of who had control of fugitives once they crossed state lines, and the agency that would soon be called the FBI had, at the time, no jurisdiction over fugitives accused of violating state crimes. But the rise of the automobile, which had transformed crimes like bank robbery into interstate offenses, contributed to what Roosevelt saw as the desperate need for the FBI to have power to track and capture fugitives, whether the underlying crime was a state or federal offense. The Fugitive Felon Act achieved that goal by making interstate flight to avoid prosecution for a state crime a federal offense in cases in which the underlying crime was, initially, an enumerated felony, such as murder, kidnapping, burglary, rape, or extortion accompanied by threats of violence.[89]

The act cleared up jurisdictional confusion. It also ended situations in which the local police in one state had to rely only on the local police in another state to apprehend a fugitive who had crossed state lines—a task that was often difficult because many local police forces were already dealing with high crime rates in their own jurisdictions. Under UFAP, the FBI is allowed to assist state and local police, at the police's request, in finding and apprehending fugitives. Also subject to arrest under UFAP are witnesses who have fled to another state to avoid testifying, creating circumstances in which "it was frequently necessary to postpone or dismiss local criminal prosecutions."[90]

The FBI's authority under the UFAP law expanded regularly since the passage of the original 1934 act, which listed the specific state felonies, such as murder and kidnapping, that had to be in play for the FBI to gain jurisdiction of the fugitive. Congress in 1946 amended the UFAP law to apply also to fugitives who had fled after a conviction for one of the enumerated felonies. Congress in 1956 added arson as an enumerated felony. And Congress in 1963 amended the act to delete the enumerated felonies "to make the act generally applicable to crimes defined as felonies by state law."[91] Under the revisions to the UFAP law, the FBI, in addition to having jurisdiction over federal fugitives, can also chase and apprehend any fugitive fleeing from prosecution for a state felony or fleeing after a conviction for a state felony, as well as any witness fleeing to avoid testifying in a state court.[92]

A fugitive is not required even to have crossed state lines for the FBI to get involved under the UFAP law. The UFAP statute, notably, does not require that a fugitive has entered another state. Rather, it prohibits, "persons from *moving or traveling in interstate commerce* [emphasis added] in order to avoid prosecution, confinement, or service of process in connection with felonies under the laws of the place from which flight is taken."[93] This legal leeway allows the jurisdiction seeking the FBI's help to show either that probable cause exists that a fugitive has fled the state or has the intention of fleeing the state—that the fugitive has taken steps that could lead to the reasonable conclusion that interstate flight is imminent. The attorney general established such a standard for the FBI in a February 21, 1995, memo on the scope of the Fugitive Felon Act, or FFA: "FBI agents have statutory authority to investigate state law fugitives whenever, as part of their evasive course of conduct, they have begun to travel on interstate highways or manifested any other reasonable indication (such as the purchase of a bus or airplane ticket to another state) that they will violate the FFA. . . . Consequently, the fact that a state fugitive has commenced evasive travel on the highways may sometimes establish that he is 'in the course' of interstate flight and therefore provide grounds for federal arrest under the FFA."[94]

The Department of Justice based its conclusion partly on its interpretation of the definition of interstate commerce as related to criminal activity. According to the memo, the "Supreme Court and lower federal court opinions . . . have adopted a flexible construction of the interstate movement element in federal criminal statutes similar to the FFA. . . . If a fugitive is 'in the course' of travel on the highways with an intent to proceed across the border, the mere failure to reach the border should not negate a violation of the statute."[95] The Department of Justice in the memo acknowledges potential issues with such an interpretation of interstate commerce as related to criminal acts, but the department said its interpretation is sound, under the correct circumstances. "Various courts have held that the crossing of state lines is a necessary element for a violation of the FFA," according to the memo. "However, the line separating a so-called 'non-federal' fugitive and a fugitive subject to federal pursuit under the FFA can be a thin one. Many fugitives will 'move' or 'travel' on interstate highways as they continue to evade arrest, even if they have not been detected crossing state lines. Under appropriate circumstances, such fugitives may be deemed to be moving in interstate commerce and there may well be a reasonable basis to believe that a violation of the FFA is in progress."[96] In any case, such an analysis could be considered academic in the end. If a fugitive who is the subject of a UFAP warrant crosses state lines, the FBI would have jurisdiction. If the fugitive does not cross state lines, the state or local police could take over jurisdiction instead and end the FBI's involvement. The Department of Justice memo outlines what needs to exist for the FBI to get a UFAP warrant to help local and state authorities find a fugitive.

The FBI also has discretion in what UFAP cases it must take. Under FBI procedures, the jurisdiction seeking a UFAP warrant, such as a county district attorney, must apply to the U.S. attorney within the judicial district where the fugitive's prosecution originated. The requester must show probable cause that the fugitive fled, and the requester must agree to pay extradition costs and to prosecute the fugitive for the underlying crime once the person is returned to the original jurisdiction. A U.S. district judge or U.S. magistrate judge then determines whether probable cause exists to issue a UFAP warrant and trigger the involvement of the FBI in the search for the fugitive.[97] The FBI typically seeks active UFAP cases by consulting with the local authorities and identifying which cases would fall under the law and "warrant FBI assistance."[98] Not all state felony fugitive cases qualify. The FBI classifies potential UFAP fugitives into four classifications, and typically works cases that involve the most serious state felonies. The categories are for violent crimes, such as murder and robbery; property crimes that involve more than $25,000 in goods or money, and narcotics investigations; parental kidnapping; and all other violations.[99]

When the FBI gets a UFAP warrant, the underlying crime still ultimately drives the prosecution of the fugitive. Under the UFAP law, a conviction for unlawful flight to avoid prosecution is punishable by up to five years in federal prison and a $5,000 fine. But U.S. attorneys rarely if ever prosecute fugitives for violating the UFAP law; indeed, prosecution for a UFAP law violation requires written approval from the attorney general, deputy attorney general, associate attorney general, or assistant attorney general.[100] Once the FBI or other agency captures a fugitive under a UFAP warrant, the U.S. attorney's office that got the warrant almost always withdraws the case even before the fugitive is arraigned on UFAP charges in U.S. District Court. The fugitive is released to the state or local authorities, who, as part of the UFAP agreement, must then pay for the fugitive's extradition and prosecute the fugitive in state court for the crime from which the person was fleeing. The UFAP law is designed not to put state fugitives in federal prison but to provide a mechanism for the FBI to use its vast resources to help local and state authorities find those on the lam.

The UFAP law has survived constitutional challenges, most of which echoed the objections to the expansion of federal law enforcement powers under President Roosevelt and Cummings, his New Deal attorney general. The federal courts have found the UFAP law's maximum penalties—five years in federal prison and a $5,000 fine—do not violate the Eighth Amendment prohibition against cruel and unusual punishment and excessive fines. And the courts have found the UFAP law does not violate the Tenth Amendment by impeding the extradition authority the Constitution grants to the states.[101] The UFAP law reflects the reliance that Congress and the courts have placed on the Commerce Clause of the Constitution to expand federal authority, whether in law enforcement or other areas.[102]

The UFAP law, in that regard, has succeeded in the fashion that Roosevelt and Cummings had hoped. Faced with a crumbling economy and rising crime, they sought ways for the federal government to come to the rescue in virtually every area of American life, including the prevention of crime. The dire circumstances, they said, warranted the expansion of federal powers beyond anything that Congress had considered. The federal government had been hindered in fighting crime, Cummings said, because most crimes were not federal offenses— even the crimes that gangsters such as John Dillinger and his crew were committing in Indiana, Ohio, Wisconsin, and other states in the Midwest.

"The desperado Dillinger, for example, whose deeds of bloodshed and violence have recently terrorized the Middle West, has, so far as we are able to ascertain, committed only one federal offense—the transportation of a stolen automobile from one state to another," Cummings said on May 12, 1934, as he continued to lobby for passage of the Roosevelt administration's package of anti-crime bills, including the Fugitive Felon Act. "The explanation for this lies in the fact that in our political system, the federal government possesses only those powers which are granted to it, explicitly or impliedly, by the Constitution. The Congress, therefore, is limited in the enactment of criminal statutes to those objects that are within the purview of the United States government, as defined in the Constitution." Cummings also said that the anti-crime bills that Congress had passed to date, including the law that made kidnapping a federal offense, showed that the federal government's efforts to fight crime were "meeting with heartening success."[103]

Five days later, on May 18, 1934, the Fugitive Felon Act became law. Also on that date, six members of Dillinger's gang—though not Dillinger himself, "the nation's No 1. bad man"[104] because he was by then America's first-ever Public Enemy Number One[105]—were suspected of using machine guns to hold up the Citizens Commercial and Savings Bank, in Flint, Michigan, of $30,000— about $560,000 in 2018 dollars. Five men stormed the bank while a woman sat in the getaway car with a machine gun on her lap. The gangster sped away and became fugitives. "With mystifying rapidity they dropped from sight," the Associated Press reported, "and a quickly organized pursuit by state police, local police and sheriff's officers was fruitless."[106]

The FBI and U.S. Marshals Service of today often work as a team, particularly when deputy marshals and FBI special agents join together on task forces. But, since the 1979 agreement that set forth their distinct fugitive-related duties, the two agencies have occasionally been at odds in Congress, as lawmakers have considered whether to shift more of the FBI's responsibilities to the marshals. The proposal came up in 1986, when the U.S. General Accounting Office issued its report that detailed the agencies' working arrangement. The report, which went to the Senate Judiciary Committee's Subcommittee on Security and Terrorism, summarized the debate in its title: "Who Should Be Responsible for State Fugitives—the FBI or U.S. Marshals?"[107]

But the 1979 agreement remains, with the FBI designated to track state fugitives under the UFAP. And the fugitive task forces bring the agencies together. The Justice Department allows FBI agents to serve as special deputy marshals and it allows regular deputy marshals to assist in the pursuit of state fugitives as part of the deputies' participation in fugitive task forces. The government has found that to have deputy marshals on these task forces but allow them only to pursue federal fugitives would be absurd and would defeat a task force's goal of having local, state, and federal agents work together. As the Justice Department found in the 1995 memo on the UFAP law, "Participation by federal marshals in cooperative federal-state task forces approved by the Attorney General to pursue and apprehend fugitive federal felons would appear to be a reasonable and necessary step to prevent violations of the FFA and other federal statutes. We do not think that such participation is rendered legally invalid, or constitutes an insupportable expansion of federal law enforcement authority, merely because it also entails the pursuit and arrest of state law fugitives as the *quid pro quo* that motivates the participation of state and local police in these operations. State and local governments cannot be expected to participate in these joint operations unless they receive reciprocal assistance in rounding up fugitives wanted under their laws and warrants."[108]

The separate but cooperative relationship between the FBI and the U.S. Marshals Service exists in another area: the agencies' promulgation of their own most-wanted lists. And though those pictured on the lists are different, the lists share the same goal: to find fugitives. As Timothy Pickering observed more than 220 years ago in the futile search for the murderers of Captain Andrew Peyton, one of the best ways to find fugitives is by advertising their names to the public.

3

THE SEARCH FOR "HANDSOME JOHNNY"

Public Enemies, John Dillinger, and the Birth of the Most-Wanted Lists

The fear of crime had grown so great in the United States by 1932 that some were calling for a return to a form of early Anglo-Saxon justice to defeat the gangsters and the bank robbers and the kidnappers. And this was even before John Dillinger's rampage in 1933 and 1934 made him a national fascination and turned him into the most influential person, next to J. Edgar Hoover, in the creation of the modern FBI, including its focus on finding dangerous fugitives. The nation had already wearied of the perception of unchecked lawlessness in 1932. President Herbert Hoover's invocation of states' rights had failed to persuade most Americans that expanding federal law enforcement powers would undermine the Constitution. So, like vigilantes, some called for empowering citizens to deal with criminals on their own. They wanted to bring back the early Anglo-Saxon custom of "outlawry"—used in the same system that featured the bot and the wite—in which someone was so wicked and incorrigible that the community declared the person outside the law and subject to summary justice, including execution. These criminals would be true outlaws—crooks so heinous as to be outside the protections of the regular legal system.

"In early English history, the proclamation of outlawry was the method of legalizing the killing by private persons of those who refused to submit themselves to the law," Gordon Evans Dean, a top official with the American Bar Association, wrote in 1932. "It was the duty of all citizens to pursue an outlaw and knock him on the head as though he were a wild beast."[1] Evans at the time was the assistant to the chairman of the American Bar Association's committee on law and criminology. He later was the head of public relations for Attorney

General Homer Cummings, who carried out President Roosevelt's New Deal war on crime and led the successful effort in 1934 to pass the Twelve Point Plan and the Crime Control Laws, such as those that made kidnapping and bank robbery federal crimes. When Dean wrote in 1932 of a desire to return to a system of outlawry, his was more of a symbolic request that expressed the general exasperation with Washington, D.C., and the wish that the federal government "do something to satisfy the public's demand for drastic action," historian Richard Gid Powers has written.[2] As Dean also wrote, in a remark that Powers noted as representative of Dean's view, "Kidnappers and other dangerous criminals have become so defiant in the United States that even conservative citizens are becoming convinced that eventually they must be suppressed summarily."[3]

Dean's type of mob justice never got the support of the federal government, though elements of outlawry—or at least elements of a popular belief that violent criminals should be publicly identified, caught, and punished—found their way into the criminal justice system in the 1930s. Instead of the outlaw, which was more of a moniker associated with the Old West, Americans got the outlaw's Depression-era equivalent: the public enemy, a category of criminal deemed so dangerous that the FBI had a special ranking for the worst of the worst: Public Enemy Number One. The first to get the top designation was John Dillinger, known as "Handsome Johnny" for his good looks, including his dimpled chin. The public enemy model of classifying and publicizing criminals would do much to influence the tools that the FBI and U.S. Marshals Service later created to find particularly violent offenders on the lam: the FBI's Ten Most Wanted Fugitives List and the U.S. Marshals Service's Fifteen Most Wanted, invented with the motto "The Hunt is On."

The creation of the term "public enemy," and especially its elevation to a universal mark of notoriety in the United States, was based both in fact and politics. The phrase is generally believed to have been coined in Chicago in 1930. The president of the Chicago Crime Commission, Frank J. Loesch, a well-known lawyer and former state's attorney for Cook County, Illinois, created a list of "public enemies" to help law enforcement curb the violence that was escalating with the likes of Al Capone. He was the top criminal on the public enemies list that the Chicago Crime Commission released in May 1930; twenty-seven other names were on the list, "most of them gaining affluence and influence during the bootleg era."[4] Also around this time, the New York newspapers began referring to the most wanted bootlegger in that city, Irving "Waxey" Gordon, as "Public Enemy Number One."[5] But the public enemies list took hold even more in Chicago, where Loesch created his ledger of lawbreakers a year after the Valentine's

Day Massacre of 1929, in which seven men believed to have been connected to Capone dressed as policemen and gunned down seven men associated with Capone's archrival, gangster George "Bugs" Moran. "The purpose," Loesch said in a letter on why he had the Chicago Crime Commission create the list, "is to keep the light of publicity shining on Chicago's most prominent, well-known, and notorious gangsters to the end that they may be under constant observation by law enforcing authorities and the law-abiding citizens."[6]

The Chicago Crime Commission, which continues to exist, formed in 1919 as a business association dedicated to stamping out violence and public corruption while supporting the police. The Chicago Association of Commerce created the commission, whose members were a hundred Chicago lawyers, bankers, and business leaders. They had their own staff of investigators, statisticians, and clerks.[7] With its large membership and firm structure, the commission represented a model for similar private crime-fighting organizations that sprang up throughout the United States before and after Prohibition (January 1920–December 1933)—an early signal that the public believed the official response to crime inadequate long before the great crime wave of 1933 and 1934. By the early 1930s, crime had become the equivalent of a public health crisis, and groups like the Chicago Crime Commission were seen as advocating for a cure—a cure that, though not quite sanctioning outlawry, still relied on public identification and pursuit of criminals as ways to keep the peace at home and on the streets. The Chicago Crime Commission and its equivalents in cities throughout the United States represented vigilantism in its most button-downed form. The members were legitimate and concerned businessmen committed to subduing their underworld brethren. "Modern crime, like modern business, is tending toward centralization, organization, and commercialization," said the director of the Chicago Crime Commission in 1919, Colonel Henry Barrett Chamberlin. "Ours is a business nation. Our criminals apply business methods. The men and women of evil have formed trusts."[8]

In addition to the Public Enemies List, the Chicago Crime Commission's most notable creation was what was known as the Secret Six, formally known as the commission's Subcommittee for the Prevention and Punishment of Crime. The identities of its members were kept secret, hence the nickname, but the Secret Six's influence on the police and public was well known. The Secret Six applied the pressure that prompted the federal government to send Eliot Ness and his "Untouchables"—a team of Prohibition agents—to Chicago to take on Capone, who famously ended up going to prison for tax evasion rather than racketeering and murder. As Richard Gid Powers has detailed, other cities developed their own groups similar to the Secret Six,[9] including the New York

City Board of Trade, which formed its Secret Six in 1931. In September of that year, in an illustration of the national hysteria over crime, Colonel Isham Randolph, the apparently not-so-secret head of the Chicago Secret Six, declared that "one large country-wide body of super-criminals" was responsible for most of the bank robberies, kidnappings, and other major crimes throughout the nation.[10] "The gang is said to include as many as 148 killers, located throughout the United States," Randolph declared.[11] The Secret Six movement went national on December 18, 1930, with the creation of the Anti-Gang Rule League of America Inc., based in New York City. Its charter declared its mission to include the development of "efficient police methods in so far as these pertain to the control and elimination of criminal, disorderly and disloyal associations, gangs and mobs and all their members."[12]

The Chicago Crime Commission's first Public Enemies List did not just feature fugitives, bail jumpers, or even those accused of crimes. Capone, at the top of the list, had yet to be charged in May 1930. His appearance, like the appearance of others on the list, recognized the influence that Capone and the others, whether under prosecution or not, had on the quality of life in Chicago, a place where the police were also under widespread suspicion for abetting or being a part of the criminal element. Also on the list were those Chicago crime figures who had violated the city's newly passed "public enemy laws," which outlawed vagrancy and other low-level crimes but were meant to force more criminals, real or suspected, out of the city, despite the questionable constitutionality of the statutes. A public enemy law that went on the books in New York in 1931, for instance, applied to anyone "engaged in some illegal occupation or who bears an evil reputation."[13] Judges usually dismissed such cases, though lawmakers could tout that they had passed the public enemy laws to do their part to clean up their communities.[14] In 1930 in Chicago, of the twenty-eight people who appeared on the Chicago Crime Commission's first Public Enemies List, seven were classified as fugitives from vagrancy warrants. Among those seven was none other than George "Bugs" Moran.[15]

By 1931, the figure of the public enemy, no matter what the crime, had turned into the newest American icon. Hollywood bestowed the status in *The Public Enemy*, released in April 1931 and starring James Cagney as Tommy Powers, a hoodlum who rises to gangland prominence in Chicago during Prohibition. Cagney's charismatic Powers is unapologetic in his lawbreaking and rage. Tommy Powers thrilled audiences, as Richard Gid Powers has observed, "because of his criminality, not in spite of it."[16] Earlier films had prepared moviegoers for the subversive anti-hero that Powers exemplified. *Little Caesar*, released in January 1931, all but invented the gangster-film genre[17] with Edward

G. Robinson's portrayal of Caesar Enrico "Rico" Bandello, a character modeled on Al Capone. Robinson's Little Caesar starts out as a small-time crook and ends up ruling the Chicago underworld and becoming more powerful than the police and other institutions that were supposed to prevent his rise. The role of Little Caesar made Robinson a star and signaled the arrival of a new American myth—the tale of the gangster, the self-made man (and the gangsters were men) who built an empire on vice and violence. *The Public Enemy* expanded the formula with even greater success, and Hollywood churned out more gangster films, despite the establishment, in 1931, of the Motion Picture Production Code, the predecessor of the current Motion Picture Association of America rating system. Not until 1934 did the Production Code develop into a moral force for regulating the content of movies. Until then, movies like *The Public Enemy* thrived and made the public enemy a familiar, if sometimes even admirable, character to millions of Americans. What they saw on the movie screens mirrored what they read in the newspapers and watched on the newsreels: Crime and public enemies were overrunning the country and outgunning the police. "The New Deal's war on crime was the moviemaker's salvation."[18]

Taking down those public enemies remained the goal of the Chicago Crime Commission and its list. The commission's success in battling the ranked criminals, combined with the continuing national concern over crime, led Loesch, the head of the commission, to make a bold request on October 7, 1933. He sent a letter to Attorney General Cummings urging the Justice Department to create a national public enemies list. Loesch's proposal included suggestions that would eventually be implemented with the FBI's most-wanted list. The national public enemies list, Loesch wrote to Cummings, "would be of great public service." He also wrote, "The Department of Justice can name a large number of professional criminals, including kidnappers, bank robbers, counterfeiters and burglars, whose operations are extensive and cover many sections of the country. This list would make available their names, criminal records, photographs and fingerprints. In this way the local authorities and the public generally would be able to join effectively in a campaign against these enemies of society."[19]

Homer Cummings's Justice Department initially did not adopt a national public enemies list, at least formally. And when J. Edgar Hoover eventually appropriated the phrase of Public Enemy Number One, he did so more as a public relations strategy than as a way to inform the public about the most dangerous criminals stalking their sidewalks, robbing their banks, and fleeing on their roads. In July 1933, when he announced plans to push Congress to pass what would become the Twelve Point Plan's Crime Control Laws, Cummings used the phrase "public enemy" to allude to a military-like force of gangsters and criminals who, much like a hostile foreign power, were enemies of the American way of life. The massive effort against racketeering, Cummings said, "is almost like a military engagement between the forces of law and order and the underworld army, heavily armed. It is a campaign to wipe out the public enemy and it will proceed until it succeeds."[20]

Months after Cummings gave his speech, the public enemy had become personified. The attorney general of Illinois by the end of 1933 had labeled John Dillinger Public Enemy Number One, using the parlance that the Chicago Crime Commission had invented, though the federal government's public enemies, unlike the commission's, had all been charged or convicted of crimes and were on the run. By the early summer of 1934, as large-scale shootouts and bank robberies continued to plague the nation, J. Edgar Hoover was said to have declared Dillinger what was then the federal Division of Investigation's[21] first-ever Public Enemy Number One. Hoover made the announcement on June 22, 1934, Dillinger's thirty-first birthday.[22] A month later, Dillinger would be killed in spectacular fashion and Hoover would replace his name with that of a new Public Enemy Number One: the bank robber Charles "Pretty Boy" Floyd. Hoover's agents gunned him down on a farm near East Liverpool, Ohio, on October 22, 1934, dubbed "The Year of the Gangster" because of his deaths and those of many other glamorous thugs.

Dillinger, Floyd, and the other notorious fugitives received more mundane numbers during the eras well. Even as the public enemies list moved to the forefront, the FBI never abandoned the system of identification orders (IOs), which it started in December 1919 to assist in the search for William N. Bishop, the Army deserter. By the 1930s, the FBI was sending IOs to police stations nationwide as tools to catch and identify those on the lam. The IOs were not as dramatic as the public enemies list, but they could be just as effective because of their thoroughness. Every major escaped criminal had an IO. Among them: Dillinger (IO 1217), Pretty Boy Floyd (IO 1194), Machine Gun Kelly (IO 1203), Baby Face Nelson (IO 1223), and Bonnie Parker and Clyde Barrow (appropriately, the pair shared an IO number: 1227).[23]

The FBI's public enemies list—and IO flyers, for that matter—seemed endless, for a time. Yet, according to the FBI, the creation and dissemination of the public enemies list stopped short of being part of an official publicity campaign to catch fugitives, even as J. Edgar Hoover readily linked the FBI to the list and though the agency never disavowed it. The FBI today acknowledges that the bureau and the Department of Justice in the 1930s made use of the term "public enemy"—which the FBI describes as synonymous with "fugitive" or "notorious gangster"—in "speeches, books, press releases, and internal memoranda. However, neither the FBI nor the Department had any type of publicity program which concentrated on a 'Public Enemy' number 1, number 2, etc."[24] Though this is the official line, Hoover nonetheless tagged Dillinger and then others with the moniker of infamy—"Public Enemy Number One"—and Hoover did so to raise the profile of both the criminal and his nascent FBI. Also clear is that the FBI's public enemies list, borrowed from the Chicago Crime Commission, eventually turned into the FBI's most-wanted list.[25]

In the end, the public enemies list appeared to be based in both fact and fiction. Hoover appropriated it for the FBI while not endorsing it; the bureau referred to having "10,000 public enemies" to battle, not just one or twenty, as if to emphasize how criminals were overrunning the country. And the press, driven to a frenzy to cover the likes of John Dillinger and the government's response to him, reveled in the creation of a criminal so larger than life that he became known as Public Enemy Number One—an unquestioned foe of the state and of law and order. The press was giving the public what it wanted, which reaffirmed its suspicions that crime in the United States had become an uncontrollable scourge: "Throughout the thirties the public believed that there *was* a public enemies list, although Cummings and Hoover, sensitive to the fact that they were ignoring the vast majority of criminals to concentrate on a few celebrities, steadfastly denied that there was a scoreboard," Richard Gid Powers has written. "All '10,000 Public Enemies,' they insisted, were being chased just as hard as Dillinger. The public enemies list does seem to be a creation of Justice Department reporters who borrowed the idea from the Chicago Crime Commission's famous list, because not until the fifties did the bureau itself begin its own 'Most Wanted Fugitive Program.'"[26]

The FBI and its most-wanted list would not exist in their modern form without John Dillinger. He gave the FBI purpose, which yielded political clout, which allowed J. Edgar Hoover to build a power base and a structure for an organization that would become the premier crime-fighting agency in the United States. Before Dillinger's crime spree, the Lindbergh baby kidnapping, and the equally infamous case of the Kansas City Massacre represented the events that had most driven Hoover and then Cummings and President Roosevelt to call for more federal authority in battling crime. Roosevelt calmed the Depression-weary nation by declaring, in his First Inaugural Address, on March 3, 1933, "The only thing we have to fear is fear itself."[27] Cummings used similar language—almost messianic in its terminology—to portray the New Deal war on crime and criminals as an epic and exhausting clash between good and evil. "We are engaged in a grim business which will tax our courage and our resourcefulness to the very limit," Cummings said in one speech. "In that sense the fight has just begun, and with your support and confidence it cannot fail."[28] And as for those who disagreed that the Constitution allowed for the expansion of federal powers, whether economic or justice-related, as part of the New Deal, Cummings said in a radio address, "In this great hour those who despair, or hang back, or lose their courage, or fail to lend aid, or seek to thwart the purposes of their government, are depriving themselves of the high privilege of rejoicing when the triumph comes and are forgetting the history of America."[29]

The Lindbergh kidnapping, known as the crime of the century, took years to solve but had an immediate effect on the nation's psyche. Charles A. Lindbergh Jr., the twenty-month-old son of renowned aviator Charles A. Lindbergh, was snatched from the family's home in Hopewell, New Jersey, on March 1, 1932, and found dead on May 12, 1932. Congress acted in June 1932. At the urging of J. Edgar Hoover, it passed the Federal Kidnapping Act, known as the Lindbergh Law, which made kidnapping a federal crime, though federal jurisdiction was triggered only if authorities proved the kidnapping victim had crossed state lines. The law was not retroactive, so the state police in New Jersey retained jurisdiction over the Lindbergh kidnapping, though the FBI coordinated the probe. It led to the arrest of carpenter Bruno Hauptmann in September 1934; he was convicted in 1935 and executed in 1936. By then, the Lindbergh Law had been strengthened with passage of the Crime Control Laws of 1934. One of the laws outlawed, on the federal level, the transportation of kidnapping victims across state lines, with the presumption that such a transfer occurs if the kidnapping victim is not returned within seven days.

The Kansas City Massacre, like the Lindbergh kidnapping, remains one of the defining moments in the history of crime in the United States. Killed in the gunfight, on June 17, 1933, were the FBI's Raymond J. Caffrey along with three other lawmen—two police officers and a police chief—as well as escaped bank robber Frank "Jelly" Nash, whose nickname was slang for the explosive nitroglycerine. Caffrey and the others were escorting Nash, by train, from Hot Springs, Arkansas, where he had been captured, to Kansas City, Missouri. From there, the contingent was to drive Nash to the federal penitentiary at Leavenworth, Kansas, thirty miles from Kansas City; Nash had escaped from Leavenworth three years earlier. The train trip went as planned. But Nash, Caffrey, and the others were killed in a spray of machine-gun fire as the group of lawmen transferred Nash from the train station in Kansas City to an armor-plated car that Caffrey was driving. Investigators suspected Nash's bank-robbery cohorts, led by underworld figure Verne Miller, were behind the shooting to silence Nash, though the identities of all those responsible that day remain a mystery.[30] Adam Richetti, a partner of Pretty Boy Floyd's, was the only person convicted in the case, and he was sentenced to death and executed. Miller and Floyd were executed in a more unofficial fashion. Floyd, who denied involvement in the Kansas City Massacre,[31] was killed in the shootout in East Liverpool, Ohio, in October 1934, and, a month later, Miller was found dead in a drainage ditch in Detroit.

Caffrey's death in the Kansas City Massacre in 1933 helped ignite the calls of Roosevelt and Cummings for stricter federal anti-crime laws, with Hoover also leading the effort. Cummings considered the killing of Caffrey, "a Department of Justice man," as "outright defiance of a governmental agency which gangdom has long respected."[32] The day after Caffrey's death, the newspapers reported how further expansion of federal law enforcement powers was the logical progression of the actions the government had already undertaken: "The government's activities against criminals have been broadened in recent years from the original endeavor to prevent counterfeiting and internal revenue evasion to cover numerous other activities."[33] With Caffrey's killing, the federal government more than ever "was moving toward stamping out racketeers and gunmen."[34]

The most prominent of those gunmen was John Dillinger, the nemesis of J. Edgar Hoover. The fiasco at Little Bohemia, Wisconsin, in which Dillinger and his crew escaped from the FBI agents on the night of April 23, 1934, nearly cost Hoover his job. He failed to help his situation by putting his hubris on full display: While monitoring the raid on Little Bohemia from his office in Washington, D.C., Hoover told reporters to prepare to write stories on Dillinger's capture.[35] Hoover had reason to be confident. An informant had told the FBI that Dillinger and his gang would be holed up at Little Bohemia, a lodge near Mercer, in northern Wisconsin, that long had been a hideout for criminal organizations. Hoover sent Melvin Purvis, the head of the FBI's Chicago office and one of his best agents, to find Dillinger. Purvis and his band of agents appeared ready to surprise Dillinger at Little Bohemia when a dog barked as the men were approaching the lodge. Purvis mistakenly thought the dog had warned Dillinger and his gang of the raid, so the agents started firing. The gunfire, not the barking dog, ended up alerting Dillinger and the rest of his gang, who jumped out of windows and escaped, firing as they fled. The fiercest member of Dillinger's crew, George "Baby Face" Nelson, gunned down FBI Special Agent W. Carter Baum. A bystander was also killed, but not John Dillinger—the most wanted fugitive in the United States at the time, and expert bank robber and prison breakout artist who once boasted that there was no jail in the country strong enough to hold him.[36]

U.S. Marshal E. D. Nix declared in 1894 that he wanted the members of the Doolin and Dalton gangs brought in "dead or alive." The federal government's response to Dillinger's escape from Little Bohemia conveyed the same grim message: As far as the Justice Department was concerned, Dillinger was better off dead. "I don't know where or when we will get Dillinger, but we will get him," Assistant Attorney General Joseph B. Keenan said after the disaster at Little Bohemia. "And you can say for me I hope we will get him under such circumstances that the Government won't have to stand the expense of a trial."[37] Homer Cummings was more direct. The policy with Dillinger, he said, was, "Shoot to kill—and then count to ten."[38]

If he were brought in alive, "Handsome Johnny" would remain a threat to the FBI because he could always escape again and could always unleash more embarrassment on J. Edgar Hoover, Melvin Purvis, and the rest of the special agents. Dillinger's inherent danger, as a fugitive, was that he would weaken the Justice Department and Americans' confidence in Hoover's vaunted crime fighters as long as Dillinger was on the lam. On March 3, 1934, less than a month before the shootout at Little Bohemia, Dillinger turned into laughingstocks the jailers, sheriff, and prosecutor in Crown Point, Indiana. He escaped from the Crown Point Jail, in Lake County, a prison that had been declared escape-proof, by using a fake gun he had made out of wood and blackened with shoe polish.

About a month earlier, in one of the most famous photographs of an American criminal, Dillinger laughed and smiled with the sheriff of Lake County, Indiana, Lillian Holley, and the man responsible for prosecuting him, Robert G. Estill. The photographer snapped the picture on January 30, 1934, when Dillinger was transported to the Crown Point Jail after being caught in Arizona, where he was wanted for the January 15 bank robbery of the First National Bank of East Chicago, Indiana, north of Crown Point. Dillinger was accused of getting away with $20,000 and with fatally shooting a local police officer, William O'Malley, whose return fire did nothing to penetrate Dillinger's bulletproof vest. With the bank robbery in East Chicago, Dillinger had also become a murderer as well as a thief. His dangerousness made his escape from the Crown Point Jail that much more infuriating and demoralizing. And his escape further illustrated the incompetence that had been immortalized in the photo that was taken when he entered the Crown Point Jail—officials of the law laughing with the heartless Dillinger as if at a picnic. The photo enraged Homer Cummings, who said he would have removed Estill and Holley from office if he had the authority to do so. "Such disgraceful conduct, such negligence, violated all canons of common sense and made law enforcement doubly hard," Cummings said.[39]

The careers of Holley and Estill were ruined. Holley resigned in April and Estill was voted out of office in May.[40]

Hoover wanted to avoid a similar fate after Little Bohemia. Dillinger's escape from the Crown Point Jail on March 3, 1934, had allowed the FBI to take over jurisdiction of his case. Dillinger was accused of fleeing in Sheriff Holley's police car, which he stole from the prison and that he and his gang drove across state lines, from Indiana to Illinois, where they headed to Chicago. The car was later recovered and Dillinger was indicted in federal court. Interstate travel in a stolen car had been a federal offense since 1919 under the Motor Vehicle Theft Act, or the Dyer Act, after its sponsor, Congressman Leonidas C. Dyer, of Missouri. Application of the Dyer Act was instrumental in the Dillinger case at a time when Congress was two months away from passing the Crime Control Laws that made bank robbery and other offenses federal crimes. The Dyer Act turned out to be Hoover's tool to get Dillinger, even as Dillinger was accused of killing the police officer in East Chicago in January and even as his gang continued to rob banks in violent fashion. Dillinger is believed to have carried out as many as fourteen bank heists in 1933 and 1934, plus three escapes from prison.

After the embarrassment at Little Bohemia, the federal government came at Dillinger hard, especially following the passage of the Crime Control Laws in May and June of 1934. Homer Cummings on June 23, 1934, announced rewards of $10,000 for Dillinger's capture and $5,000 for the capture of Baby Face Nelson, wanted for killing Special Agent Baum at Little Bohemia. (The $10,000 reward is the equivalent of about $187,000 today.) Cummings was authorized to act under the Federal Reward Bill, which President Roosevelt signed on June 6, 1934, and which allowed the Justice Department to offer rewards of up to $25,000 for assistance in capturing anyone charged with violating federal laws. The act was informally known as the "The Public Enemy Bill,"[41] but Congress officially described it as an Act to Authorize an Appropriation of Money to Facilitate the Apprehension of Certain Persons Charged with Crime.[42]

By putting up the rewards (some considered them to be bounties[43]), Cummings had turned Dillinger and Nelson into the most wanted fugitives in the United States. The announcement made the front page of the *New York Times*. The report declared, "By this action, taken under crime curb legislation adopted by Congress in its closing days, the Department of Justice hopes to give new impetus to the hunt for the two fugitive outlaws, trace of whom has been lacking for several months. This is the first time, according to officials, that the Department of Justice has taken such a step."[44] Dillinger and Baby Face Nelson, whose given name was Lester M. Gillis, were described as "desperadoes" and the worst of the criminal element. "Dillinger is held to be the most desperate outlaw of his time and Nelson one of the most dangerous members of his gang," the article stated. "For these reasons the first rewards under the new act are offered for their capture."[45]

The Justice Department circulated five hundred thousand wanted posters, dated June 25, 1934,[46] notifying the public of the rewards. Though the first of their kind for the FBI, the posters recalled the most-wanted placards that were fixtures when marshals and others searched for fugitives in the Old West. J. Edgar Hoover's name was on the bottom of the Justice Department's posters, which featured photos of Dillinger and Nelson and which detailed what Cummings had stated in the newspaper articles. The Justice Department and the FBI were offering $10,000 for information that led to Dillinger's capture, $5,000 for information that led to Dillinger's arrest, $5,000 for information that led to Nelson's capture, and $2,500 for information that led to Nelson's arrest. The posters and newspaper articles also described the fugitives and listed their crimes, establishing a template that continues to this day. The description for Dillinger: "Age, 31 years; height, 5 feet 7½ inches; weight, 153 pounds; build, medium; hair, medium chestnut; eyes, gray; complexion, medium; occupation, machinist; marks and scars: ½ inch scar back left hand, scar middle upper lip, brown mole between eyebrows; mustache."[47] For Nelson: "Age, 25 years; height, 5 feet, 4½ inches; weight, 133 pounds; build, medium; eyes, yellow and gray slate; hair, light chestnut; complexion, light; occupation, oiler."[48]

Though Cummings and the press emphasized the groundbreaking aspect of posting reward money for Dillinger and Nelson, Cummings and the press, oddly, played down the idea that Dillinger and Nelson were public enemies. On June 22, 1934, according to a number of accounts, J. Edgar Hoover declared Dillinger Public Enemy Number One, and so did Cummings.[49] But a *New York Times* article published on June 24, 1934, made no mention of Hoover's appellation of Dillinger and suggested that such a "public enemy" designation would be contrary to federal practice, as would any call for the government to bring in a fugitive "dead or alive." According to the *Times*, "The announcement by Attorney General Cummings refrained from any mention of the men as 'public enemies,' as this phrase was deleted from the law by which Congress authorized the offer of rewards, aggregating $25,000. The department announcement also carefully avoided using the term 'dead or alive,' stating that the rewards were for arrest."[50] Cummings and others in the Justice Department were known to have called for Dillinger to be killed if necessary. But making such a plea in private and announcing it in public are two different matters, and Cummings, even working with a compliant press, likely would have never considered telling the public that the federal government endorsed treating Dillinger like a true outlaw and subject to summary execution. Perhaps Cummings dealt with the public enemy designation the same way: He had no qualms with Hoover labeling Dillinger as a national threat but did not want to trumpet the designation too much and risk sounding desperate or defeated at the hands of Dillinger. The media played a role as well, of course. Because even if J. Edgar Hoover never publicly identified Dillinger as Public Enemy Number One, the newspapers did so, contemporaneous to when Cummings announced the $10,000 reward: "Newspapers," according to one account, "began calling Dillinger 'Public Enemy Number One' because the law Cummings referred to was dubbed informally the 'Public Enemy Bill.'"[51]

In any case, by declaring Dillinger the first-ever national Public Enemy Number One on June 22, 1934, Hoover raised Dillinger's profile, which made his attempts to hide more difficult. But the designation also added to Dillinger's burgeoning reputation as a kind of criminal folk hero who robbed from the same banks whose practices, in the popular imagination, had contributed to a much larger evil—the Great Depression. In addition, a personal injustice is said to have motivated Dillinger. When he was twenty-one years old, he was charged with helping in the armed holdup of a grocer in Dillinger's hometown of Mooresville, Indiana, near Indianapolis. Though Dillinger confessed and pleaded guilty, he got a stiffer sentence than his accomplice, who fought the charges and was convicted at trial. Dillinger was furious while he sat in prison, where he learned to rob banks and plotted a life of crime once he was paroled in 1933, when he was thirty years old.[52]

Dillinger robbed banks, which were villains to ordinary people during the Depression. Dillinger believed the justice system had wronged him. For these reasons, Dillinger went on to become, like Jesse James and even Robin Hood, a "noble robber" or "a social bandit," a widely admired criminal who engendered sympathy while he was on the run.[53] By putting Dillinger's face on most-wanted posters, and even on targets[54] at the FBI's shooting range, Hoover made Dillinger even more notorious. A fugitive's appearance on a most-wanted poster signifies two things: that the fugitive is dangerous and that the fugitive is smart enough and quick-witted enough to outmaneuver law enforcement, including the FBI's fleet of special agents. In this regard, Dillinger was like Al Capone, the Chicago Crime Commission's first-ever Public Enemy Number One. By giving the powerful gangster and racketeer such a notable if not inglorious title, the Crime Commission elevated Capone's status. The label Public Enemy Number One, as applied to Capone, "struck a chord in a nation racked by the Depression, and Capone now became the scapegoat for all sorts of social ills," Capone biographer Laurence Bergreen has written. "No longer was he indulged as a symptom of these ills; he was now perceived as the *cause*. Thanks to Loesch's publicity stunt, Al Capone became the first great American criminal of the twentieth century, and as befits a modern criminal, he was an organization man, not a highway robber or a lone killer, but a racketeer, the leader of an illegal fraternity."[55] Thanks to J. Edgar Hoover and the FBI's publicity stunt—adopting a national public enemies list, and making John Dillinger the first Public Enemy Number One—Dillinger became the second great American criminal of the twentieth century, whose notoriety was even greater than Capone's. The peerless gangster had a stranglehold on one city, Chicago. Dillinger, with his gang of bank robbers serving as another illegal fraternity, plundered the entire Midwest.

Dillinger's expanded fame changed his behavior in radical fashion. He tried to erase his features. He wanted to avoid being recognized as *the* John Dillinger, the "Handsome Johnny," whose face was plastered all over the most-wanted posters. Dillinger, if caught, also wanted to avoid being identified as the most famous bank robber in the country. On May 27, 1934, Dillinger traded in vanity for survival. He and one of his closest partners, Homer Van Meter, had two underworld-connected doctors perform plastic surgery on them at the home of underworld figure Jimmy Probasco in Chicago. Dillinger and Van Meter each paid $5,000 to undergo the back-alley operations, which included the obliteration of their fingerprints; one of the doctors cut off the skin on their fingertips and treated the remains with hydrochloric acid.[56] The work on Dillinger's face was just as drastic. The doctors removed the mole between his eyes, "cut the cheek along the ear and the edge of the jaw and transported some of the flesh to the dimple on the chin. Finally they tightened up the cheeks with kangaroo tendons."[57]

Dillinger had reason to undergo the transformation. The public was watching for him, even outside the United States. In one case, which occurred around June 19, 1934, the landlord of an inn at Stratford-on-Avon in England told authorities that four new American lodgers were Dillinger and his gang. They turned out to be Americans visiting England as Rhodes scholars at Oxford University.[58] Dillinger was still at large, and still robbing banks. On June 30, 1934, he and his crew, including Homer Van Meter and Baby Face Nelson, stole $29,890 from the Merchants National Bank in South Bend, Indiana; killed was a South Bend police officer, Howard Wagner, a murder attributed to Van Meter.[59] It was Dillinger's first bank robbery since his plastic surgery. It would be his final heist overall.

The cosmetic changes failed to make Handsome Johnny disappear. They might have made Dillinger less recognizable to the public, but they did nothing to prevent an informant, a person who knew him well, from alerting police and triggering Dillinger's demise. The informant was the madam of an Indiana brothel who went by the name Anna Sage and whose real name was Ana Cump-anas. Seeking some of the reward money for Dillinger's capture, and to avoid deportation to Romania, she tipped off the authorities; one of her boarders was a waitress named Polly Hamilton, who was Dillinger's girlfriend. Sage said she, Hamilton, and Dillinger planned to see the gangster-themed movie *Manhattan Melodrama*, starring William Powell, Clark Gable, and Myrna Loy—Gable plays a gangster who dies in the electric chair in the end—at one of two Chicago theaters the night of July 22, 1934. Melvin Purvis was still heading the FBI's Chicago office and had help in finding Dillinger from Special Agent Samuel A. Cowley, whom Hoover had assigned to lead the task force to find the world-famous fugitive. Purvis, Cowley and other agents, working undercover, staked out the two theaters and quickly determined that Dillinger was at the Biograph Theater. Purvis saw Anna Sage outside "wearing an orange skirt that looked blood red in the lights of the marquee."[60] Sage, who betrayed the first national Public Enemy Number One, would be forever known as "the woman in red."[61] She stayed in the United States and received $5,000 from Cowley on behalf of the government.[62]

The capture of Dillinger immortalized Purvis as well. He and Cowley and the other agents had the Biograph surrounded when Dillinger, Sage, and Hamilton left the theater at about half past ten on the night of July 22, 1934. Dillinger got suspicious and started to run and refused to surrender when Purvis yelled at him. The Justice Department said Dillinger pulled out his .38-caliber Colt automatic pistol and was shot to death when three special agents—Charles B. Winstead, Clarence O. Hurt, and Herman E. Hollis—opened fire. Two bullets grazed Dillinger. Another struck him in the left side, and another in the neck, with that bullet exiting just under his right eye—the fatal wound.[63] Two bystanders, both women, were shot and injured. Purvis finally got his man, and so did Hoover, who got word of Dillinger's death in a phone call from Purvis shortly after the shooting. "The most determined and wary killer on the continent," according to one report of the shooting, "had paid his last debt to society."[64]

Though he was in Washington, D.C., Hoover forever saw himself as an active participant in the capture of America's most wanted criminal and fugitive. From that point on, and until he died, while FBI director, on May 2, 1972, Hoover had a death mask of Dillinger's face on display at the FBI's headquarters in Washington. D.C.[65]—a 2.8 million square-foot structure that Congress named after Hoover in October 1972. The massive building was the house that J. Edgar Hoover built using the political power he accrued over forty-eight years as head of the FBI. If Hoover was at risk of losing his job when Dillinger escaped at Little Bohemia, when Hoover was in his tenth year of heading what would become the FBI, Hoover regained his stature with Dillinger's death. And he never stopped talking about Dillinger and other public enemies whose capture burnished the FBI's image. Hoover did all he could to dismantle what he considered the Dillinger myth, built around the injustice that the bank robber and killer was said to have experienced when he was sentenced for the armed holdup of the grocer at age twenty-one. "After the demise of John Dillinger," Hoover said, "many trusting souls came to his defense on the basis that he had been embittered by a long sentence for burglary while his companion in crime was given a shorter one. This was not true. Dillinger was a cheap, boastful, selfish, tight-fisted pug-ugly who thought only of himself."[66] Dillinger, for Hoover, was in no way handsome. And the head of the FBI was just as obsessed with Dillinger when the Public Enemy Number One was dead as when he was alive.

"Hoover had a thing about Dillinger," one of his assistant directors said. "If he were alive today and you went to see him, he would tell you about Dillinger, Ma Barker, and all those old cases of the thirties."[67] Another assistant director told Richard Gid Powers how critical the Dillinger case was to the FBI's success under Hoover. "We did the job," the assistant director said. "We got the Dillingers and the Machine Gun Kellys."[68]

Though it publicly said it did not endorse the creation of a public enemies list, the FBI played up its success in capturing fugitives like Dillinger; the pursuit of public enemies became embroidered into the bureau's image. A two-page *New York Times* story about the FBI that was published on October 28, 1934, and clearly had Hoover's cooperation, heralded in its headline the "Men Who Track Down the 'Public Enemy.'"[69] The agents are near mythic in their abilities. "They have shot down so many gangsters that the representative of the genus homo whom Hoover calls 'a yellow coyote' is beginning to fear them more than anything in the world," wrote the reporter, Russell Owen. He then quoted Hoover as saying, "The only thing these gangsters fear is death. They don't mind jails, because they can get out of them or be released on parole—the biggest racket in the country. But they fear a man who meets them with a gun and can shoot quicker and straighter than they do. People said I gave orders not to bring in Dillinger alive. I did not. Dillinger tried to pull a gun. Only three shots were fired and every one hit him in the head."[70]

Hoover in the article emphasized innovations he introduced to the FBI: fingerprint and handwriting analysis and other scientific-based methods of crime detection; the structure that stressed the importance of the organization over the individual; the education of special agents, whom Hoover characterized as unassailable in their ethics and their commitment to justice. The special agents, according to the secondary headline for the *New York Times* story, "Are Trained to Think, Also to Shoot, and They Employ All Modern Scientific Aids."[71]

Hoover's push for organization and records collection ranked as one of his greatest achievements while he headed the bureau, and it culminated to a large degree with the creation, in 1967, of the FBI's National Crime Information Center (NCIC), a nationwide clearinghouse for outstanding warrants and other data. The FBI and police departments enter the information into the NCIC's computer database, and the police have access to those records immediately to check a suspect's criminal history during a traffic stop, for example. The NCIC has become one of the most effective tools for the FBI and other federal and local police agencies to identify fugitives, and the idea for it was born in the days when Hoover created the training programs in the 1930s—the gangster era—that employed "all modern scientific aids" in what was still called the Department of Justice's Division of Investigation.

At a time when the automobile had quickly allowed any criminal to cross state lines and turn into an interstate fugitive, "The only agency which is obviously qualified to pursue criminals from one jurisdiction to another is the division," the *New York Times* continued in its report about the men who track down the public enemy, "and Congress gave it power to fill the gaps between local police authorities."[72] Thirty-three years later, Hoover viewed the creation of the NCIC, called the FBI's computer information bank, in the same context of what he considered the FBI's constant drive to innovate to catch fugitives and other criminals. The creation of the NCIC, Hoover said in January 1967, represents "a new era in law enforcement" and he said the NCIC's information network "will grow and expand and take its place as a major landmark in the annals of law enforcement."[73]

In 1934, as the newspapers fawned over the FBI and its new tools, Hoover could not have written the FBI's story better himself, though Hollywood soon did. As *The Public Enemy*, with James Cagney as its star, glorified the gangster, so another movie, *G-Men*, with Cagney again the star, but this time playing a lawman, glorified the FBI. Released in May 1935, *G-Men* tells the story of James "Brick" Davis (Cagney), who trains as a special government agent, or a G-man, after his friend, already an agent, is killed while trying to arrest a gangster. Davis goes on to track down a number of criminals modeled after the most notorious public enemies of the day, including Dillinger and Pretty Boy Floyd. Even the Lindbergh kidnapping and the Kansas City Massacre are fictionalized. *G-Men* serves as a cinematic counterpoint to *The Public Enemy*, making the government agent, rather than the gangster, the true hero. That Cagney, over a period of a year, starred as both the bad guy and the good guy was yet another example of how deeply embedded the gangster and the G-man had become in the American psyche during the Great Depression, when the public yearned for a winner, whether on the wrong or right side of the law. And Hollywood had no problem with Cagney's G-man killing gangsters. The Motion Picture Production Code was now in effect and banned gratuitous violence such as had been on display in *The Public Enemy*, made before the code existed. But the violence in *G-Men* was acceptable under the Production Code. FBI agents were firing the guns.[74]

G-Men was the first movie to focus on the FBI, and though the Justice Department did not provide technical assistance or other official input, *G-Men* portrayed the FBI as Hoover would have wanted: as a scientifically advanced and incorruptible agency that was American society's only hope against gangsters and fugitives and chaos. It was one of the most popular films of 1935 and his credited with helping to create the popular image of the FBI as the preeminent law enforcement agency in the land and an agency that, though part of the Justice Department on paper, was seen as nearly autonomous as well as omnipotent.[75] It was an agency that could be trusted because it was, after all, the FBI.

A book published about the same time as *G-Men* furthered the romanticized version of the FBI. In *Ten Thousand Public Enemies*, freelance writer Courtney Ryley Cooper, who for years had written articles about the FBI, crafted an entire nonfiction saga about Hoover's agency and its near-flawless capabilities of finding the lawbreakers and fugitives who were leading the United States to moral ruin. Cooper, more of a hagiographer than a journalist, borrowed the title of his book from a phrase that he calculated, most likely with Hoover's approval: ten thousand was the number of criminals, among a total of 3 million criminals in the United States, who were particularly dangerous. "[Out] of these three million," Cooper wrote, "there were ten thousand whose capture means that raiding officers must be prepared with machine guns, automatic rifles, and perhaps tear-gas guns. . . . These are America's Public Enemies."[76] In Cooper's telling, the United States was inundated with criminals and fugitives, a grim scenario that not only justified the FBI's existence but required its special agents and the director to be godlike in their courage and sagacity. In *Ten Thousand Public Enemies*, Cooper let unfold the story arc that made the fugitive the creator of the FBI. Without those on the lam, and especially without the likes of John Dillinger, the FBI had no reason to exist. Fugitives and special agents were doppelgangers, just as J. Edgar Hoover and John Dillinger were forever linked, each giving shape to the identity of the other: "*Ten Thousand Public Enemies* showed that the FBI was the negative image of the criminal army it was designed to fight."[77]

The tropes in *G-Men* and *Ten Thousand Public Enemies* became so powerful and so synonymous with the FBI that the agency soon used them in authorized projects, including newsreels, documentary-style short films, and movies, most of which came off more like propaganda than cinema verité portrayals of J. Edgar Hoover and his special agents. In its title alone, one of the documentary-style films, *"You Can't Get Away With It!"* from 1936, serves as a warning to would-be criminals and those on the loose.[78] The twenty-six-minute short feature by Universal, directed by Charles E. Ford, was presented with the permission of Homer Cummings and the cooperation of Hoover; it takes the viewer, as a subtitle states, "Behind the Scenes with the G-Men." *"You Can't Get Away With It!"* features a tour of the FBI operations—its fingerprint files, the switchboard for its kidnapping hotline, its shooting ranges—and includes shots of Cummings, Hoover, and assorted criminals, most notably John Dillinger, shown, in live action, sharing laughs with Sheriff Holley and Prosecutor Estill outside the Crown Point Jail. The narrator, Lowell Thomas, one of the best-known broadcasters of the day, intones throughout about the FBI's integrity and crime-fighting prowess in the war on gangsters. "This is a bureau of scientific crime detection," Thomas says, "new, modern, up-to-the-minute, day and night. The FBI never sleeps. The G-men have become a legend."[79]

The star of the short is J. Edgar Hoover, then forty-one years old and riding a surge of public praise following the capture of Dillinger, Pretty Boy Floyd, Machine Gun Kelly, and so many others in the legion of doom. Speaking in a rat-tat-tat fashion, almost seeming to mimic one of the machine guns that his agents use throughout the film, Hoover makes no secret of the FBI's mission. An FBI special agent, he says, must, among many other things, "be a good marksman and have the courage to shoot it out with the most venomous of public enemies."[80] The special agent also must be well-trained in methods of evidence detection and realize that "science is the bulwark of criminal investigation."[81] Hoover is also seen at a "war map," a large map of the United States, where he and his longtime assistant director Clyde Tolson decide where to move agents as if the agents were infantrymen getting assignments on the front. For as Lowell also says at the start of *"You Can't Get Away With It!,"* the FBI special agents are "soldiers in war while the world is at peace—the victorious war that the G-Men have waged against organized crime."[82]

By 1937, the Chicago Crime Commission had stopped releasing its Public Enemies List,[83] and the popularity of the list, as unofficial as it supposedly was, had waned at the federal level by then as well. In some ways, the FBI had made the need for the list obsolete. After Dillinger's death, the bureau, sometimes with Hoover's direct involvement, had killed or captured one Public Enemy

Number One after another: Pretty Boy Floyd (shot to death on October 22, 1934, on the farm near East Liverpool, Ohio), Baby Face Nelson (shot to death on November 27, 1934, near Barrington, Illinois, in which Nelson killed Special Agent Cowley and another special agent, Herman Hollis, who had fired at Dillinger outside the Biograph), Ma Barker and her son Fred (killed on January 16, 1935, in Ocklawaha, Florida), and the last Public Enemy Number One, Alvin "Creepy" Karpis, Ma Barker's surrogate son (arrested May 1, 1936, in New Orleans, with Hoover present, and the 325th prisoner of Alcatraz,[84] another creation of the federal government during the great crime wave).

The undeniable violence of the period is reflected in the list of FBI special agents who were killed while pursuing gangsters and bank robbers—Hollis and Cowley, in the gunfight with Nelson; Raymond J. Caffrey, in the Kansas City Massacre; and W. Carter Baum, in the failed raid of the Dillinger gang at Little Bohemia. Killed on August, 16, 1935, was another special agent, Nelson B. Klein, gunned down by bank robber George W. Barrett in College Corner, Indiana. Barrett was the first person to be executed under a new federal law that made killing an FBI agent a capital offense.[85] Congress passed the law on May 18, 1934, as part of the package of Crime Control Laws; Congress on that date also passed the Fugitive Felon Act, or the UFAP law (Unlawful Flight to Avoid Prosecution). And two years later, on February 8, 1936, Congress amended the death-penalty law that listed FBI agents as victims to include U.S. marshals and deputy U.S. marshals, among other federal law enforcement officers. Of the thirty-six FBI agents killed in the line of duty, five were slain between 1933 and 1935; all are listed on the FBI's Wall of Honor, which is featured in an opening shot of *"You Can't Get Away With It!"*[86]

Also during this period, the bank-robbing duo of Bonnie Parker and Clyde Barrow were gunned down on May 23, 1934, near Shreveport, Louisiana. Their pursuers were members of a posse whom the Texas governor had commissioned. The FBI was not involved in the ambush, though federal agents got jurisdiction in the pursuit of the pair in May 1933, when the two robbers were accused of driving a stolen Ford V-8 across state lines in violation of the Dyer Act. Bonnie and Clyde were not listed as public enemies; their deaths predated Hoover's designation of Dillinger as Public Enemy Number One on June 22, 1934—two days after President Roosevelt signed the law that gave FBI special agents the authority to carry firearms and make arrests. But these facts did not prevent Hoover from linking the FBI to the deaths of Bonnie in Clyde. In one scene in *"You Can't Get Away With It!"* Hoover oversees a group of FBI agents who are opening fire with their machine guns on a car sitting in a field. Riddled with bullets, the car eventually explodes. "This is what happened to Bonnie Parker and Clyde Barrow in a battle with local officers," Lowell Thomas says.[87]

By 1937, despite the ends to the careers of so many high-profiled criminals and fugitives, Hoover and the FBI continued to extol how the agency was in a battle for the country—Hoover starting in May 1936 even had the bureau collaborate on a newspaper comic strip called "War on Crime," that depicted the G-men in battles with real criminals, such as Dillinger and Baby Face Nelson.[88] But these public enemies were long gone by then, and the nation and world soon would be caught up not in a war on crime but World War II. Who needed public enemies like John Dillinger when the Allies were protecting the world against the likes of Adolph Hitler and Benito Mussolini? The FBI still went after fugitives in the late 1930s and beyond, but the public enemies list had gone from an active accounting of gangsters, killers, and racketeers to a reminder of the FBI's exploits during the gangster era.

Five years after the end of World War II, the FBI resurrected and repackaged the public enemies list. Hoover once more saw his agents in a fight with a criminal element at home. The FBI initiated its Ten Most Wanted Fugitives list, commonly known as its Ten Most Wanted list, in 1950. The list, whose format the U.S. Marshals Service would adopt in 1983, was not solely an invention of the FBI. Like the public enemies list, the Ten Most Wanted List was a product of pragmatism but also public relations. The FBI had a role in creating the list. So did the newspapers.

PART II
HUNTED AND HUNTER

4

INFAMOUS AND
ELUSIVE
On the Trail of the Top Ten

The call came from a reporter on deadline who was searching for copy: something, anything to help fill the newspaper. In a twist, the bureau's Ten Most Wanted Fugitives list originated not with J. Edgar Hoover or Clyde Tolson or any of Hoover's other top assistants. None of them, the FBI said, contacted the newspapers or wire services and pitched a story idea that would recreate the media glory and public adulation that the FBI enjoyed when the special agents were capturing public enemies in the 1930s. This time, the FBI said, the idea came from the media, albeit a media likely most fully aware that the FBI, under Hoover, was a publicity machine that needed only a slight push to roar into operation.

The call came from a United Press International reporter, who, in February 1949, needed copy. He called an agent he knew at the FBI and asked for a list of the "toughest guys" that the FBI wanted to bring to justice.[1] The information was fashioned into a ground-breaking piece that appeared under the byline of James F. Donovan, a United Press correspondent in Washington, D.C. Donovan's account first appeared on the front page of the *Washington Daily News* on February 7, 1949, and was immediately published in newspapers throughout the country that subscribed to the United Press, the predecessor to United Press International, or UPI. "FBI's 'Most-Wanted Fugitives' Named," read the headline in the *Washington Daily News*, a headline so large that the reader might have thought the United States had declared war. The article included mug shots of ten fugitives, all men, with descriptions of the charges against them— why the FBI was so interested in their capture.[2] As the FBI had done with the most-wanted posters for John Dillinger, Pretty Boy Floyd, and the other high-profile criminals from more than a decade earlier, the bureau in the newspaper article also provided information on the fugitives' physical appearances, including their height and weight. The FBI wanted none of these ten newly minted high-profile crooks and swindlers to go unnoticed.

Donovan's article provided no clues for the why the FBI had decided to create and release such a list of the infamous. But Donovan wrote that the FBI and the police needed the public's help. His story opened as follows:

> The FBI today listed 10 men as the most-wanted fugitives now at large. They are two accused murderers, four escaped convicts, a bank robber, and three confidence men.
>
> There are about 5,700 fugitives from justice in this country. Of these, the FBI considered these to be the 10 most potentially dangerous.
>
> The FBI does not label any one of them as "Public Enemy No. 1." But in response to a United Press inquiry, it compiled the list in the hope that this may lead to their arrest. Anyone knowing the whereabouts of these men should communicate immediately with the nearest FBI office or the local police.
>
> The FBI picks up an average of 9,416 fugitives a year. Here are the names and records that the FBI would particularly like to include in the 1949 quota.[3]

Donovan's story turned into a recurring feature—for the FBI. The piece generated so much publicity that J. Edgar Hoover became enamored with the idea of an official top-ten list of fugitives.

"It was a story that took off," FBI historian John Fox said of Donovan's story. "It was almost immediate. There was so much positive feedback and once it started being picked up across the country, we were getting leads—obviously most of them turned out to be dead ends—but enough of them were positive that they thought they had a real hit on their hands."[4]

Hoover had the FBI introduce its official list on March 10, 1950, the date that the Ten Most Wanted Fugitives program "was born."[5] The FBI made the list available to newspapers, magazines, television, and radio, and arranged to have most-wanted posters sent to police stations and displayed at post offices, gas stations, and other places the public frequented. Just as Hoover appropriated the public enemies list for the benefit of the FBI, he transformed the most-wanted fugitives list from a spur-of-the-moment newspaper feature into one of the FBI's most enduring and recognizable publicity campaigns. Some questioned the FBI's motives with the creation of the most-wanted list, claiming that the bureau used it largely to polish its image by loading the list with fugitives whose arrest the FBI believed was imminent.[6] Yet the list has thrived because of its simplicity and its directness: Here are the nation's most dangerous at-large criminals, and you, the everyday citizen, can help catch them. You, too, can be like a G-man. With the Ten Most Wanted Fugitives program, the FBI expanded its scope on an exponential scale. FBI special agents would get lots of help looking for fugitives. "If we can put that information out across America, all of the sudden, we've got several hundred 100 million eyes," Fox said. "It is a very different prospect."[7]

Even more so than the public enemies list, which the FBI neither fully disavowed nor completely embraced, the creation of the FBI's Ten Most Wanted list showed how the bureau was still able to cultivate relationships with the public, the media, and local and state law enforcement. Who, after all, doesn't want to help catch a thief? The most-wanted list, as one FBI official described it, is "part of Americana."[8]

Its creation brought together two approaches that had proven beneficial for the FBI for years. The most-wanted program melded the staid system of the identification orders (IOs), invented in 1919, while the FBI was still called the Bureau of Investigation; and the public enemies list that generated so much publicity for the FBI during the gangster era, even as J. Edgar Hoover said the FBI never officially identified John Dillinger or anyone else as the top public enemy in the United States. With the Ten Most Wanted Fugitives program, the FBI combined the fact-based strategy of the IO with the flair of the public enemies list. An appearance on the most-wanted list transformed a fugitive—no matter what his or her number—into a dark celebrity not unlike Dillinger, Pretty Boy Floyd, or Machine Gun Kelly. But the most-wanted program's goal was identical to that of the sober IO system: to provide enough reliable information to the police and the public to thwart the fugitive and protect the community. With the Ten Most Wanted Fugitives program, the FBI finally appropriated the public enemies list, though with the IO system providing the framework as well. A poster for the most-wanted program was like a charged-up IO notice. The poster was designed to get the attention mainly of the public rather than—as was the case with IO notices—primarily the police.

With the creation of the formal most-wanted fugitive program, including the posters, the FBI also bridged two eras of law enforcement in the United States. The most-wanted posters recalled the vigilantism of the Old West, where angry and injured settlers were able to pursue thieves and murderers with impunity, sometimes killing them. Echoes of that era of lawlessness and outlawry survived well into the twentieth century, with the creation of the public enemies lists to counter the great crime wave of the Depression-crushed 1930s. The Chicago Crime Commission and groups such as the Secret Six were made up of vigilantes in shirts and ties, frustrated at the Old West–type of violence that had over-whelmed Chicago, New York, and other metropolises due to the double plague that descended upon them after Prohibition: more criminals and ineffective or corrupt local police forces. By labeling a person a public enemy—sometimes even when the person had yet to be accused of crime—the Chicago Crime Commission and its brethren nationwide were all but encouraging a return to frontier justice, in which the morality of taking someone dead or alive was never in question. The FBI, through its tacit embrace of the public enemies list, could be said to have never discouraged frontier justice as a way to rid the nation of the Dillingers, Pretty Boy Floyds, Machine Gun Kellys, and so many other so-phisticated and deadly criminals.

The FBI never broke its link to the public enemies list. It formalized it—made it more civilized—by creating the Ten Most Wanted Fugitives program and its corresponding list. The FBI certainly never gave anyone approval to capture someone dead or alive, but the most-wanted program nonetheless promoted a kind of citizen involvement—not quite vigilantism, but not quite acquiescence, either—that flourished in the Old West in a more activist and often bloody form. The most-wanted lists, whether a product of the FBI or the U.S. Marshals Service, represented the modern iteration of the battle between the outlaw and the law. And with the emergence of the Ten Most Wanted Fugitives program in 1950, the FBI could turn to a new tool, but still a tool based in the past, to prove the government's commitment to making sure the law won.

The Ten Most Wanted Fugitives program and its soon-to-be ubiquitous list also signaled how deeply consolidated law-enforcement operations had become under the FBI. From the post-Revolutionary era to the Old West, searching for fugitives in the United States had been a largely isolated affair. A U.S. marshal might rush down to Norfolk, Virginia, to search for a wanted murderer in 1797, or a sheriff or marshal in the Old West might set out on horseback to find a criminal on the lam. But they were largely alone in their endeavors, cut off from others in law enforcement due to the localized technology of the time. They operated "without the national data and communications networks so familiar today. Western sheriffs and police departments had to communicate by mail, telegraph, and telephone, spreading the news of wanted fugitives to their known haunts and along likely paths of escape: roads and railway lines."[9] The creation of the Ten Most Wanted Fugitives program nationalized, to a great degree, a critical aspect of law enforcement—finding those who are dangerous.

The FBI's Ten Most Wanted list made a difference from the start. Of the ten fugitives on the first list, on March 10, 1950, eight were caught that year.[10] And since the creation of the official list a total of 521 have appeared on it as of October 2018; only 10 have been women.[11] A total of 486 of the fugitives have been captured, for a success rate of 93 percent, and apprehensions of most-wanted fugitives have occurred in every state except Alaska, Delaware, and Maine.[12] In FBI parlance, anyone who makes the list, no matter how long the duration or the crime, is known as a "top tenner."[13] But those on the list are not ranked in the pattern of Public Enemy Number One, with the worst put first. Once a person is taken off the list due to an arrest or a limited number of other reasons, the FBI adds a new fugitive to fill the slot. The FBI considers each person on the list to be dangerous; none is considered to be more dangerous than another. The standing minimum reward for information leading to the capture of any fugitive is $100,000, though the amount can go higher. The highest award, as of mid-2018, was $20 million for accused Mexican drug lord Rafael Caro Quintero, charged with overseeing the kidnapping and murder of a special agent with the Drug Enforcement Administration in 1985.[14]

The number of fugitives on the list can go higher than ten. The FBI allows for "special additions"—fugitives whose capture is urgent enough that the bureau must get them on the list immediately and without waiting for another criminal to be removed. Since March 1950, thirteen "special additions" have appeared on the Ten Most Wanted Fugitives list. They include James Earl Ray, the 277th person to appear on the most-wanted list, who assassinated Martin Luther King Jr. in Memphis on April 4, 1968, and was caught two months later; and Ramzi Ahmed Yousef, No. 346 on the most-wanted list, the mastermind behind the World Trade Center bombing on February 26, 1993. The FBI added him to the list on April 12, 1993, and he was caught two years later in Pakistan. Yousef was the thirteenth and most recent "special addition." Ray was the second.

The criteria the FBI uses to place a fugitive on the list in regular fashion have changed little since the list's inception. The bureau's Criminal Investigation Division at FBI headquarters in Washington, D.C., seeks candidates by canvassing the FBI's fifty-six nationwide field offices and the FBI's legal attachés overseas. Two sets of FBI special agents—in the criminal division and the public affairs office—sign off on the selections, with final approval from the FBI's executive management, including the director.[15] Nominees must have a record of committing serious crimes and must be wanted on federal charges, including unlawful flight from prosecution, which allows federal authorities to pursue fugitives running from state crimes. Also, nominees must, in the words of the FBI, "be considered a particularly dangerous menace to society due to current criminal charges."[16] And the FBI must determine that additional publicity will help lead to the nominees' capture. If a fugitive is already well known, he or she might never make the most-wanted list, though, as shown in the cases of the "special additions," even the most infamous criminals of the day can appear on the list. The list does not necessarily include the fugitives that the FBI believes are the most dangerous. It includes the fugitives the FBI believes are dangerous *and* more susceptible to capture with extra media attention.

"There's a lot of people that we want, and there's a lot of people that are wanted," once explained Mark Giuliano, who was the FBI's deputy director, or chief operating officer, from December 2013 to February 2016. "While there are a lot of folks that are out there, we may have leads on them, we may have sources into them, we may have other ways to capture them. But this is one in which we believe that the media attention through this program is one that will help us capture them. There are a lot of other folks out there that we want to capture. This is one where that media attention, we feel, brings a unique perspective to it."[17]

Perhaps the most infamous top-ten fugitive of all time—the focus of one of the world's biggest manhunts and publicity campaigns—was Osama bin Laden, No. 456. He made the list before he orchestrated the terrorist attacks of September 11, 2001. He was first placed on the list on June 7, 1999, and was wanted on 224 charges of murder in the bombings of the U.S. embassy in Nairobi, Kenya, and Dar es Salaam, Tanzania, on Aug. 7, 1998.

The criteria for getting off the list also have gone unchanged over the years. A top-ten fugitive must die, be captured, have the case against him or her dismissed (a decision of prosecutors, not the FBI), or be removed because the FBI determines the person no longer meets the criteria for appearing on the list. The FBI has taken only ten people off the list for the third reason, and each time determined that the fugitive is no longer "a particularly dangerous menace to society."[18] Removal from the list for failure to meet its criteria does not mean a fugitive is no longer at large. It means that the FBI believes publicity will no longer aid the fugitive's apprehension, and that the bureau is ready for another fugitive to assume the spot on the list.

One of the most recent removals came on June 27, 2018, in the case of William Bradford Bishop Jr., who had been the 502nd fugitive to appear on the Ten Most Wanted list. Bishop, a U.S. foreign service officer, was wanted on charges he used a hammer to kill his mother, wife, and three sons—five, ten, and fourteen years old—on March 1, 1976, in Bethesda, Maryland. He was also accused of driving the victims' remains to North Carolina, burying them in a shallow grave, and setting the remains on fire. "A family annihilator," is how investigators described Bishop.[19] He was last seen the day after the slayings, buying sneakers at a sporting goods store in Jacksonville, North Carolina. The FBI placed Bishop on the Ten Most Wanted list on April 10, 2014. Officials said Bishop was believed to be still alive, and they said they hoped that adding his name to the most-wanted list would boost publicity and generate the tip that would lead to Bishop's arrest wherever he might have used his foreign-service experience to travel. The most-wanted poster for Bishop included a digitally enhanced photograph designed to show what he would look like in 2014, when he would have been seventy-seven years old.

"When Bishop took off in 1976, there was no social media, no 24-hour news cycle," the special agent in charge of the FBI's Baltimore field office, Steve Vogt, said in announcing Bradford's addition to the list in 2014. "There was no sustained way to get his face out there like there is today. And the only way to catch this guy is through the public."[20]

"No lead or tip is insignificant," Vogt said. "If Bishop is living with a new identity, he's got to be somebody's next-door neighbor. Don't forget that five people were murdered. Bishop needs to be held accountable for that."[21]

The accountability has yet to happen. When the FBI removed Bishop from the list in June 2018, authorities said they believed he was still alive. But they said they had concluded that the increased publicity would no longer benefit the case, that Bishop was no longer considered to be a danger to the public, and that the FBI could better use Bishop's spot on the list. So Bishop, still on the lam, disappeared from the ranks of the Ten Most Wanted. If still alive, he would be eighty-one. At the time, he was the oldest person to have appeared on Ten Most Wanted list.

"There have been no confirmed sightings of Bishop since his initial disappearance," the FBI said in a statement that explained Bishop's removal. His continued presence on the list, the FBI said, "is not expected to result in any additional information that would lead to his capture."[22]

Many times, publicity, in any number of forms, has led to the apprehension of top-ten fugitives. Of the 486 fugitives on the list who were captured, a total of 130 were caught because of publicity, according to the FBI.[23] The most-wanted notices generated the key tips in fifty of the cases, followed by newspapers, with thirty-three; television, twenty-eight; magazines, thirteen; the internet, four; and the radio, two.[24] Another fourteen of the fugitives were found to have died. Information gleaned from the FBI's National Crime Information Center, which has hundreds of thousands of outstanding warrants on file, led to two apprehensions. The other fugitives were caught through police work or from tips that were not the result of publicity. The FBI caught 238 of the fugitives and the local police caught 99, with another 75 captured due to the work of joint task forces. Twelve of the fugitives on the list were killed during capture. Twenty-five surrendered, and police and other authorities in other countries caught another thirty-four.[25]

The FBI keeps all these statistics from the list on its website, which it updates regularly, creating something like a real-time and grisly Guinness Book of World Records for those on the lam. The statistics include the number of top-ten fugitives caught each year (the high of thirty-three was recorded in 1968, and four years yielded no arrests: 1993, 2005, 2010, and 2015) as well as the number of fugitives who were removed from the list when their cases were dismissed (fifteen), plus the number of people who have appeared on the list twice (six, including James Earl Ray, in 1977, when he escaped from prison and was later caught).[26] The length of time spent on the list is another area rich in data and characters.

The shortest time a fugitive spent on the list was two hours. The quarry was Billie Austin Bryant, the 295th top-ten fugitive to appear on the list and the third special addition. He was a convicted bank robber and federal prison escapee who was listed as soon as he fatally shot FBI Special Agents Anthony Palmisano and Edwin R. Woodriffe after surprising them while they searched for him in an apartment building in Washington, D.C., on January 9, 1969. Palmisano and Woodriffe had gone to the apartment building, where Bryant's wife lived, to pursue a lead that the twenty-nine-year-old Bryant had robbed a Maryland bank earlier that day. Bryant escaped from the apartment building, but after a massive manhunt that included placing him on the most-wanted list, he was found in the attic of a nearby apartment two hours later; an alert resident of the apartment building had called the police. Bryant was later sentenced to two consecutive life terms.[27] He died in federal prison at age sixty-nine on March 3, 2009.[28] Palmisano and Woodriffe were added to the FBI's Wall of Honor, a tribute to the thirty-six special agents killed in the line of duty since 1925.

The fugitive on the most-wanted list the longest was Victor Manuel Gerena, who occupied a spot from March 14, 1984, to December 15, 2016—nearly thirty-two years. Gerena, top-ten fugitive No. 386, was wanted for the 1983 armed robbery of about $7 million from the Wells Fargo armored car service where he worked in West Hartford, Connecticut. The heist was the largest robbery of cash in the history of the United States at the time. Gerena, who was twenty-five years old when he fled, is still at large. The FBI took him off the most-wanted list in December 2016 once he was determined to be living in Cuba.[29]

As the fugitive on the run for the longest period of time, Gerena replaced a top-ten fugitive who had become a fixture on the most-wanted list for more than eighteen years. He was Donald Eugene Webb, No. 375, a jewelry-store thief with mob ties who was wanted for the killing of the police chief in Saxonburg, Pennsylvania, north of Pittsburgh, on December 4, 1980. Webb had been in town to rob a jewelry store as part of his connection to organized crime. After shooting the thirty-one-year-old chief, Gregory Adams, during a traffic stop, Webb, then fifty, fled to his native New England, where his abandoned car was found in Warwick, Rhode Island, with blood from a gunshot wound to Webb's leg covering the inside of the car. The FBI placed Webb on the most-wanted list on May 4, 1981, and he became the longest tenant on the list at the time on September 4, 1999—a total of 6,705 days—more than eighteen years.[30] The FBI removed Webb from the list on March 31, 2007—not because he was caught, but because leads had dwindled and he was believed to have died.[31] He was the only fugitive on the list wanted for killing a police chief.

Webb did die, but in 1999. The FBI in July 2017 announced that Webb's remains had been discovered on July 13, 2017, buried on the property of his former wife's house in the southern Massachusetts town of Dartmouth.[32] Authorities said Webb's wife confessed to helping to hide him in a secret room inside her house when he was alive, and she said he granted his wish that she bury him in the backyard after his death, in 1999, of a stroke.[33] Police came across the secret room in the house during an investigation into illegal gambling in 2016; the search for Webb's whereabouts intensified from there.[34] The FBI knew Webb so well that agents included in his most-wanted description such details that he was flashy dresser who left big tips and liked dogs.[35] The FBI described Webb as a "career criminal and a master of assumed identities" who had worked as a butcher, car salesman, jewelry salesman, and vending-machine repairman.[36] Once Webb went underground, and despite rewards of as much as $100,000 for his capture, he remained a fugitive until death.

Every fugitive who makes the most-wanted list has a story. In many cases, such as those of Donald Eugene Webb and Victor Manuel Garena, their crimes are more local in nature; their appearance on the Ten Most Wanted list is designed to make their notoriety national. In other cases, the fugitives who made the list were already known across the United States before their mug shots, biographical sketches, aliases, personal characteristics, and shape and locations of their tattoos became reading material on the bulletin board at the post office. The crimes of and accusations against these large-than-life fugitives—Osama bin Laden, the serial bank robber Willie Sutton, the serial killer Ted Bundy, the mobster James "Whitey" Bulger, the radical Angela Davis (who was acquitted of the charges against her)—have become part of American history. So have the ways in which they were captured.

The fugitive that headed the first official top-ten list was among the most famous criminals of his day, both because of his offenses and the fellow criminals with whom he was accused of associating. They included Verne Miller, Alvin "Creepy" Karpis, and Frank "Jelly" Nash, of the Kansas City Massacre. Top-ten fugitive No. 1 was fifty-one-year-old Thomas James Holden, known as "Tough" Tommy Holden, a train robber and lead member of the Holden-Keating Gang of bank robbers during the great crime wave of the1930s.[37] He appeared on the most-wanted list on charges that he murdered his wife and two brothers-in-law in his native Chicago in June 1949.[38] But he had been on the lam before. With help from fellow inmate Machine Gun Kelly, Holden and fellow bank robber Francis Keating escaped from the federal prison at Leavenworth, Kansas, on February 28, 1930; Holden and Keating handed phony trusty passes to a new guard, who let them leave the penitentiary.[39] Holden and Keating had been at Leavenworth serving twenty-five year sentences for stealing $135,000 from a U.S. Postal Service truck that they had held up in suburban Chicago in 1926.[40]

While he was at large after the prison break, Holden in 1932 helped rob the Citizens National Bank in Fort Scott, Kansas, of $47,000. Also involved in the heist were Keating, Karpis, Miller, and master bank robber John Harvey Bailey, who knew Frank Nash. The robbery was well planned. The robbers kidnapped three women from the bank and placed them on the running boards of the getaway car. Bailey learned the strategy during his gangland days in Chicago, where the bank robbers correctly guessed that the police would not fire on their getaway cars for fear of shooting the women riding on the outside.[41]

Holden and Bailey and Keating also liked to golf, which was their undoing. As the three were wearing knickers and walking the links on the Old Mission Course, near Kansas City, Missouri, FBI agents arrested them on July 7, 1932.[42] The agents had been hiding behind trees.[43] Holden was eventually sent to Alcatraz on September 7, 1934, where he served time with his partner-in-crime Frank Keating.[44] Holden was among the first inmates sentenced to Alcatraz, or "The Rock," which the federal government opened on August, 1 1934, in response to the rise of gangsterism.[45] Attorney General Homer Cummings was behind the effort to create Alcatraz as an escape-proof federal prison designed especially for criminals like Holden, convicts with "advanced degrees in crime."[46]

Holden was transferred from Alcatraz to Leavenworth in March 1944 and in 1947 he was paroled to Chicago, where he had a loyal wife.[47] He did not stay out of trouble for long. On June 5, 1949, in what police said was a drunken rage after a family party, Holden fatally shot his forty-five-year-old wife, Lillian. Her two brothers came to her defense and Holden shot them too. He killed Ray Griffin, thirty-seven; and his wife's half brother, John Archer, thirty-five.[48] A fourth bullet grazed the cheek of Griffin's wife, Elva, who identified Holden to the police as the killer who gunned down three of her relatives inside a fourth-floor apartment on Chicago's south side.[49] Police arrived at the apartment after getting a call about the murders. Investigators discovered the bodies and found, on a dresser, a .38-caliber revolver with four spent cartridge and four loaded shells. Tommy Holden had disappeared after killing his family, including a wife who had stood by him while he was locked up at Alcatraz and waited for his return.[50]

Eight months later, Holden's name and mug shot occupied the top spot on the first Ten Most Wanted Fugitives list on March 14, 1950. The FBI announced Holden's inclusion on the list with language that likened the fight against crime to a kind of existential battle. And the FBI's references to Holden echoed J. Edgar Hoover's booming condemnations of John Dillinger and other public enemies decades earlier. The top-ten list formally extended the FBI's fight against crime to the tracking of fugitives. "Crime we have had with us always," the FBI wrote. "We will continue to have crime as long as man's basic passions and instincts survive. Crime can, however, be minimized. The devastating effects of crime are to some extent reduced by quick apprehension of those engaged in criminal activity. Thomas James Holden is one man whose freedom in society is a menace to every man, woman, and child in America."[51]

Holden was free for two years before the FBI caught him, though the most-wanted program undeniably contributed to his apprehension. Holden after the shootings withdrew $2,000 from his bank accounts and was last seen in Cedar Lake, Indiana, just south of Crown Point, whose jail John Dillinger had made infamous with his escape fifteen years earlier. Holden's flight to Indiana prompted police in Chicago to seek assistance from the FBI, and agents on November 4, 1949, issued a UFAP (Unlawful Flight to Avoid Prosecution) warrant against him, accusing him of crossing state lines to avoid prosecution for murder.[52] From Indiana, Holden headed west, to Phoenix, Arizona; Butte Montana; and finally to Portland, Oregon. Along the way, he worked as a carpenter, dishwasher, and construction helper. By the time he settled in Portland, he was a fifty-five-year-old plasterer for the Cascade Concrete Products Company, where he was known as a quiet and reliable laborer who went by the name John R. McCullough. He lived in a small rented cabin outside of Portland.[53]

Holden had almost been caught, twice, before he found his way to Portland. In Montana, a police officer stopped him to check the ownership of a radio. The other time, he was stopped while driving a friend's car without a driver's license.[54] Holden, relying on his skill at keeping a straight face and keeping his mouth shut, got away in the era before computers, when online links to the National Crime Information Center would provide police officers, in an instant, access to criminal records nationwide.

Holden's cover was blown through the FBI's use of the dominant media platform of the time—the newspaper. On Wednesday, June 20, 1951, the Portland *Oregonian* ran Holden's photo and an article about him under the headline, "FBI Admits Triple Killer Wily Prey, Lists Description, Habits of Criminal."[55] The writer was James Lee, with the International News Service; his story represented the latest example of the FBI generating publicity for those on its most-wanted list by cooperating with wire services to get stories on the fugitives in newspapers throughout the country. Lee's story on Holden was the second article in an International News Service series called "The FBI's 'Ten Most Wanted Criminals' of 1951."[56] Holden, though the first No. 1 fugitive to appear on the list, by then was occupying the second spot because of other top-ten fugitives the FBI had apprehended before him. Holden, by then on the lam for more than two years, was proving to be a tough catch. "The FBI," according to Lee's article, "admits that Holden is one of the wiliest desperadoes in its archives."[57]

In the accompanying photo, Holden stares straight at the camera. His box-shaped head features a high forehead, creating a face that must have been hard to forget, a face that, as one observer has written, looked like the actor Boris Karloff's when he played the lead role in the movie *Frankenstein*.[58] The *Oregonian* article, setting the tone for so many newspaper articles and most-wanted posters to come, detailed Holden's personal attributes. A reader could think he or she knew Holden just by perusing the three paragraphs at the end of the story:

> Habits—Likes to play bridge and is considered an expert, sometimes does landscape painting, is a heavy eater, has a nervous motion around the mouth, causing lips to be drawn tightly over teeth.
>
> Description—Age, 55; height, 5 feet, 9 ½ inches; weight, 142 pounds; build, slender; hair, dark brown, auburn tint, wavy; eyes, blue; wears glasses when reading; complexion, medium florid; occupations, auto salesman, laborer, steamfitter; scars, left middle finger and left wrist.
>
> Warning: Armed and considered extremely dangerous.[59]

The tip came in on June 23, 1951. The FBI never identified the person, but someone noticed that the most-wanted suspect featured in the *Oregonian* two days earlier resembled John McCullough, a plasterer helping to remodel an unoccupied house near Beaverton, outside Portland. The FBI agents first checked with John McCullough's boss to make sure the worker fit the profile of Thomas Holden; the FBI agents wanted to avoid confronting an innocent person.[60] They then went to McCullough's work site, where they captured a startled Thomas James Holden.

Holden had not seen the newspaper story; had he read it, he told the FBI, he would have fled. If he had read the story, he also would have understood why his fellow employees for the past few days had been remarking on how much he looked like the fugitive Thomas James Holden. The employees, picking up on the line that described Holden as an avid bridge player, kept asking McCullough if he wanted to play bridge after work. Holden had declined.

"I don't know how he missed the story," said Charles Robinson, Holden's boss. "The paper was staring him in the face all day Wednesday."[61] Robinson also described Holden—or McCullough—"as an exceptionally hard worker."

"I never asked him where he was from," Robinson said. "I never cared."[62]

Holden at first insisted to the FBI that he was really McCullough, but he confessed to being Holden after he realized how much information the FBI had on him. Agents later used fingerprints to identify Holden.

"I knew the jig was up when I saw the agents and they said they were from the FBI," Holden is reported to have said some time after his arrest.[63]

His days as a fugitive were over. He had to abandon his reinvented life as John McCullough, who had been known as one of the best laborers on his crew, and who had liked to keep to himself at his home in his rented cabin in a trailer park near Beaverton. Holden had been in the area for three months before the FBI apprehended him.

"He was a model tenant," Holden's landlord, identified in the *Oregonian* only as Mrs. Wayne Drake, said after his arrest. "I suspect a lot of people about being crooks, but not this one. I'm a little shocked. I took his rent every week. He always was happy and singing Irish folk songs. He had a good enough voice to be in opera."[64]

Drake's eight-year-old son, Frankie, said Holden was kind to him and once gave him two nickels because he had been "a good boy."[65] One of Holden's neighbors in the trailer park praised Holden as the considerate, mild-mannered man who lived next door.

"He was a very good neighbor," said Mrs. Garnet Scott. "I just can't understand it. I stayed here night after night alone while my husband was at work and he and I used to talk through our windows. He was a quiet man who lived alone and cooked for himself. We only had one argument. One night he had his radio on late and I asked him to turn it down. He did, right away."[66]

Holden became a local celebrity. His apprehension was the top story on June 24, 1951, in the *Oregonian*, which also featured a photo of him getting booked at the sheriff's office. But Holden's arrest was not unique to the area. As the *Oregonian* also reported, another fugitive on the FBI's newly christened most-wanted list had been captured on a chicken farm near Portland more than a year earlier.[67] He was Orba Elmer Jackson, a former farmer from Missouri who had escaped from Leavenworth while serving a twenty-five-year sentence for armed robbery of a store that included a post office in Missouri; Jackson got no money, but he pistol-whipped the store's owner, and the presence of the post office in the same building made the robbery a federal offense.[68] Jackson had been on the lam for three years when he became top-ten fugitive No. 7 on the most-wanted list released on March 21, 1950, a week after Holden made the list at No. 1. But Jackson, unlike Holden, was also on the FBI's first, unofficial list, which appeared in the *Washington Daily News* on February 7, 1949.[69]

The FBI in 1951 first got a tip about Jackson's whereabouts from the postmaster in Tualatin, also near Portland, who noticed his photo on the most-wanted poster that the FBI had circulated. The postmaster thought the fugitive was a handyman who worked on a chicken farm in nearby Aloha. As it would in the case of Holden, the *Oregonian* published a wire-service story on Jackson's status as a most-wanted fugitive; the story, also by International News Service reporter James Lee, appeared on March 21, 1950.[70] A tip from a reader helped the FBI find Jackson on the chicken farm, where agents arrested him on March 23, 1950, two days after the FBI had placed him on the most-wanted list. Jackson, forty-three years old, had been using the name of Kenneth Van Kempen. He was not known to be violent, and his coworkers on the chicken farm liked him so much that they launched a campaign to get him clemency. The effort failed for Jackson, whose coworkers described as "a perfect gentleman."[71] Jackson denied being the same person as the one featured on the most-wanted list.

"To put me on the list of the ten worst criminals is the silliest thing I ever heard of," he said. "I haven't done anything very bad. The paper said I was dangerous and probably armed. Hell, I haven't had a gun since I got out. What do I want with a gun? I got enough trouble without one."[72]

He was returned to Leavenworth and later released when his sentence expired. He died at age eighty-six in California in 1993.

Following Jackson's apprehension, Holden's arrest marked the second time within two years that the FBI had captured a top-ten fugitive in the Portland area, with the help of newspaper articles that had become a key part of the new most-wanted fugitive program. Four days after Holden's arrest, the *Oregonian* noted how the two most-wanted designees had run out of time and luck in the state.

"The fact should disprove a theory held by some criminals that a quiet, comparatively sparsely populated community makes the best hideout," the newspaper said on its opinion page. Its editorial also stated that "an individual's face stands out in greater detail in a small crowd than a large one, and publication of their pictures made them marked men."[73] The *Oregonian* wondered if Holden would have been more successful had he tried to hide out in Chicago, where "one face among four million must be quite remarkable to command a second look."[74]

The flood of most-wanted fugitives in Oregon did not last. As of mid-2018, a total of four most-wanted fugitives had been found in Oregon since the FBI started the official list.[75]

Holden, the first most-wanted fugitive to make Oregon famous, declined to fight extradition. He was sent to Illinois and convicted at trial in Chicago for the murders of his wife and two brothers-in-law. The testimony of his sister-in-law, whose cheek had been grazed in the shooting, proved pivotal. Holden was sentenced to life at the Illinois State Prison. He died at age fifty-seven after only two years of incarceration. A heart condition caught up to him.[76] A news story on his death listed the lowlights of his life: Holden was "a wife killer, train robber, prison breaker and once listed as one of the FBI's ten most wanted men."[77]

Holden's capture exemplified a pattern that would mark the arrests of so many other top-ten fugitives after him. The FBI puts a name on the most-wanted list, circulates the information, and a tip comes from an ordinary citizen who takes a special interest in person who appears to be as regular as anyone else but is really a criminal or a suspect on the run. If Tommy Holden or Orba Elmer Jackson had been loud or rambunctious or had otherwise attracted attention, they never would have escaped justice as long as they did. As for the role of the citizens, J. Edgar Hoover knew the FBI was only as strong as the confidence the public had in it—a realization Hoover cultivated through films like *"You Can't Get Away With It!"* and through many other public-relations efforts. If the public did not trust the FBI, the public would not help the FBI, and no one would ever come off the list of top ten most wanted fugitives. With its offer of rewards in exchange for tips to find fugitives, the FBI lubricated the system of public cooperation. Special agents, in delivering those rewards—a process that remains secretive—express their gratitude to those who provided tips. The practice started with Hoover, who "himself would congratulate any citizen who played a part in the apprehension in the early years, but he also did it privately, so as to not subject them to any retaliation by the fugitives or the fugitives' friends—a tradition that survives today."[78]

The U.S. Marshals Service, like the FBI, also reached into the past to create one of its signature efforts: the Fifteen Most Wanted fugitive program and its list. In 1982, top officials of the agency were exploring ways to publicize high-profile fugitive cases. They decided to "bring back the feeling of the wanted posters of the past"[79]—posters that marshals and their deputies used to their advantage in the Old West. The director of the U.S. Marshals Service, William Hall, developed the Fifteen Most Wanted fugitive program along with Howard Safir, the service's associate director of operations, and its inspector, Robert Leschorn. They came up with the idea in July 1982, three years after the landmark memorandum of understanding between the U.S. Marshals Service and the FBI delineated their responsibilities for capturing fugitives—the marshals adopted less of an investigative role than the FBI and took on finding fugitives who had already broken the law: escaped federal prisoners, federal bail jumpers, witnesses who failed to appear in court, federal offenders who had violated probation and parole. The U.S. Marshals Service launched the Fifteen Most Wanted fugitive program in 1983.

The U.S. Marshals Service created the program to "prioritize investigation and apprehension of high-profile offenders who are considered to be some of the country's most dangerous fugitives," according to the service.[80] The marshals' most-wanted program resembled the FBI's most-wanted program in many ways, including the use of posters with photographs and other identifying information; the Fifteen Most Wanted fugitive program can trace its lineage, in the United States, to the marshals' operations in the Old West as well as to the FBI's identification orders and the public enemy campaigns of the Depression. The programs of the FBI and the U.S. Marshals Service's both serve the same functions and generally use the same tools; the main difference is the types of fugitives each agency is charged with pursuing.

"We're two different kinds of agencies," said David S. Turk, the historian for the U.S. Marshals Service. "They are primarily an investigative agency, while we are primarily a protective one (with some investigative powers). We patterned the Fifteen Most Wanted in 1983, four years after [the] memorandum of understanding with the FBI for federal prison escapes and failure to appear at trial. The Top Ten was already in existence for some time, and although both include violent individuals or fugitives, there are different criteria to measure for inclusion on either."[81]

The invention of the Fifteen Most Wanted fugitive program had a do-it-yourself feel, even at an agency as large and established as the U.S. Marshals Service. As Turk also said, Leschorn, who was an inspector in the agency's Enforcement Operations Division, "actually created the draft of the very first

Fifteen Most Wanted in February 1983. He literally . . . glued or taped thumb-nail pictures on letterhead to show the draft appearance. The agency created publication USM-132 for display purposes in district offices, post offices, and other venues. Each form was printed on heavy stock, as they had to stand in Fifteen Most Wanted boards at each district office with interchangeable slots. As to the actual wanted poster, this was a tie to the historical wanted posters of the Old West. This was because it attracted attention and stood out from other types of similar programs."[82]

And why fifteen fugitives on the list rather than ten?

"We wanted to differentiate our listing from that of the FBI," Turk said. "One factor was the number on the listing."[83]

The U.S. Marshals Service's criteria for placing a fugitive on its most-wanted list resemble the FBI's standards, though the marshals typically pursue those criminals who have already been charged and have jumped bail or violated probation or parole. Only one out of every 1,000 fugitives makes the fifteen most-wanted list, and those who do, according to the U.S. Marshals Service's original guidelines for the most-wanted program, "have a history of violent be-havior and are wanted for such heinous crimes that their continued status as a fugitive would pose a serious threat to the public."[84]

The Fifteen Most Wanted fugitive program got a boost in 1985, when the U.S. Marshals Service supplemented it with its Major Case Fugitive Program. In an evaluation of the worst of the worst, the marshals prioritized the capture of "high-profile offenders who tend to be career criminals whose histories of violence pose a significant threat to public safety. Current and past fugitives targeted by this program include murderers, violent gang members, sex offend-ers, major drug kingpins, organized crime figures, and individuals wanted for high-profile financial crimes."[85] Since its inception in 1983, and including the results of the major case program, the Fifteen Most Wanted fugitive program has led to the capture of 241 fugitives as of fiscal year 2017.[86] The number is low compared to the other fugitives the U.S. Marshals Service has captured during that time, but only because the service is charged with finding so many people. In fiscal 2017, when the service made arrests in or otherwise cleared the cases of 84,048 fugitives, three were on the fifteen most-wanted list.[87]

Local and state police also have most-wanted lists. So do other federal law-enforcement agencies. The Bureau of Alcohol, Tobacco, Firearms, and Explosives has a list. So do the Drug Enforcement Administration, the Secret Service, and the Air Force Office of Special Investigations and the Naval Crimi-nal Investigations Service, both of which use the lists to find fugitives from the military.[88] And in 1985, the FBI created the Violent Criminal Apprehension

Program, known as ViCAP. It is designed to help local police and other law enforcement agencies capture serial killers and other violent criminals by creating a database for major violent crime cases throughout the country. ViCAP collects and analyzes data in homicides, sexual assaults, missing-person cases, unidentified-person cases, and other investigations. Police can access the information to examine whether any crimes they are investigating resemble those in the database.

A secure internet connection for ViCAP is a key tool for the program. But, no matter how modern in its techniques, ViCAP, like the other most-wanted programs, grew out of the same event: reporter James F. Donovan's call to the FBI in February 1949. His newspaper article, replete with the booming headline and mug shots of ten wanted men, started it all.[89] From then on, fugitives had a new fear: getting on a list, whether the FBI's, the U.S. Marshals Service's or another agency's. "They can't be terribly happy about it when they see their names on the list, because we're are going to put some effort on it," an FBI official once said. "It's like going on *America's Most Wanted*," he said, referring to the popular true-crime television show that ran from 1988 to 2011. "That's a bad thing for a fugitive."[90]

But do the lists work? Does publicizing the name of a fugitive, particularly on the FBI's Ten Most Wanted Fugitives list, the most prominent most-wanted list in all of America, prove effective? The first scholarly study to examine these questions determined that the use of the lists helps the FBI catch fugitives, but the lists advance another purpose as well: They allow the FBI and other law enforcement agencies to signal their priorities by whom they place on the lists. Instead of filling its lists with fugitives who might be easy to catch, according to the 2008 study by law professor Thomas J. Miles, the FBI populates its list with fugitives who have been difficult to find—that is one of the primary reasons, after all, that they are on the list.[91] But those fugitives who are most elusive are often those who are wanted for high-profile crimes, or crimes in which the FBI has taken a strong interest, usually because of new federal legislation.

But the two-pronged purpose of the list can create a tension with the FBI Ten Most Wanted list. Miles does not dispute that the list is often successful in achieving both purposes—the apprehension of fugitives and the dissemination of the FBI's priorities in fighting certain crimes—but he also writes, "When an enforcement agency assigns a high priority to the pursuit of fugitives who are sensitive to publicity, wanted posters and lists furnish the benefits of both faster apprehensions and priority announcement. However, when an enforcement priority includes offenders whose apprehension probabilities are insensitive to publicity, the choice of which kind of offender to feature on a wanted list presents a tradeoff between hastening apprehension and announcing priorities."[92]

Though such a tradeoff can exist, it has not detracted from the use of most-wanted lists: "Despite the common perception that wanted lists are anachronisms, police agencies increasingly issue wanted posters and lists of wanted fugitives," according to Miles.[93] The reasons for the lasting use of the posters seem obvious: On the most basic level, how else would the FBI or any other police agency be expected to publicize fugitives?

The main challenge for law enforcement, no matter what the effectiveness of most-wanted lists, is the number of fugitives, which makes catching all of them a virtual impossibility. One investigative report found "an often overlooked reality for U.S. law enforcement: For all the advances police and prosecutors have made in their ability to solve crimes, they still struggle with the basic step of making sure that the people they arrest show up to answer the charges."[94] As shown by the number of fugitives the U.S. Marshals Service alone catches year after year, the total number of fugitives on the loose at any time, at every level of law enforcement, is almost unfathomable. As of November 1, 2018, the number of active warrants on file with the National Crime Information Center, was 2,482,546—1,305,049 felony warrants and 1,177,497 misdemeanor warrants.[95] The number of warrants nationwide is much higher because states are not required to enter information into the National Crime Information Center (NCIC) database.

In 2000, Senator Strom Thurmond, of South Carolina, captured the essence of what has become an almost interminable problem. At the time, the number of outstanding felony warrants in federal cases was about 45,000, and the number of fugitives accused of felonies and other serious crimes numbered more than 500,000, according to the database for the National Crime Information Center. Thurmond, a Republican who died in 2003, recounted the figures on June 22, 2000, at the hearing on fugitives before the Senate Subcommittee on Criminal Justice Oversight, which Thurmond chaired. Thurmond acted out of concerns that too many fugitives were on the loose. Out of the hearing grew the Presidential Threat Protection Act of 2000, which expanded the authority of the U.S. Marshals Service to operate regional fugitive task forces. "Fugitives represent not only an outrage to the rule of law, they are also a serious threat to public safety. Many of them continue to commit additional crimes while they roam undetected," Thurmond said. "Fugitives are the Achilles heel of law enforcement today. As the number of warrants rise, the problem can almost be overwhelming for law enforcement. Indeed, no one knows exactly how many fugitives there are."[96]

5

FLIGHTS OF FANCY

The Fugitive in American Popular Culture

The hero of one of the best-known manhunts in the history of the United States turned out not to be the person who caught and killed the fugitive. That person, Bob Ford, become the villain. No one disputed that his victim, Jesse James, was a bank robber and a train robber and a killer. But James became a legend after Ford, seeking a reward of as much as $10,000, shot the thirty-four-year-old to death while James was hiding out under the assumed name of Thomas Howard in St. Joseph, Missouri, on April 3, 1882. Sixteen days later, none other than Oscar Wilde, the poet, playwright, and peerless conversationalist from England, observed the public fascination with Jesse James during a stop in St. Joseph during Wilde's heralded speaking tour of America. Wilde noted that James had been killed, and Wilde wrote that he had seen what he characterized as a throng of visitors descend on James's house to retrieve whatever they could from the estate of the newly deceased outlaw. "They sold his dust-bin and foot-scraper yesterday by public auction, his door-knocker is to be offered for sale this afternoon, the reserve price being about the income of an English bishop," Wilde, in tongue-in-cheek fashion, wrote to his friend Norman Forbes-Robertson on April 19, 1882. "The citizens of Kansas have telegraphed to an agent here to secure his coal-scuttle at all hazards and at any cost, and his favourite chromo-lithograph was disposed of at a price which in Europe only an authentic Titian can command, or an undoubted masterpiece. The Americans are certainly great hero-worshippers, and always take their heroes from the criminal classes."[1] And in another letter he wrote to a different correspondent on April 19, 1882, Wilde remarked, "The Americans, if not hero-worshippers, are villain-worshippers."[2]

Decades later, with the advent of first the public enemies list and then the Ten Most Wanted of the FBI and the Fifteen Most Wanted list of the U.S. Marshals Service, the American public would get even more fugitives to read about, wonder about, and, in some instances, celebrate, much like some Americans of Jesse James's era came to lionize him. Of all criminals, fugitives often offer the most potential to be seen as heroes or at least noble lawbreakers despite the trails of mayhem and even death that they often leave behind. Homer S. Cummings and J. Edgar Hoover early on recognized the possibility that Americans, weary of the Great Depression and looking for any type of hopeful diversion, might come to regard John Dillinger and other gangsters and fugitives as somewhat honorable. The Justice Department and FBI countered the public enemies of the movies with the creation of the real-life G-men, and, through the introduction of the fugitive lists, the FBI and U.S. Marshals Service emphasized the risk the fugitives posed, particularly because a criminal on the run could be almost anywhere. But the conception of the fugitive as a folk hero has endured in American culture, with many of those on the run from the law—Jesse James, Bonnie and Clyde, and Willie Sutton among them—given continued iconic status in popular literature and the movies.

The fugitive, for better or for worse, is interwoven into the identity of America. "The lam story," as crime writer William Beverly has observed, "is surely one of America's great minor genres. From slave narratives to *Light in August* and *Beloved*, tales of flight occupy central places in its literary canon. Of the American Film Institute's 1998 list of '100 Greatest American Movies,' four are fugitive stories, depicting a criminal's flight: *Bonnie and Clyde, Double Indemnity, North by Northwest,* and *Butch Cassidy and the Sundance Kid*."[3] For Hollywood, fugitive movies were on par with gangster movies in terms of public fascination in the 1930s. As Beverly also notes, Paul Muni in March 1932 starred in *Scarface*, a landmark film that glamorized the criminal underworld with a lead character not unlike Al Capone. (The movie was remade in 1983 as the famously violent *Scarface*, starring Al Pacino.) In November 1932, Muni starred in *I Am a Fugitive from a Chain Gang*, which was nominated for Academy Awards for best picture and best actor and continues to be recognized as a noir classic that made a strong impression in its day.[4]

The national admiration for fugitives and outlaws, particularly as reflected in movies and literature through much of the twentieth century, is a reflection of the national character—a character of a populace that, in general, is suspicious of governmental authority, roots for the underdog, and is wary of injustice, including a disregard for due process, even for outlaws. Though summary execution—

sanctioned with the capture of fugitives "dead or alive"—might have been necessary to guarantee order on the frontier, its use in more civilized realms, such as
post–Civil War Missouri, generated dissent, even if the outlaw was a Jesse James
who was clearly guilty of crimes for which he had never been prosecuted. Public
sympathy is understandable for a truly innocent fugitive, a person, who, like the
protagonist in the movie and television series *The Fugitive*, is on the run for a
crime he or she did not commit. But the reasons are more complicated for public
sympathy for a genuine outlaw, though the movies and popular fiction certainly
play a role in many cases. Every culture, though, has its Robin Hood; its Rob
Roy, the Scottish rogue; its Dick Turpin, the English highwayman. All are "social
bandits" considered to be friends of the people despite their crimes. The robbers
argued, or posterity determined, that they stole from the rich and from wealthy
institutions, such as banks, for the benefit of the poor. In terms of Jesse James, the
influential historian Richard Maxwell Brown has linked his romantic legend to
his status as a "resister gunfighter"—"a notable lawbreaker paradoxically widely
admired by law-abiding members of society."[5] As Brown also has written, "In the
post-1865 era, social bandits, in the James tradition of crime, looted banks and
railroads, institutions whose rapacious economic exactions caused resentment
among peaceable western farmers, ranchers, and townspeople."

Such sentiments for outlaws and fugitives are rooted in the founding of the
United States, in which the colonists revolted against the British Empire. From
the start, revolutionaries and rebels were viewed as heroic when their foes were
unfair governments and overreaching central authority. For the Americans of
the Revolution, being free meant breaking the law and defying the overlord. The
suspicious attitude toward power as well as the national inclination toward chal-
lenging authority became further pronounced with the Civil War. The North
opposed slavery, the South opposed the North, with each claiming the superior
view. The federal government was caught in the middle and thus weakened. As
Leland Tracy, an academic and essayist, has observed, "Early in the country's
history, the federal government found itself challenged both by the moral and
religious authority of the northern abolitionists and by the military and political
authority of the southern slave states. The federal structure of the United States
guaranteed considerable sovereignty for each state, creating real ambiguity over
who has the authority over certain aspects of American life."[6] Even the U.S.
Marshals Service, the nation's oldest law enforcement agency, saw its standing
diminished by its pursuit of runaway slaves. In the Civil War, the North's hero
was the South's outlaw, and vice versa. What was criminal and legal was, in
many ways, a matter of perception, with one's opinion of the federal government
driving much of the evaluation.

The American acceptance and even fondness for the outlaw and fugitive flourished in the Old West. The vastness of the territory on the other side of the Mississippi River made hiding out from the law easy for most fugitives, who often found that lawmen were either nonexistent or scarce. As more settlers moved to the West, creating more opportunities for criminals, the lack of law enforcement and the wide-open landscape benefited fugitive thieves and other crooks. And, as Tracy deftly observes, even as a more structured justice system arrived to join U.S. marshals, the fledgling operations were often called into question: "Local law enforcement and judges in these areas often had no clear legal legitimacy; and while some judges and sheriffs were elected, many were appointed and paid for by local economic interests."[7] These local economic interests included private security firms, such as the Pinkerton detectives. They worked for their employers, not the public, creating a private system of enforcement that was answerable to no one.[8]

The ambiguity emboldened criminals like Jesse James, which caused more organized yet still quasi-legal forces to try to take control of the legal chaos. Frontier justice reigned in the form of vigilantes and posses intent on capturing fugitives dead or alive. Outlaws truly became outside the law, even as the Constitution allowed for no citizen to be without legal protections. Especially because of summary executions, such as lynchings or "prairie necktie parties," the good and the bad became further blurred, as Tracy has also written: "Such expedient justice was obviously meant to have a dissuasive effect on criminal activity, and may have been unavoidable given the enormity of the continental United States and the still nascent criminal justice system, but it also undermined the moral foundation of the legal authority which permitted this type of frontier justice, allowing a degree of sympathy for these criminals that they probably would not have otherwise deserved."[9]

The moral and legal fluidity created situations in which the hunter and hunted switched places. Grat and Bob Dalton rode as deputy U.S. marshals before they turned to robbing banks as members of the Dalton Gang; their badge-wearing patrols of what was then known as the Indian Territory and what is today Oklahoma surely aided them when they were looking for places to hide while on the run in the 1890s. They settled on Dalton's Cave, in the area which is today west of Tulsa. Like many who had gravitated to the Indiana Territory and other areas of the Old West, the Daltons started with good intentions but turned to crime as a way to make a living. Farmers and ranchers made the same jump after blizzards and other difficulties plunged them into financial distress. Everyone was trying to survive in the West, on both sides of the law. "In many instances," as one writer has observed, "the man who filled the noose and those who tied it had gone to the West with similar motives. All wanted freedom from the restraints they felt farther east."[10] Not much separated the lawmen and the criminal or the fugitive. Heroes could be villains and villains could be heroes, depending on your point of view.

Jesse James's death provided plenty of opportunities for interpretation. Only James's most fervent sympathizers would have argued he never broke the law. Between 1866, when he was eighteen years old, and 1882, when he died, James and his gang robbed or attempted to rob as many as eleven banks in five states. They carried out as many as twelve train robberies and four stagecoach robberies, among other crimes, netting them as much as $350,000, or more than $6 million today.[11] James and his gang were also part of multiple murders. But the manner in which James was caught and killed became a matter of debate, creating divisions about who was really on the right side of the law. The ambiguity allowed James to grow into a legendary figure, a "social bandit" in the same league as Robin Hood. James's death featured a convergence of two themes—suspicion of a central government and intolerance for injustice, particularly denial of due process. The death of Jesse James and the mixed reaction to it showed how Americans eventually saw outlaws as fellow citizens worthy of constitutional rights, even in areas such as Missouri, where a legitimate justice system was in place. James's death, to many, was nothing less than a summary execution in which the ends in no way justified the means.

If the manner of James's death engendered posthumous sympathy for him, it undercut the reputation for the man who pleaded for his apprehension—Missouri Governor Thomas T. Crittenden. He all but arranged James's death by offering a reward for the capture of him and Frank James, his brother, at $10,000 each, with half delivered upon capture and the other half upon conviction.[12] Crittenden made the proclamation on July 28, 1881. Bob Ford claimed the reward less than a year later when he killed Jesse James by shooting him in the back of the head in St. Joseph. The house was in Clay County, Missouri, where the Jameses were raised and where they and the Younger brothers had enraged Crittenden and many others by roaming the countryside as Confederate guerrillas and terrorizing Union sympathizers, including those who owned banks, during and after the Civil War. Frank James surrendered to Crittenden in Jefferson City, the capital of Missouri, on October 5, 1882. He was acquitted of train robbery in 1883.

At least Frank James got a trial. Crittenden never stated that the rewards for the James brothers would be payable whether they were brought in dead or alive; indeed, that half of the reward for each brother was due upon conviction shows that a death clause was not formally part of Crittenden's offer. Crittenden nonetheless indicated that the capture of the James brothers, to be legitimate, need not follow the regular rigors of the law. The size of the rewards was outside the bounds of the governor's legal authority. Missouri had a $300 statutory limit for bounties—that was how much the state was allowed to put up. To get around that restriction, Crittenden in late July 1881 arranged a deal with railroad magnates to supply the money for the full $10,000 in rewards for each James brother; small handbills distributed throughout Missouri advertised the amounts.[13] The railroads' involvement was not unlike how railroad-hired detectives and other employees of private interests searched for outlaws and fugitives before a reliable and trusted apparatus for criminal justice found its way to the Indian Territory and other unorganized western lands.

In another concession to the railroads, Crittenden agreed that the rewards for the James brothers would be delivered even if the evidence showed that neither was connected to the incident that spurred the push to establish the rewards—a train robbery near Winston, Missouri, on July 14, 1881. Jesse James was accused of killing the conductor, though most likely by accident.[14] The incident prompted Crittenden to travel to St. Louis on July 25, 1881, to meet with the railroad officials about what to do about the Jameses and to request that the railroads fund the rewards. What mattered was not whether Frank and Jesse James were captured to answer charges that truly applied to them. What mattered was that they were caught along with every other "desperado and outlaw,"[15] as a participant in the meeting with Crittenden said. The goal, the participant said, was to establish a reputation for Missouri so that "the class of ruffians abroad would as soon think of committing suicide as to undertake such an outrageous crime as that recently perpetrated."[16]

The Winston robbery, in which Frank James was also accused of participating, gave Crittenden the impetus to fulfill a promise he made when he took office as governor of Missouri in January 1881. He vowed to rid Missouri of its bandits and outlaws, proclaiming that the state "cannot be the home and abiding place of lawlessness of any character."[17] Crittenden with those words had declared war on outlaws such as the James brothers, and for good reasons. The Jameses and their gang members were real threats to the peace and prosperity in Missouri; the railroads' posting of the reward money, as the participant in the meeting relayed, showed how worried private interests were that Missouri's reputation as a haven for criminals such as the James brothers would make the state a national backwater for development. Yet Crittenden's war-on-crime rhetoric also encouraged the type of state-sanctioned vigilantism that led to the death of Jesse James and that later contributed to his legend. As the historian

T. J. Stiles has written about Crittenden's reward proclamation for the James brothers, "The offer has often been misrepresented as 'dead or alive'—though that is how it was applied."[18]

By coincidence or design, Crittenden announced the rewards at an opportune time. Death and age had weakened the Jameses' gang by the early 1880s, stripping the brothers of many longtime fellow bandits whose loyalty the Jameses never questioned. As more newcomers joined the gang, the chance for betrayal grew, especially with as much as $20,000 in rewards greasing the duplicity. By March 1881, Frank James had moved to the East, leaving as Jesse James's only remaining gang member Charley Ford, Bob Ford's older brother, whom James had befriended in 1880. In March 1882, at James's request, Bob Ford moved in with his brother and the James family at the Jameses' new house in St. Joseph, Missouri. James welcomed Bob Ford even as he had confided in Charley Ford that he did not fully trust Bob. Unknown to James, Charley and Bob Ford had agreed in that last week of March 1882 that they would kill Jesse James and seek the reward money. By then, as T. J. Stiles has written, "Jesse James had only two followers remaining, and both were plotting to kill him."[19]

Jesse James was a victim of betrayal—another aspect of his death that gained him sympathy. If a U.S. marshal had caught James, perhaps that sympathy would have never materialized. And perhaps even if a U.S. marshal would have killed James during a gunfight, the manner of the death would have been acceptable. Jesse James was a deadly criminal, and he above all knew that he was wanted. His capture was inevitable. If taken down fairly, the fugitive Jesse James would have met, for all but his most committed apologists, a just demise. But James lost his life at the hands of two of his closest friends, with Bob Ford pulling the trigger and Charley Ford helping to set up the plot. James was not even armed when Bob Ford shot him on April 2, 1882. James had spent some of the morning discussing a possible bank robbery with the Fords, and then he and Charley Ford left the house to take care of the gang's horses. When the two returned to the house, James took off the holsters that held his two six-shot revolvers; he had complained of the heat and was wary that someone might spot him with the guns in his yard and blow his cover as Thomas Howard. James—in a scene that, all these years later, seems incongruous with the daily activities of a killer and bank robber—stepped up on a chair in his house's living room to use a brush to dust a painting.

Bob Ford took advantage of the opening. He knew that no one, including him, could outdraw Jesse James, so an unarmed James had to be his target. "We waited a long time to catch Jesse without his revolvers," Bob Ford later said of him and his brother, "knowing that unless he put them off we could not fetch him."[20] As if their betrayal was not enough, Ford shot Jesse James in the back of the head. As Charley Ford later testified at the coroner's inquest, "Then he went to brush off some pictures and I gave my brother the wink and we both pulled out our pistols but he, my brother, was a little the quickest and fired first. I had my finger on the trigger and was just going to fire but I saw his shot was a death shot and did not fire. He heard us cock our pistols and [was about] to turn his head. The ball struck him in the back of his head and he fell."[21]

James's wife, Zerelda, known as Zee, entered the room and saw her husband collapsed on the floor. Charley Ford said he told her, "a pistol had accidentally gone off."

"Yes," Zee James replied. "I guess it went off on purpose."[22]

Two thousand mourners attended the funeral of Jesse James on April 6, 1882, in his hometown of Kearney, Missouri, where his body was put on public display. The Ford brothers, after working together to shoot an unarmed man in the back of the head, were indicted on murder charges on April 17, 1882. They pleaded guilty that day and were sentenced to hang on May 19, 1882. Governor Crittenden gave them an unconditional pardon the same day that they pleaded guilty[23] and arranged for them to get a share of the reward money, though details of the payment were never made public.[24] Crittenden was unrepentant in how Jesse James died and his role in it. The Ford brothers, according to the coroner's report on James, said that Crittenden had sanctioned the slaying.[25] Crittenden's comments on James's death did little to dispel any belief that the governor might have been culpable. "I am not regretful of his death and have no words of censure for the boys who removed him," Crittenden said. "They deserve credit is my candid, solemn opinion."[26] He also said, "I have no excuses to make, no apologies to render to any living man for the part I played in this bloody drama. . . . The life of one honest law-abiding man however humble is worth more to society and a state than a legion of Jesse Jameses."[27]

As T. J. Stiles and others have detailed, many agreed with Crittenden that Jesse James got the fate he deserved. He had terrorized Missouri during and after the Civil War, and his elusiveness made him a constant threat to banks and trains as well as Missouri's standing as a law-abiding state. Crittenden had acted with noble intentions, according to this view, and his heroism came with risk: In the days after James's death, rumors circulated that Frank James had assassinated Crittenden out of revenge. The rumors were so strong that the newspapers printed stories to debunk them.[28] But many others were upset at what they considered James's unlawful death. Much of the push for sympathy for James came from John Newman Edwards, a Missouri newspaper editor who turned into the outlaw's hagiographer and defended him without pause or reason. "We called him outlaw, and he was; but fate made him so," Edwards wrote in James's obituary in the *Sedalia Democrat*. He called James's death "cowardly and unnecessary," and, targeting Crittenden, wrote "this so-called law is an outlaw."[29] Some of the criticism was based in politics, as the governor's foes attempted to use James's death to discredit him.[30]

But more objective forces also railed against James's death and Crittenden's role in it. These critics were upset over what they considered the "'legalized murder' of even so murderous a desperado as Jesse James."[31] To catch Jesse James, editorialized the *Daily Register*, in New York, Crittenden "took an adroit and reckless Western way of meeting an outlaw with outlawry."[32] The newspaper continued: "The satisfaction of the community at being rid of a desperado is a poor offset for their permitting such measures to be taken in the name of law. It is the worst form of lynch law, for it borrows the garb of justice itself. The repetition of such measures would be a graver symptom of the decay of justice than the repetition of such a career as that which was then brought to an end."[33] *The American Law Review*, which cited the *Daily Register* editorial in its examination of the James case, took a similar approach. The journal neither defended James nor called for Crittenden to be punished. But it advised that the governor or anyone else would be best, from then on, to let the regular justice system deal with the likes of a Jesse James. "In brief, a Governor of a State like Missouri is committed to civilization," according to *The American Law Review*. "Attacked by barbarism in its midst, the community may pardon or approve, or even applaud, his recent acts. But we do not believe that the civilized forces of the State of Missouri are so weak as to stand aside after this and to have the Governor directly or indirectly plan assassination to keep the peace. While we defend Governor Crittenden from punishment if he is liable to any, we cannot approve of his act; and we are reminded of the ironical but serious verdict of a sympathetic but sensible jury,—'Not guilty; but do not do it again.'"[34]

In the case of Jesse James, the popular class and the intellectual class agreed: Despite his murderous ways, he had been treated unfairly due to the overreach of the government. As America's original outlaw, the first outlaw with a truly national reach and reputation, Jesse James set a standard, in his life and death, in how the nation might view criminals and fugitives. While their crimes would most definitely be part of the calculus of setting popular opinion, so would be the government's response. Governor Thomas Crittenden and Bob Ford, more than anyone else, allowed the legend of Jesse James to flourish, a legend that to this day gives him the benefit of the doubt beyond what he should truly receive.

"Murdered by a traitor and a coward whose name is not worthy to appear here," reads the inscription on Jesse James's tombstone. Well before the era of the movies, the ballad, a prevalent form of popular entertainment in the 1880s, further enshrined Jesse James as a fugitive for the ages. The "Ballad of Jesse James," written shortly after his death, is still sung today. Its stanzas include the following:

> Jesse James was a lad that killed many a man.
> He robbed the Glendale train.
> He stole from the rich and he gave to the poor,
> He'd a hand and a heart and a brain.

> It was Robert Ford, that dirty little coward,
> I wonder how he does feel,
> For he ate of Jesse's bread and he slept in Jesse's bed,
> Then he laid Jesse James in his grave.

> Jesse was a man, a friend to the poor.
> He'd never see a man suffer pain,
> And with his brother Frank he robbed the Chicago bank,
> And stopped the Glendale train.[35]

Bonnie Parker and Clyde Barrow saw themselves as their era's Jesse James, and, since their deaths in May 1934, the popular conception of the murderous duo has only further idealized them more as anti-heroes than villains. A ballad that Bonnie wrote, and which newspapers throughout the country published after she and Clyde were ambushed and gunned down, established the trope: Bonnie and Clyde, like Jesse James, were killers and fugitives, but were also largely misunderstood in their ways and were, in the end, victims of treachery. Like Jesse James, Bonnie and Clyde were mythologized because they were able to outwit the law for so long and so well. Bonnie called her ballad "The End of the Line," though it is popularly known as "The Story of Bonnie and Clyde." Its sixteen stanzas include these words:

> You've read the story of Jesse James –
> Of how he lived and died;
> If you are still in need
> Of something to read
> Here's the story of Bonnie and Clyde.

> Now Bonnie and Clyde are the Barrow gang.

I'm sure you have all read
How they rob and steal
And those who squeal
Are usually found dying or dead.

There's lots of untruths to those write-ups;
They're not so ruthless as that;
Their nature is raw;
They hate the law –
The stool pigeons, spotters, and rats.

They call them cold-blooded killers;
They say they are heartless and mean;
But I say this with pride,
That I once knew Clyde
When he was honest and upright and clean.

They don't think they're too smart or desperate.
They know the law always wins;
They've been shot at before,
But they do not ignore
That death is the wages of sin.

Some day they'll go down together;
And they'll bury them side by side,
To a few it'll be grief –
To the law a relief –
But it's death for Bonnie and Clyde.[36]

    Like Jesse James, Bonnie Parker and Clyde Barrow deserved no accolades for what they did in reality. James' brutality at least had a political motivation, however misguided and inexcusable. Bonnie and Clyde, both natives of Texas, robbed and killed for the thrill in the lower Midwest and the Southwest in 1933 and 1934. They mostly robbed grocery stores and gas stations; the banks they hit were mostly in small towns and the take was limited. No matter what their targets, Bonnie and Clyde, and especially Clyde, left behind a trail of blood. Clyde is believed to have committed most if not all of the murders attributed to the couple and their gang—at least thirteen slayings across Missouri, Oklahoma, Arkansas, and Texas. Seven lawmen were among the victims, including two whose deaths spurred the most outrage. Clyde and his newest gang member at the time, Henry Methvin, killed two motorcycle police patrolmen near Grapevine, Texas, outside of Dallas, on April 1, 1934, which was Easter. The victims were E. B. Wheeler, who was twenty-six years old, and a twenty-two-year-old rookie named H. D. Murphy, who was to have been married in twelve days.

From then on, Bonnie and Clyde were marked as they never had been. But even well before then they had few allies, even among the criminal class. Their killing ways and what other killers considered their amateurish style of robbery earned them the enmity of none other than John Dillinger, who viewed the couple as more like sloppy punks than professional thieves and fugitives who ranked alongside professional criminals like him. "They're giving bank robbery a bad name," Dillinger is reported to have said.[37] Criminals and law-abiding citizens came to despise Bonnie and Clyde during their lifetimes. "They were, in short, not only outlaws but outcasts," the historian John Toland wrote in *Dillinger Days*, his influential biography of Dillinger.[38]

And yet Bonnie and Clyde continue to be associated with more than a touch of glamour and sympathy. Much of the ambiguity is due to *Bonnie and Clyde*, director Arthur Penn's stylish 1967 hit film that made stars out of Warren Beatty, who played Clyde, and Faye Dunaway, who played Bonnie. Reflecting the counter-culture of the times, Penn portrayed Bonnie and Clyde more as rebels and outliers than ruthless killers, though the film never looked away from their violent careers. The Bonnie and Clyde of Hollywood were anti-authoritarians doing their best to survive in the Great Depression by robbing banks, the scourge of the economic collapse that had wiped out the savings of so many common folk. Bonnie and Clyde were fugitives, but their flight, according to the movie, had something of a noble element. In the movies, as in real life—as evidenced by Bonnie's ballad—Bonnie and Clyde knew that their running would end only in death. Who could blame anyone for wanting their flight to last as long as it possibly could?

At the same time, the mythmaking of Penn's film was based, to a degree, in the facts. Begrudging admiration was not out of line for Clyde Barrow because of his mastery in using his powerful and stolen Ford V-8 to elude police throughout a cluster of states. As Leland Tracy has written, "In addition to the speed these cars gave him, Barrow's knowledge of the roads linking the contiguous states of Texas, Oklahoma, Kansas, Missouri, Arkansas, and Louisiana, combined with his remarkable driving skills, made it possible to cross quickly from one state to another after a robbery."[39] Bonnie and Clyde, in addition to possessing the practical skills needed to be fugitives, possessed a level of self-awareness that made the more than simpleton thieves. Bonnie's poetry, though far from literary, conveyed the couple's sense of doom and fate. And the couple left behind a trove of photographs that proved they were more than cognizant of how images and public relations could bend reality.

Whether Bonnie and Clyde ever wanted the photos published will forever be a matter of debate. They were on a roll of undeveloped film that police seized during a raid of the house where Bonnie and Clyde were hiding in Joplin, Missouri, on April 13, 1933. Two lawmen died in the firefight. Authorities developed the roll of film and the photos were distributed to the newspapers, which published them nationwide. For nearly a year, up until their deaths in May 1934, Bonnie and Clyde were the most famous bank robbers and fugitives in the United States. The photos, which they took of each other and others took of them, made them so: Bonnie smoking a cigar and holding a pistol while leaning against the getaway car; Bonnie pointing a shotgun at Clyde in jest; the two of them kneeling in a clearing in the woods, where Clyde is cleaning his submachine gun; the two of them hugging and looking straight at the camera—she is wearing a dress and he is wearing a suit and tie and holding a fedora—as they stand against the back of the getaway car, with the license plate clearly visible. None of these photos made Bonnie and Clyde blameless or erased their crimes. The snapshots still created a mystique and added an allure—Bonnie and Clyde were bank robbers, but the photos made them more human. They were bank robbers and killers and fugitives with personalities. And, based on the photos, they clearly loved each other in a kind of star-crossed romance of the criminal kind. They even died young: She was twenty-three years old and he was twenty-five.

Bonnie and Clyde became fugitives of the footlights, known for their image as much as their crimes. Decades later, Warren Beatty and Faye Dunaway would play Bonnie and Clyde in a movie, but the two were matinee idols in their own right, especially as their bank-robbing exploits were captured in newsreels that came after the photos. As biographer Jeff Guinn has written of Bonnie and Clyde and the photos,

> Few real-life villains had the roguish charisma that Jimmy Cagney and Edward G. Robinson brought to the movie screen. Al Capone was clearly a barbaric thug. Ma Barker was a dumpy middle-aged woman. John Dillinger had matinee-idol good looks and Pretty Boy Floyd has the best possible nickname, but the Joplin photos introduced new criminal superstars with the most titillating trademark of all—illicit sex. Clyde Barrow and Bonnie Parker were young and unmarried. They undoubtedly slept together—after all, the girl smoked cigars. Whether they'd heard the term or not, the Freudian implications did not escape journalists or their readers. That made it easy, when writers exaggerated Clyde's and Bonnie's exploits, for readers to buy into far-fetched stories about these young criminal lovers.[40]

Guinn's interview with Jim Wright, the former speaker of the U.S. House of Representatives and a well-known Texan, further explained why Bonnie and Clyde became a popular attraction. Wright said he was eleven years old when he first saw the photos and newsreels of the bank robbers and their fellow gang members. "Their whole image was one of glamour," Wright said. "You rather imagined them holed up in some upscale hotel. They always dressed perfectly, wielding guns in a deadly manner, coolly evading capture against all odds. It was a very romantic existence we felt they must enjoy. And even if you did not approve of them, you still would have to envy them a little, to be so good-looking and rich and happy."[41]

The way Bonnie and Clyde died only helped their posthumous cause. Like Jesse James, the two were so adept at staying on the lam that the law had to rely on betrayal to catch and kill them. In the case of Bonnie and Clyde, their Bob Ford was Ivy Methvin, the father of Henry Methvin, one of their gang members. Ivy Methvin arranged to tip off a posse about Bonnie and Clyde's whereabouts in exchange for the state of Texas granting a full pardon to his son, who had been convicted of an assault with intent to murder. That was Ivy Methvin's reward: his son's freedom.

Texas Governor Miriam "Ma" Ferguson approved the deal in mid-March 1934. Ferguson earlier had had commissioned a decorated retired Texas Ranger, Frank Hamer, to find Bonnie and Clyde. The FBI had also been searching for the pair, using the authority under the Dyer Act, which made driving across state lines a federal offense.[42] Though Congress in early May passed the landmark crime bills, including, on May 3, 1934, the law that made bank robbery a federal offense, they were not retroactive. Hamer in any case was pursuing Bonnie and Clyde mainly for a state crime—the murder of the two police patrolmen three weeks earlier. Hamer created a six-member posse, with lawmen from Texas and Louisiana, who failed to track down Bonnie and Clyde until they got help from Ivy Methvin. On May 23, 1934, shortly after nine in the morning, the posse ambushed Bonnie and Clyde and gunned them down in their V-8 on the outskirts of Gibsland, Louisiana, north of Shreveport. Bonnie and Clyde were heavily armed; inside the car police found three rifles, two sawed-off shotguns, nine pistols, and three thousand rounds of ammunition.[43] But they never had a chance against the posse. And they certainly never got a trial. The outlaws, like Jesse James, were all but summarily executed. Bonnie was shot with fifty rounds, Clyde with forty. As Leland Tracy has written, "the extrajudicial killing of Bonnie and Clyde by Frank Hamer and his posse provided a mitigated circumstance that relativized the brutality of the young couple's crimes."[44]

As was the case with Jesse James's death, the perception that the law over-reached in the capture of Bonnie and Clyde stirred up popular dissent and helped transform the two into folk heroes after their deaths. If they had been fugitives caught fairly, perhaps they would never have turned into myths. Ten thousand to twenty thousand people attended the visitations at two Dallas funeral homes for Bonnie and Clyde. Not long after their burials, their legend started to take shape, culminating, in 1967 with the release of Arthur Penn's film *Bonnie and Clyde*. The text for their story was published in the fall of 1934. It was a nonfiction book that writer Jan I. Fortune fashioned from remembrances of Clyde's sister Nell Barrow and Bonnie's mother, Emma Parker. Bonnie and Clyde are portrayed as intelligent, misunderstood, and fated. The name of the book is *Fugitives*.

Its foreword captures the intersection of myth and reality that propelled Bonnie and Clyde to their twisted celebrity. In several paragraphs, Fortune puts Bonnie and Clyde in the class of the ordinary and the extraordinary—desperate fugitives on the run who, because betrayal preceded their deaths, were like Jesse James and others, and who, because of their love for each other, were like no criminals the United States had ever seen or was likely to see again. As Fortune made clear, Bonnie and Clyde were criminals, but also criminals who rose above the rest. She wrote,

> There is nothing in these pages that would attract any normal person to the life of the outlaw. The two years which Bonnie and Clyde spent as fugitives, hunted by officers all over the Southwest, were the most horrible years ever spent by two young people. They were on the road constantly; they lived from hand to mouth; they never knew the happiness of safety and security; they had no home and they rarely had enough money.
>
> Never for one instance did they experience a joy or a thrill which could possibly compensate them for the living hell which made up their lives. In the last accounting, all they had left was each other and the pleasure of occasionally sneaking home to see their people. There never was a time, after the chase began, when they would not have traded places with the poorest and humblest couple on earth if they could have had peace and ordinary happiness.
>
> They trusted but few fellow beings and even here as always that trust was betrayed. Bonnie and Clyde were betrayed by one they considered a friend. This was also true of Jesse James, of Cole Younger, of Pancho Villa, of John Dillinger, of Machine Gun Kelly. It will always be true of those who steal and kill and prey upon decent law-abiding society.
>
> There was only one thing that Bonnie and Clyde possessed which the above mentioned did not own: Clyde and Bonnie had a love which bound them together

in life and went with them to their graves. We believe that no two people ever loved more devotedly, more sincerely, and more lastingly than Clyde Barrow and Bonnie Parker.[45]

Other fugitives failed to receive such treatment after their deaths. The type of extrajudicial killings that bolstered the popular appeal of Jesse James and Bonnie and Clyde worked against other well-known fugitives, mainly because they also engaged in the kind of vigilante justice that was so objectionable when the government practiced it. To be sure, James and Bonnie and Clyde were ruthless killers who committed crimes with impunity and with no sense of justice for their victims. But because their deaths involved treachery and a lack of due process, the public bestowed a degree of posthumous glory upon them. One of the more famous fugitives in American history, the master bank robber and prison escapee Willie Sutton (No. 11 on the FBI's Ten Most Wanted list), would have received just as many accolades, and an even more celebrated posthumous reputation, had his final capture in 1952 not been connected, three weeks later, to the death of the innocent bystander who had recognized Sutton from an FBI most-wanted photo and tipped off police about his whereabouts. And James "Whitey" Bulger, (No. 458 on the FBI's Ten Most Wanted list), the mobster and killer who was on the lam for sixteen years until his capture in 2011, is seen as a murderous thug rather than a wily and resourceful crook at least admired for his ability to stay on the run for so long. Being an informant and getting convicted of participating in the murders of eleven people has done little to add a mythic or folk-like element to Bulger's flight.

Sutton, who died at age seventy-eight in 1980, is remembered primarily for a saying that he maintained he never uttered but that he appropriated without complaint. "That's where the money is," he is purported to have said when asked why he robbed banks.[46] The remark conveyed a message so indisputable in its obviousness that it became transformed into a medical term, Sutton's Law, coined in 1960. It refers to the theory that physicians should first explore their hunches, or what seems obvious to them, in pinpointing the cause of an illness. Sutton also possessed an air of likeability because of the way he robbed banks—as many as sixty in two and a half years alone, according to one estimate, though determining a precise amount is difficult because of the length of Sutton's career, which ran from 1920 to 1952. He is believed to have stolen as much as $2 million.[47] Sutton, known as "Slick Willie" and "the Actor," for his smooth manner and wide array of disguises—police officer, postal worker, deliveryman—was not violent during the bank robberies; he carried a gun, but was disinclined to use it, instead relying on directness and a courteous nature to get the bank employees to turn over the money. According to the FBI, "One victim said witnessing one of Sutton's robberies was like being at the movies, except the usher had a gun."[48]

Sutton rarely got caught, and when he did, he broke out of prison. He used a makeshift ladder to escape from one, in 1932, and he tunneled out of another, in 1945. In 1947, while serving a life sentence at the Philadelphia County Prison, in Holmesburg, Pennsylvania, Sutton and four other inmates dressed as prison guards and escaped by using ladders to climb over the penitentiary walls. That escape landed Sutton on the FBI's newly created top-ten list on March 20, 1950. Eleven days earlier, on March 9, 1950, Sutton was accused of robbing a bank of $64,942, in Long Island City, New York. Sutton was committing more crimes as a fugitive, making his lack of apprehension doubly embarrassing to the authorities.

Sutton's appearance on the Ten Most Wanted list meant he likely could not stay undercover forever. The FBI had circulated his photo to police departments and other locations, including the shops of tailors. Sutton, according to the FBI's description on the most-wanted list, "dresses neatly and conservatively," and was also known to buy tailored clothes.[49] On February 18, 1952, a twenty-four-year-old clothing salesman and pants-presser and Coast Guard veteran by the name of Arnold Schuster told police in Brooklyn that he had spotted someone who looked like Sutton riding the subway. By Sutton's own account, Schuster had been looking for him: Schuster worked in his father's tailor shop, where, on the wall near the presser, Schuster had posted the FBI most-wanted flyer on Sutton. It included six photographs, Sutton said, of him "with five different kinds of mustache drawn in. Including the pencil mustache I was wearing at the time. . . . How he could have made me during those few seconds, without my noticing, is something I will never understand."[50] After noticing Sutton, Schuster told police, he followed the man to a service station. The information led police to track Sutton to a street in Brooklyn, where he was trying to fix the dead battery in his car.

Sutton at first denied being the famous bank robber but admitted his identity once police said they planned to take his fingerprints. "OK, you got me," Sutton said. "I'm Willie Sutton."[51] He was armed but put up no fight. The police trumpeted his apprehension. "Well, we've got Willie Sutton. We've got Willie Sutton," declared the New York City police commissioner, George P. Monaghan. "This culminates one of the greatest manhunts in the history of the department. Sutton was the most-sought criminal in the United States. We've caught the Babe Ruth of bank robbers."[52]

Sutton turned into a villain on March 8, 1952, when Schuster was fatally shot—once in each eye and twice in the groin—while he was walking in the neighborhood. After Sutton's arrest, Schuster's name had appeared in the news as the person who helped track down the elusive thief. Sutton was in prison and denied involvement in Schuster's death, but the tipster's demise and his role in fingering Sutton were too closely linked to be unquestionably coincidental. Schuster's murder was never solved, though a prime suspect was Frederick J. Tenuto, a mobster who had escaped from prison twice with Sutton and was No. 14 on the FBI's Ten Most Wanted list (added March 24, 1950).

Tenuto was never captured and is believed to have been the victim of a mob hit, leading the FBI to remove his name from the most-wanted list on March 9, 1964.[53] Whether Sutton was connected to the death of Schuster was never determined; police never solved the case. Sutton felt the sting of the murder. Sutton acknowledged that Schuster's death stripped him of the perception that he was a different kind of criminal—a gentleman bank robber. "The public's attitude toward me turned completely around," Sutton said. "They had viewed me as a little guy who had outwitted the authorities without hurting anybody, and there was now a young man, a Coast Guard veteran, who had been gunned down in the street, gangster-style, because he had tried to be a good citizen. I could understand their attitude very well. Even as I said, 'That sinks me,' my heart had gone out to that poor kid whose life was over because he had happened to see me on a train."[54]

The rest of Sutton's life was quiet. He was convicted in 1952 of bank robbery and sentenced to 30 to 120 years in prison, though, suffering from emphysema, he was released early, on December 24, 1969. He capitalized on his lingering notoriety in 1970, when he filmed a commercial for a new photo credit-card program for a bank in Connecticut—the "face card," in which the photo on the credit card was meant to prevent theft. "Now when I say I am Willie Sutton, people believe me," a smiling Sutton says as he displays his photo on his credit card.[55] A decade later, Willie Sutton was dead, leaving behind an unforgettable saying that will always be his legacy, along with the murder that came after his capture.

Whitey Bulger became as famous a fugitive as Willie Sutton. But his crimes made him more heartless than Jesse James and Bonnie and Clyde. Bulger, the mob boss from Boston, was also the subject of a movie, *Black Mass* (2015), in which Johnny Depp, as big a star as Warren Beatty was in 1967, played Bulger as a coldhearted and duplicitous killer who was relentless in his efforts to control the rackets in South Boston and beyond. Bulger was also the inspiration for the mobster played by Jack Nicholson, another box-office star, in the 2006 Martin Scorsese film, *The Departed*. As the movies detailed, Bulger took the law into his own hands by murdering his rivals; he also informed on them to the

FBI. He exhibited the same traits—unrestrained vigilantism and treachery—that tarnished the reputations of Bob Ford and Governor Crittenden and the posse that gunned down Bonnie and Clyde. Bulger's criminal exploits and betrayal of his peers made him a fugitive that most of the public wanted caught, even if he was able to stay ahead of the FBI, U.S. marshals, and others for sixteen years, between 1995 and June 2011. As the *New York Times* reported when Bulger was finally captured, Bulger "shared top billing on the most-wanted list with Osama bin Laden and drew the largest reward—$2 million—that the bureau ever offered for a Top 10 domestic fugitive."[56]

Bulger was as meticulous in planning for his life as a fugitive as he was in controlling the underworld in South Boston. When he was getting ready to go on the run, Bulger was said to have taken out safe deposit boxes in cities throughout the United States and in Montreal, London, Dublin, and Venice; each box would serve as a kind of way station for Bulger to hide and retrieve cash, jewelry, and other valuables.[57] To prepare for his time as a fugitive, Bulger and his longtime girlfriend, Catherine Greig, also underwent plastic surgery.[58] They traveled often while on the run, including to Las Vegas and Boston, but they eventually became recluses in their own home: an apartment near the Pacific Ocean in Santa Monica, California. They were captured there when he was eighty-one and she was sixty—they called themselves Charlie and Carol Gasko—and after the FBI launched a publicity campaign that focused on Greig more than Bulger. The FBI doubled the reward to $100,000 for tips leading to Greig's arrest on charges that she was harboring a fugitive, and the bureau emphasized in television public-service announcements that Greig, like Bulger, was believed to have had plastic surgery. The FBI believed that tips on Greig's whereabouts were likely to be more plentiful than tips on Bulger's: "She was a person with the kind of idiosyncrasies—a devotion to animals, the beauty parlor and monthly teeth cleanings—that might make her easier to find."[59]

The FBI was not specific in what kind of tip agents received that led them to Bulger and Greig's apartment on June 22, 2011. But the FBI said the tip resulted from the publicity campaign, in which the bureau aired the TV spots in fourteen cities during daytime shows that appealed to older women.[60] Bulger and Greig, in the parlance of the police and crime reporters, surrendered without incident. Inside their apartment, whose rent they paid in cash, agents found more than $800,000, more than twenty guns and knives, and false IDs. The fugitive couple had lived in the apartment since 1996 and were known to hang a sign on the front door: "Please do not Knock at Any Time."[61]

Greig pleaded guilty to helping hide Bulger and was sentenced in June 2012 to eight years in federal prison and fined $150,000. Bulger on August

12, 2013, was convicted in federal court in Boston of a number of racketeering charges, including participating in eleven murders. At eighty-four years old, he was sentenced to two consecutive life terms, plus five years, in federal prison on November 14, 2013. U.S. District Judge Denise J. Casper, who sentenced Bulger, took aim at his image that had made him, for some, a protector of insular South Boston and its proud but sometimes criminal ways. Casper sought to undermine any chance that Bulger somehow, even in South Boston, could be viewed as a folk hero. "You have over time and in certain quarters become the face of this city, and that is regrettable," the judge said. "You, sir, do not represent this city."[62]

Bulger's alliance with a corrupt FBI special agent, John Connolly, made his case more sinister and damaged the reputation of the FBI, especially in Boston. Connolly, who handled Bulger as a confidential informant, was convicted in 2002 of federal charges including racketeering, for protecting Bulger and tipping him off to police investigations. Connolly was sentenced to ten years in federal prison in that case. He was sentenced to another forty years in prison for his 2008 conviction for second-degree murder in Florida. He was found guilty of leaking information to Bulger that led Bulger and his mob partner, Stephen Flemmi, to kill a gaming executive, John Callahan, who was found dead in the trunk of a Cadillac found at the Miami airport in 1982. Connolly was convicted of telling Bulger and Flemmi that Callahan might testify against them.

Adding to the FBI's shame in the Bulger case was that he was able to elude the bureau as a fugitive for so long. Connolly, after all, was also accused of allowing Bulger and Greig to go on the run by tipping them off about their imminent arrests in December 1994. Upon Bulger's sentencing, the head FBI special agent in Boston pledged to rebuild the integrity of the office that Bulger had undermined while he was in his hometown and when he was on the lam. "I realize that the actions of a small percentage of law enforcement many years ago caused some people to lose faith and confidence in us," said Vincent B. Lisi, who had taken over as the new special agent in charge of the Boston office. "Our job now is to make sure that we can regain the faith and confidence of those people who may have lost it years ago."[63]

Bulger's life ended in prison on October 30, 2018. He was beaten beyond recognition at the Federal Correctional Institution at Hazelton, in Bruceton Mills, West Virginia, east of Morgantown. Bulger hours earlier had been transferred to the prison from a federal penitentiary in Florida. He was eighty-nine years old. Bulger's killing had the markings of a mob hit. His eyes were nearly gouged out, and the initial suspects were linked to the Mafia.[64] For most of his life Bulger had managed to elude his enemies and cheat the kind death that he had imposed on so many other people as a mob boss. While in prison, he was no longer wanted by the law. But he was still wanted. His murder made that clear.

   While Bulger was on the run, the only other fugitive that got more attention in the United States was Osama bin Laden, who was on the FBI's Ten Most Wanted list from 1999—for the terrorist attacks that predated 9/11—until Navy SEALS killed him during a raid of his hideout in Pakistan on May 2, 2011. Bin Laden, of course, was killed without a trial and he was buried at sea, both by orders of President Barack Obama. Such actions, if applied to a fugitive with popular appeal, such as Jesse James, Bonnie and Clyde, or even Willie Sutton, would have the potential to transform the fugitive into a legendary victim of the state. But not bin Laden. The unfathomable sweep and brutality of his crimes guaranteed that he would never be the object of sympathy in the United States. He was more of war criminal than a criminal fleeing prosecution.
   Times had also changed. Particularly after 9/11, American society became more prone than ever to cheer for the police, the firefighter, and other first responders than give any show of support to fugitives and other lawbreakers, accused or convicted. The fugitive, after 9/11, in many respects became an object of scorn. In post-9/11 America, "It is difficult to imagine any modern criminals receiving the kind of sympathy, not to mention admiration, that some of the more colorful outlaws of the Wild West or the Depression era enjoyed," Leland Tracy has written. "From now on, only thoroughly fictional outlaws in extenuating circumstances will draw sympathy. When contemporary fugitives are on the run, the hearts and minds of the public will be rooting for the law, and cheering on the hounds."[65]

   If, as Tracy suggests, fiction is the last refuge for the truly sympathetic fugitive, then the fugitive whom Americans can be said to have embraced with near universal consent is a fictional creation—Dr. Richard Kimble. He became part of the culture via two media platforms. Kimble was the main character in *The Fugitive*, the landmark television series (1963–1967) and the blockbuster movie of the same name (1993).
   As played by David Janssen on TV and Harrison Ford in the film remake, Kimble is the source of sympathy because he is indeed innocent, as the audience knows. He is falsely accused of killing his wife but is convicted and sentenced to death. He escapes and goes on the run after the train on which he is a passenger accidentally derails on the way to deliver him to a prison and death row. For the rest of the TV series, and throughout the course of the movie, Kimble tries to achieve two goals: to stay ahead of his would-be captor, Lieutenant Philip Ge-

rard (Barry Morse) in the TV series and Deputy U.S. Marshal Samuel Gerard (Tommy Lee Jones) in the film; and to find the person who murdered his wife, an assailant described as the mysterious one-armed man. In the TV series, each episode brings Kimble to a different city with a different set of problems for him to face. The audience roots for Kimble because of the desire for justice on two fronts: Kimble's exoneration and the one-armed man's capture. Kimble is so emotionally attractive as a fugitive because he has done nothing wrong, unlike most fugitives in real life. The accidental train wreck and Kimble's decision to flee to seek justice, rather than to run away from justice, made him into a hero because he possessed "willed irresponsibility without a concomitant sense of guilt," the creator of the TV series, Roy Huggins, once said.[66] In another analysis, "TV viewers felt perfectly at ease with this particular 'outlaw' because what was happening was not his fault."[67]

The Fugitive TV series held an added fascination. It resembled real life, though in real life the main character was not a fugitive. Huggins's inspiration for the TV series was said to be the ordeal of Jean Valjean, the unjustly accused fugitive in Victor Hugo's classic novel *Les Misérables*, which also features Javert, the relentless police detective who tracks Valjean. But the plotline of *The Fugitive*, as so many commentators have shown, closely resembled the case of Sam Sheppard, the Cleveland doctor charged in the beating death of his wife, Marilyn Sheppard, who was four months pregnant, at their home on July 4, 1954. In one of the most sensational cases of the era, Sheppard was initially found guilty of murder on December 21, 1954, despite telling police that a "bushy-haired" intruder had broken into his house the night his wife was murdered. Sam Sheppard appealed his conviction, and whether he was guilty or innocent turned into a matter of intense national interest. With Sheppard's appeals pending, *The Fugitive* premiered on ABC on September 17, 1963, and by its second season had become the fifth-most popular program on television.[68]

With Sheppard's guilt in doubt, *The Fugitive* not only mirrored real life. It mirrored real life as real life was unfolding. The United States Supreme Court, citing lack of due process at his trial, set aside Sheppard's conviction on June 6, 1966. At his second trial, he was acquitted on November 16, 1966. On television, *The Fugitive* still had one season to go. Unlike Sheppard's, Kimble's innocence was never in dispute, making him a figure of admiration. But he was also portrayed as a genuinely kind-hearted individual who had to rely on the help of strangers nationwide to stay free and beyond the reach of Gerard. Even the pursuer contributed to Kimble's role as he hero: over time, in both the TV series and the movie, Gerard comes to doubt that Kimble killed his wife. In one of the best-known scenes in the movie, Kimble, before escaping from Gerard by jumping off a dam, says, "I did not kill my wife!" To which Gerard replies, "I don't care."[69] By the end of the movie, Kimble has saved Gerard's life in a shootout, and Gerard has become convinced that Kimble really did not kill his wife. "I thought you said you didn't care?" Kimble says to Gerard in the movie's final lines. "I don't," Gerard replies. Then he laughs. "Don't tell anyone, will you?" Gerard says.[70]

The movie was a critical and commercial success. It was nominated for the Academy Award for best picture (*Schindler's List* won), and Tommy Lee Jones won the Academy Award for best supporting actor. Made for $44 million, *The Fugitive* grossed $369 million worldwide, including $184 million in the United States.[71] Three decades earlier, the TV series had proved just as successful. It grossed $30 million over four years and was consistently a ratings winner: The final episode, the second part of a two-part finale, aired on August 29, 1967, and drew the highest TV rating (72 percent) up to that point, with 78 million viewers; it was the most-watched TV episode in history until November 21, 1980, when 90 million Americans tuned into *Dallas* to find out who shot J.R.[72] Called *The Judgment*, the final episode of *The Fugitive* (Episode 120) concludes with Kimble tracking down the one-armed man in California, and Gerard fatally shooting the one-armed man just as the one-armed man is about to kill Kimble. The final episode marked the time when, after four years, "the running stopped," intoned the narrator of *The Fugitive* TV series, Robert Conrad, at the start of the finale.

The end of the chase ended a TV series but imprinted on American culture the iconic, if unrealistic, image of the fugitive: An innocent man on the run for his life. Richard Kimble was fiction. But what made him so popular was that he was the ideal fugitive, if such a character could ever exist. He was blameless.

"Everybody's fantasy as a little kid is, what would you do if you were falsely accused?" once recalled Michael Zagor, one of the writers of the final episode for TV's *The Fugitive*. "Where would you go? Where would you run?"[73]

The Fugitive also succeeded because Kimble's plight transcended that of a criminal on the run. By trying to stay free, Kimble lived out the deeply American concept of self-reliance. He never gave up as he battled circumstances beyond his control. The viewer roots for Kimble because he is innocent, of course, but also because he is noble in his quest for personal justice. Kimble, as a fugitive, embodies, as the literary critic Stanley Fish has written, "a man who wants nothing but to be free—free not merely from the physical constraints of prison and the death penalty, but free from anything and everything."[74]

Left: As the third secretary of state, serving under President George Washington and President John Adams, Timothy Pickering directed U.S. Marshals and their deputies as they searched for fugitives and conducted other duties. Congress created the posts of U.S. Marshals—what would become the U.S. Marshals Service—in the Judiciary Act of 1789. Courtesy of the Library of Congress.

Right: The Fugitive Slave Acts often put U.S. Marshals at odds with an angry populace in the North who wanted runaway slaves to be free. Under the laws, marshals were required to search and capture runaway slaves, wherever they were found. Courtesy of the Library of Congress.

Left: The fatal shooting of Jesse James on April 2, 1882, ended one of the most celebrated manhunts in the history of crime in the United States. James's body was displayed after his death, as if to prove to the public that the infamous fugitive really had been caught. Courtesy of the Library of Congress.

Left: John Dillinger (right center) went on the lam for the last time after he broke out of the Crown Point Jail in his native Indiana on March 3, 1934. This photo, taken at the Crown Point Jail on January 30, 1934, shows Dillinger with Lake County Sheriff Lillian Holley (far left) and prosecutor Robert G. Estill (center). The two were heavily criticized for posing with Dillinger in one of the best-known photos of the soon-to-be fugitive. Courtesy of Everett Collection Inc./ Alamy Stock Photo.

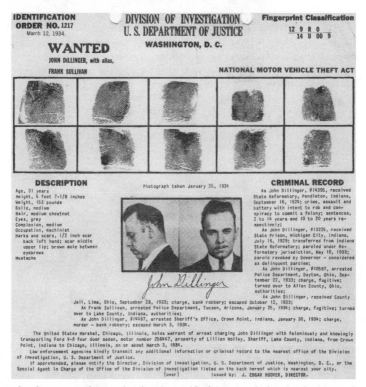

Above: The Federal Bureau of Investigation intensified its search for the fugitive John Dillinger by issuing an identification order for him on March 12, 1934, nine days after he escaped from the Crown Point Jail in Indiana. Identification orders were the FBI's precursors to official most-wanted posters. The FBI issued its first most-wanted poster for a fugitive on June 25, 1934. The fugitive was Dillinger. The FBI gunned him down in Chicago a month later. Courtesy of the Federal Bureau of Investigation.

Above: FBI Director J. Edgar Hoover made the bureau's special agents into highly trained fugitive catchers, and he was never shy about publicizing the FBI's advances. He is seen here (center left) in 1939, fingerprinting Vice President John N. Garner (center right). Courtesy of Library of Congress.

Right: In the movie *The Public Enemy* (1931), James Cagney glorified gangsters in his portrayal of Tom Powers as he uses his ruthlessness to control the underworld in Prohibition-era Chicago with allies like girlfriend Gwen Allen (Jean Harlow) by his side. The use of public enemies lists, which labeled certain crooks Public Enemy Number One, become a model for the FBI as it created its Ten Most Wanted Fugitives list decades later. Public enemies were often fugitives. Courtesy of Moviestore collection Ltd./Alamy Stock Photo.

MILLIONS

have waited for this world-acclaimed picture! Thousands suffered the tortures of the damned that it might be made! Now here's the original, authentic truth about a present day hell-on-earth, written in blood by a convict who is *still in flight* from the horrors he dared expose! His escape made front-page history—and so will this blazing real-life picture of Robert E. Burns' amazing life and desperate loves!

Now see the great star of "Scarface" in an entirely DIFFERENT role!

"I AM A FUGITIVE FROM A CHAIN GANG"

with

PAUL MUNI

With more than 40 featured players including Glenda Farrell.

See how the fury of a scorned woman sent him back to hell!

Directed by Mervyn LeRoy of "Five Star Final" fame.

Based on the famous book you've heard about.

I am a FUGITIVE from a CHAIN GANG! BY ROBERT E. BURNS

WARNER BROS. HIT OF HITS!

SIMULTANEOUS WORLD PREMIERE

TODAY—NOV. 12th

IN HUNDREDS OF LEADING THEATRES THRUOUT AMERICA

Above: The figure of the fugitive in American culture took on greater depth in 1932 with the release of the hit movie *I Am a Fugitive From a Chain Gang*, based on the bestselling memoir *I Am a Fugitive from a Georgia Chain Gang!* Paul Muni was nominated for an Academy Award for his portrayal of Robert Elliott Burns, a fugitive who escaped horribly unfair treatment in a Georgia chain gang. In this case, the fugitive's flight was justified. Courtesy of Walter Oleksy/Alamy Stock Photo.

Above: FBI Director J. Edgar Hoover countered Hollywood's popular portrayals of gangsters and fugitives by undertaking a massive public-relations campaign in the 1930s. The effort included the 1936 documentary *"You Can't Get Away With It!"* The film showed Hoover and his FBI agents, or G-men, at war with fugitives and other criminals. The fugitive helped shape the image of the FBI. Courtesy of Everett Collection Inc./Alamy Stock Photo.

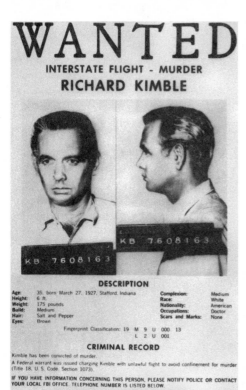

WANTED

INTERSTATE FLIGHT - MURDER
RICHARD KIMBLE

DESCRIPTION

Age:	35, born March 27, 1927, Stafford, Indiana	Complexion:	Medium
Height:	6 ft.	Race:	White
Weight:	175 pounds	Nationality:	American
Build:	Medium	Occupations:	Doctor
Hair:	Salt and Pepper	Scars and Marks:	None
Eyes:	Brown		

Fingerprint Classification: 19 M 9 U 000 13
L 2 U 001

CRIMINAL RECORD

Kimble has been convicted of murder.

A Federal warrant was issued charging Kimble with unlawful flight to avoid confinement for murder (Title 18, U. S. Code, Section 1073).

IF YOU HAVE INFORMATION CONCERNING THIS PERSON, PLEASE NOTIFY POLICE OR CONTACT YOUR LOCAL FBI OFFICE. TELEPHONE NUMBER IS LISTED BELOW.

IDENTIFICATION
ORDER NO 2771

UNITED STATES DEPARTMENT OF JUSTICE
WASHINGTON 35, D. C.
TELEPHONE NATIONAL 8-7117

Left: One of the most popular fugitives in American culture is a fictional one: Dr. Richard Kimble, who goes on the lam after he is wrongfully convicted of killing his wife. David Janssen (shown here) played Kimble in the hit TV series *The Fugitive* (1963–67), the basis for the blockbuster 1993 movie of the same name, starring Harrison Ford. Kimble in both iterations is innocent, which heightened his appeal as the ideal fugitive. Courtesy of AF archive/Quinn Martin Productions/United Artists Television/Alamy Stock Photo.

FBI TEN MOST WANTED FUGITIVE

Racketeering Influenced and Corrupt Organizations (RICO) - Murder (19 Counts), Conspiracy to Commit Murder, Conspiracy to Commit Extortion, Narcotics Distribution, Conspiracy to Commit Money Laundering; Extortion; Money Laundering

JAMES J. BULGER

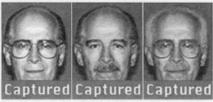

Captured   Captured   Captured

Photograph taken in
1994

Photograph Age
Enhanced in 2008

Photograph Age
Enhanced in 2008

Multimedia: Images Video | Audio

Above: The sixteen years on the lam for one of the FBI's most notorious fugitives, Boston mobster James "Whitey" Bulger, ended with the capture of him and his girlfriend at their apartment in Santa Monica, California, on June 22, 2011. Bulger was later sentenced to two consecutive life terms for participating in eleven murders. He was beaten to death in a federal prison in West Virginia on October 30, 2018. Courtesy of the Federal Bureau of Investigation.

6

A MIND AT UNREST
The Psychology of Living on the Run

An existential crisis had gripped the mind of this fugitive. Life on the lam had become so wearing that he turned to one of Dostoevsky's greatest characters to explain what was churning through his thoughts as he stayed on the run and, for the sake of survival, remained cut off from friends and relatives. For the fugitive, every person is a potential threat, so every person is a stranger; intimacy, especially of the romantic kind, can get you caught. In the case of this fugitive, nothing could stop the possibility of the world closing in, like a hell, like something out of the Grand Inquisitor segment in *The Brothers Karamazov*.

"Images of myself: eyes bugged out, arms extended before me, running as fast as [I] can to escape the steam-roller which is almost on top of me, and casting an occasional glance from side to side to see if I can help someone who's out of breath or who's stumbled and about to succumb to destruction, all the while screaming in a hoarse, inaudible voice for help," the young fugitive wrote a friend around 1970.

"Waiting for that unseen hand which will snatch me away to safety before I heave head first into the pit[;] the Grand Inquisitor's steaming hot moving walls are pushing toward me," the fugitive wrote. "These are desperate images. That's not altogether true. Sometimes the steam-roller breaks down or gets gummed up with the bones of more intentional victims. Or I begin to think I'm imagining the whole thing and it's surrealist fantasy."[1]

With the Vietnam War raging, the fugitive considered whether going into battle would be a better option than fleeing the law. Being a soldier carried with it a certain degree of certainty and order. Death was always lurking, always a possibility, on the battlefield. But at least there you could expect to see death coming. On the lam, you never knew when the end would arrive and you would be led away in handcuffs.

"Is this why they call it the human race?" the fugitive wrote. "Because we have to move so fast to preserve ourselves from the phantoms that pursue us? Much better to be involved in a mass charge under a hail of bombs and artillery and small weapons fire! Then, at least, you can see what your death looks like. Here you don't dare peek over your shoulder for fear the lack of attention to the path ahead will cause you to trip on the unseen rock and be crushed."[2]

Also during this era—a time when many young Americans were intent on finding themselves and bonding together—another young fugitive expressed similar feelings of helplessness and dread, along with the frustration at how a life on the run foiled the need for human companionship.

"There's this woman in Chicago I hoped to marry," the fugitive said. "But of course I can't contact her at all, or, naturally, my family either, because that's the first place the cops would look. That's really hard for me because I'm an extremely sensitive person. So I'm looking for a female companion now, but whenever I find one I tend to freeze up because I wonder whether I could promise her anything beyond the minute we have together. If I ever had a meaningful relationship, I couldn't tell her who I was; for her protection and for mine, the less she knows the better. And that makes me lonely."[3]

No matter how sensitive, fugitives are most often criminals, so fugitives typically possess characteristics of the criminal kind, including those associated with antisocial personality disorder. They can be deceitful and compulsive, show a lack of remorse,[4] and, in many instances, possess a penchant for behavior that is, in the words of psychologist H. J. Eysenck, by turns "sensation-seeking" and "foolhardy."[5] Combined with these traits can be a sense of invincibility as well as a deep desire, no matter what the potential for a blown cover, to stay connected to society.

This paradox runs throughout the careers of many fugitives: A need to stay hidden—and out of prison—competes with a need to enjoy some kind of human companionship.

Willie Sutton was a fugitive who was as introspective as he was disciplined. He was too much of a professional thief and fugitive to get caught easily. But he was too much of deep thinker to ignore how much the constant need to stay in hiding, and to stay mostly alone, grinded on his well-being.

Had Arnold Schuster, who spotted him on the subway, not been so careful an observer of the FBI's most-wanted gallery of photos, Sutton most likely would have been able to stay on the lam for longer than five years before his final capture. He probably would have been able to change his car battery uninterrupted instead of having police nab him on the street in early 1952. Without Schuster's tip to the police, Sutton would have gone back to his rented three-foot-by-ten-foot furnished room in Brooklyn, where he lived for $6 a week and was known as John Mahoney. The location of the room was evidence of Sutton's diligence and extreme discretion as a fugitive. It was four blocks from the Brooklyn police station. He had lived in the room, in what the *New York Times* called "miserly obscurity," for nearly two years before he was caught, with a gun, at about two o'clock in the afternoon on February 18, 1952. Police converged on the Chevrolet he had bought a month earlier, and which he had left parked, with its hood up, in front of his boarding house at 340 Dean Street, in a Puerto Rican neighborhood.[6] The apartment was a mile from where Sutton was born and a block from the subway station, the place from which Schuster would depart to tell the police he had seen Willie Sutton.[7]

After his arrest, Sutton shrugged when reporters asked him how he felt about his capture after being on the run for so long. One reporter said Sutton's mood took "a philosophical turn" before he answered the question.

"I've been expecting it," he said.[8]

A life on the run had darkened the mood of Sutton, who upon his capture revealed a fraught state of mind that had left him on edge mentally for five years. Sutton had found that robbing banks gave him energy and affirmation. "Why did I rob banks?" he said. "I enjoyed it. I loved it. I was more alive when I was inside a bank, robbing it, than at any other time in my life."[9] And he got a similar thrill from escaping from prison and after years of careful planning. "Like nothing else in the world," he said.[10] But no matter how skilled he was as a bank robber and a fugitive, Sutton could never evade the deep loneliness and wariness that dogged him while he was trying to stay ahead of the law. He had cut himself off so much from regular interactions with those on the outside world that he had no idea whether his mother was alive or dead until he asked the authorities after his arrest. She was still alive. His wife, however, had died while he was in prison, leaving him further isolated. While he was on the lam, Willie Sutton had no one but himself. And sometimes, he said, he was not even sure of his own true identity; donning so many disguises over the years seemed to have eroded his sense of self. Upon his arrest, Sutton, at fifty-two years old, seemed almost relieved to be able to talk to strangers—the reporters—about what was termed as "the problems that come to fugitives."[11]

"Extreme loneliness does things to a man," he said hours after his arrest. "I went to church at least once every week. I read a lot of psychology and psychiatry. I found it strange to change my identity every time someone seemed to be catching up with me, and when a man changes his identity he begins to think more deeply.

"It's hard to be somebody different, over and over again. You're never sure of who's around you. In restaurants and other public places, you study faces and actions—anyone might betray you. That study becomes a habit."[12]

Sutton also had a habit of reading the newspaper stories about him, partly to make sure the police were not closing in and partly for amusement. He said some of the stories accused him of being involved in bank robberies that he had nothing to do with. He had another habit: he made sure he never ate at a restaurant too often. "I kept changing around," he said. "I thought that was wiser."[13]

Sutton came to realize that he had been living as if he was paranoid. So many people truly were looking for him. In one of the more insightful reflections of a fugitive, Sutton explained how gaining too much confidence could doom someone on the run, who could never be so confident as to slip up and get caught. Sutton wrote,

> Confidence: a very good thing to have if you're up to bat with the bases loaded in the ninth inning and a very bad thing to have if you are a fugitive. If you set out to draw the ideal profile for a fugitive, you'd find yourself describing the classic paranoiac.
>
> What, after all, is a paranoiac? He is the man who is perpetually on the alert, whose guard is always up. He feels "they" are out to get him, and since he isn't exactly sure who "they" are, he has to see everything, hear everything, protect himself against everybody. The only difference with a fugitive is there is nothing imaginary about it.
>
> They *are* out to get him. The police, the FBI, the law, the government. The massed power and resources of the state. He had damned well better see everything, hear everything, protect himself against everybody.[14]

Much like other fugitives on the FBI's Ten Most Wanted list, such as Thomas William Holden and Orba Elmer Jackson, who had both blended into daily life as laborers in Oregon, Sutton succeeded while on the run because he was able to make himself seem so ordinary. As Whitey Bulger would do decades later, Sutton gave up a career as a flashy and powerful criminal to become a boring everyman who was calm on the outside but at a permanent state of mental turmoil. Sutton's Spanish-speaking landlord and her family had no idea who Willie Sutton was, let along that Willie Sutton was really living among them, keeping to himself in his tiny room when he was not out in the neighborhood.

He liked to go to bed early, around ten o'clock, to avoid being out on the streets late at night, when the police were on their beats. And when he was out during the day, he avoided the police. "I'm no dunce," he said. "I kept away from cops. I walked around them."[15]

He bought his landlady roses at Christmas and Thanksgiving. His largess, as well as his rudimentary Spanish, which he taught himself using a Spanish grammar book, helped ease a strain that developed about a month before he was caught, when his landlord scolded him for having another boarder, a Puerto Rican girl, over to his room for whiskey. Other than that incident, the landlord told police, Willie Sutton—known to her as John Mahoney—was an ideal tenant, "a nice gentleman" and "a good man in this house."[16] To stay ahead of the police, Sutton also kept another apartment, on Fifty-seventh Street and Madison Avenue in Manhattan, where he said he was known as Arthur Buckley. Sutton said he stayed at that apartment during the day and slept at the Dean Street apartment at night. "You might think that having two apartments would give me two sets of neighbors, and therefore twice as many people who would recognize me," Sutton recalled of the arrangement. "Quite the contrary. If I had spent all my time holed up in one apartment, the neighbors might have started to wonder about me. By having two apartments I was able to keep regular hours. To the people around me on Dean Street, where I was known as John Mahoney, I worked the day shift. To the people at Fifty-seventh, who knew me as Arthur Buckley, I worked nights."[17] Of the two apartments, Sutton considered the furnished room on Dean Street his "hideout" because he slept there.[18]

This is what the police found in Sutton's furnished Dean Street room, the room of a man always ready to pack up on a moment's notice, if necessary: three thousand dollars in cash locked in a briefcase that was locked in a valise; six suits; a second pair of black shoes, which, like the suits, were inexpensive, which would have been difficult to wear for someone like Sutton, who was known to like tailored clothes; a table radio; a chess set; the Spanish dictionary; and a .38-caliber revolver like the one Sutton was wearing when he was arrested. Police found that gun loaded and stuck inside a homemade holster that was positioned in the front of his trousers. Sutton, who had a reputation as a gentleman bank robber, cultivated that image as a fugitive, even if he had sworn off wearing flashy clothes to avoid the attention of police. He even shined his own shoes and darned his own socks. Sutton said he always carried a gun, but never planned to fire it. He only wanted to be able to show it to anyone who got too curious so he could scare them and run away before he was identified. Flashing the gun and freezing the onlooker, he said, would give him a "head start."[19]

Otherwise, at least according to the news accounts when he was arrested, Sutton did not appear to be imposing, not while he was in handcuffs standing five feet, eight inches tall and weighing 150 pounds. He was described in pathetic terms. He was a criminal so celebrated that he became trapped in a prison of his own making. He could not go far from his furnished room. He made no effort to go overseas or cross the border because of the risk of getting caught. Sutton, who would have endured a restricted life while in prison, experienced a restricted life while he was on the lam. Whether in prison or not, Sutton really had no way out. The weariness showed. "An insignificant little man in a tieless but neat blue shirt in blue suiting striped gray," reported the *New York Times* of how Sutton looked after his arrest. "His brown hair was dyed black and glinted in the harsh illumination. The brown in his mustache was betrayed in the glare and the light brought out the gray at his temples, too."[20]

Also in Sutton's room, police found his library, a small collection of books whose topics pointed both to his intelligence and his desire to learn more about himself and human nature. If you did not know the occupant of the apartment was the nation's most accomplished bank robber, you would have thought he was a middle-aged man who might be down on his luck but trying to improve himself. The titles on his bookshelf were *First Aid and Emergency Treatment*; *Peace of Soul*, by Bishop Fulton J. Sheen; *The Basic Writings of Sigmund Freud*; *You Can Change the World*, by the Rev. James Keller; and *A Business of Your Own*, by Larson, Johnson, and Teller. The bookshelf held one more title. It was an autobiography of the novelist Meyer Levin, who had taken to nonfiction to explore his pursuit of how to be an authentic person. The name of the book was *In Search*.[21]

Willie Sutton lived in a constant fear of getting caught and going back to prison, but at least his conviction and sentence were justified. He had indeed robbed banks and escaped from prison. In the rare case in which a fugitive is either wrongly accused or treated unfairly, the mind is at a greater, more intense unease. The TV series and movie *The Fugitive* used fiction to convey the desperation of such a scenario. Decades earlier, the fugitive Robert Elliott Burns, in the 1932 memoir *I Am a Fugitive from a Georgia Chain Gang!* described how he endured the reality of injustice during his life on the lam. For a time, and because of the hit movie that was based on his book, Burns was the most famous fugitive in America—not because what he had done to society, but because of what he said society had done to him. The circumstances that Elliott faced, or so he wrote, would have made any reasonable person want to flee.

Elliott was sentenced to six to ten years of hard labor on a chain gang in Fulton County, Georgia. He got tricked into conspiring with two other armed robbers to hold up a grocery store of $5.80 in Atlanta in February of 1922. Burns, an Army veteran born in Brooklyn, had been wandering around Georgia, suffering from shell shock and looking for work, after the close of World War I.[22] He said the robbers were acquaintances, and one of them threatened to shoot him if he failed to go along with the heist.[23] After he was caught in the robbery, he pleaded guilty, hoping, as he wrote, to get a minimum sentence. He got at least six years on the chain gang instead. By that June, he had decided that he would only survive if he escaped.

"Not that I wanted to cheat justice," Burns wrote. "I leave that to the reader. If I had been sentenced to one year—which under the condition of the chain gang and the extenuating circumstances of my crime, would have been plenty—I would have tried to make it. But six years—that was plain vengeance and also complete destruction."[24]

Burns first went on the run when he was thirty years old. One day in June of 1922, another convict agreed to slam a sledge hammer into Burns's leg shackles, misshaping them enough so that Burns could slip them off. He did so while on a work detail on June 21, 1922, the "longest and hottest day of the year."[25] The guard on duty started firing at him as soon as he broke into a sprint. "Never in my life did I run as I did that day," Burns recalled. "Ten minutes later the dogs were at my heels, howling, barking, and snapping. But instead of being afraid of them, I called them and tried to make them think I was playing with them. I kept to the woods and fields using the sun as my guide to point north."[26]

So began Burns's extraordinary odyssey of flight. It is unique not only because of the circumstances—Burns would end up a national celebrity—but also because of Burns's ability to articulate his life on the lam so well. "Uncommon is the criminal who takes the reins of authoring his own story," William Beverly, the crime writer, has observed of Burns. "Even more so is the fugitive who manages, even while running, to become master of his own narrative, drowning out legal categorizations with his own justifications of his crime, his flight, and his defiance of law."[27] With his story, Burns joined the ranks of famous, and sometimes legendary, noble fugitives from throughout history. "The story is told with vivid concreteness yet has a mythic universality that transcends the particulars of the Depression-era South," historian Matthew J. Mancini has written of Burns's memoir. "The figure of the haunted, doomed fugitive unjustly condemned to years of wandering and exile has resonated with audiences in many times and cultures. If not as Odysseus or Aeneas, he was thought of by many as a 'modern "Jean Valjean,"' and the contemporary popularity of the film and television series *The Fugitive* certainly owes something to Burns as one of its originals."[28] Mancini, while vouching for the accuracy of Burns's memoir, writes that *I Am a Fugitive from a Georgia Chain Gang!* is also noteworthy because "it caused sectional rancor [between the North and South], it became a great motion picture, and it stands as one of the key documents of the Great Depression."[29]

Burns was white, but as Beverly has pointed out, his story evoked the fugitive-slave narratives that were in wide circulation before and during the Civil War. Burns rightfully viewed the chain gang as a form of involuntary servitude, and he considered himself a seeker of justice. As the enslaved persons were justified in heading to the North to flee an unconscionable system, so Burns saw himself, in a vision that others soon joined, as justified in escaping from the chain gang. Just as a slave was always worried about getting captured and returned, with punishment, to the harsh conditions of the plantation, so Burns feared what would happen if he was shipped back to the chain gang. His knowledge that he was fleeing an unjust system intensified his desire to escape, but the righteousness of his cause did nothing to alleviate his anxiety about getting spotted and getting caught.

Shortly after his initial escape Burns was sitting in a barber's chair in Atlanta when a police officer walked into the shop talking about "a New York gunman"[30] who had gotten away from another chain gang and who now was the quarry of several posses. Burns, who was getting a shave, listened in terror. "I couldn't see the speaker as I lay flat on my back, my face full of soap lather," he wrote. "A nervous tremor ran through my body, beads of perspiration started to roll down me, but I just sat tight."[31] Burns listened more as the policeman described the fugitive to the barber. Burns hoped the policeman did not pose any questions to him or even notice the style of his hat, which he described as a "prison hat." "And there I sat in the chair, staring at the ceiling," Burns wrote. "Fear clutched every nerve and muscle. If I attracted suspicion I was done for. . . . My legs were trembling and I was a nervous wreck."[32] Burns finally left without the policeman chatting with him. "If he had asked me any question, I think I would have collapsed," Burns wrote. "How I got out of that barber shop without creating any suspicion I don't know. I was in a daze when I reached the street. I kept turning corners zig-zag fashion, and did not breathe freely until I got about five blocks away."[33]

From Atlanta, Burns made his way, by train and with sixty cents in his pocket, to Chicago, where he eventually became a businessman and publisher of some renown. In an era before the interconnectedness of the electronic mass media, and even before the creation of the FBI and its most-wanted list, Burns was able to keep his fugitive status a secret. He lived a double life, until a betrayal revealed his criminal past. When he reached Chicago, he first worked in the stockyards and then as a landlord for apartments that he had refurbished. In 1925, with little capital and lots of ambition, he launched the *Greater Chicago Magazine*, which was thriving in three years and which, Burns wrote, "became a force in the civic affairs of Chicago."[34] "And I, the founder," he continued, "became prominent and successful. I had many friends. I believe I was respected and honored by thousands. I delivered an average of five lectures a week during this period. An average of at least one hundred persons attended each lecture. My message was always one of inspiration, achievement and courage, both to face and master the problems and difficulties of life."[35]

One of Burns's difficulties, particularly because of his fugitive status, concerned matters of the heart. He was cautious about becoming too close to any person, including a woman, fearful that, if anyone learned his secret, his freedom would be in jeopardy. But then a woman fell in love with him and, despite his insistence that the feeling was not mutual, he ended up marrying her because, to some degree, he felt trapped. The woman, Emilia Del Pino Pacheo, known as Emily, learned about his past through deceit. He said she opened a letter addressed to him from his father, whom Burns had asked, along with Burns's brother, to try to resolve the situation in Georgia so that he might return someday without going back on the chain gang. Until Pacheo opened the letter, Burns had been able to evade her questions about his past. After reading the letter, and still committed to marrying Burns, she pledged not to betray him. "Your secret is safe with me," Burns said she promised. "Never, never, never will I tell a single soul."[36]

Burns continued to resist Pacheo, but finally relented. In Burns's telling, Pacheo blackmailed him into marrying her. In August of 1926, he wrote, Pacheo told him that she would publicly expose his escape from Georgia if he did not marry her that day. Burns, whose memoir is filled with ruminations on the comforts of true love, said he had no choice but to make Pacheo his wife. He found his situation reprehensible. As a fugitive, he could never truly be himself, and now he was being forced to wed a woman whom he did not love. Burns was cursed. "What could I do? What should I do?" he wrote. "She knew my secret. My God! Must that ghost of the past always rise up before me; would it haunt me the rest of my days? Time was pressing and I needed a clear head for the day's activities. I pleaded, I begged for a time, for anything but exposure or marriage. But she was adamant."[37]

The marriage failed to save Burns. He soon fell in love with another woman and asked his wife for a divorce—he promised to pay her $25 a week in alimony—and pleaded with her not to report his whereabouts to the authorities in Georgia. Pacheo initially agreed to the terms, Burns said, but on March 28, 1929, she sent a letter to Georgia, informing on him. Burns had transformed himself into a successful magazine editor earning $20,000 a year in the late 1920s. But his livelihood and his freedom were about to vanish.

The prospect of returning to prison would be difficult for most fugitives to face. But in the case of Burns, the possibility of having to return to the chain gang was too much to contemplate. Indeed, the conditions of the chain gang, combined with what he considered an unfairly long sentence, provided him and his allies with justifiable reasons for him to go on the lam in the first place. Georgia had no state prison system; convicts were leased to chain gangs in what amounted to a form of state-sanctioned slavery. The results of the system "were horrific," Mancini has written. "Prisoners were scattered all over the state in small squads and large gangs, on plantations, coal mines, sawmills, and brickyards. There the mostly black workforce endured foul shacks, putrid food, backbreaking labor, brutal punishment with whip and stocks, and sometimes literal torture."[38]

The chain-gang system, in a cruel twist, was an outgrowth of one of the greatest results of the North's victory over the South in the Civil War: the Thirteenth Amendment, which outlawed slavery and involuntary servitude "except as a punishment for crime whereof the party shall have been duly convicted." With slavery abolished, the owners of plantations and other businesses in the South turned to a new form of forced labor to stay viable: the convicts, such as Burns, who were sentenced to the chain gangs. "The link between prison labor and slavery is not merely rhetorical," author Shane Bauer, who went undercover to report on prisons in the United States, has written. The Thirteenth Amendment, for Bauer, "opened the door for more than a century of forced labor that was in many ways identical to, and in some ways worse, than slavery."[39]

In Union General William T. Sherman's March to the Sea, in 1864, Georgia's penitentiary burned, and it later fell into such disrepair that the property was cleared in the 1870s and the prison was gone by 1874.[40] Georgia would not have another prison until 1938. In the meantime, chain gangs were the norm. By the time of Burns's ordeal, Georgia's penal system had become a national shame. "Several times during recent years," the *New York Times* wrote in 1932, "the American public has been horrified by accounts in newspapers, magazines and books of the antiquated and inhuman methods employed by the State of Georgia in the management of convicted criminals."[41]

Burns's personal reformation and the conditions of the chain gangs in Georgia combined to create popular opposition to his return to the South. The Burns Citizen Committee was one of several groups formed to support his cause by petitioning government officials. "Once having experienced penal servitude marks many men for perpetual membership in the ranks of the enemies of society," the committee wrote. "Not so in the case of Robert E. Burns."[42] His wife opposed his requests for relief, calling him "a menace to society."[43] Burns considered fighting extradition, but voluntarily surrendered to the authorities in Georgia on a promise that the state would grant him a quick pardon and release from incarceration. Georgia prison officials instead ordered him "to the worst gang in the state,"[44] where he would have to serve at least a year. The promise of a pardon disappeared, and Burns was once more in the grip of "the heavy hand of unfeeling law."[45] Within fourteen months, and after the Georgia Prison Commission had rebuffed his appeals, Burns escaped again, in September of 1930, by leaving the chain gang and bribing a motorist in a passing car to drive away. The only way to save his life, he believed, was to flee. Employing the calculus of a would-be fugitive, he concluded that staying on the chain gang would mean he would be a broken man, with no future. "What good would life be for me then?" Burns wrote. "What I wanted, what I earned, what I deserved right now was freedom, while I still had the force, the character, and determination, to become an efficient, creative member of society. What I wanted was life, not living death."[46]

Burns fashioned another new life while on the lam, and that new life, like Burns's first foray as a fugitive, was remarkable. He became the rare fugitive who ultimately shed his disguise and let the public know where he was. He also became a celebrity fugitive—the author of a best-selling book, which was made into a popular movie. But before reaching those achievements, Burns remained a more ordinary fugitive, constantly on the lookout. After his escape, he took a bus out of Georgia and ended up in New Jersey, to live near his brother, Vincent, a Unitarian minister who had been trying to get the state of Georgia to let Burns go free. Burns assumed the name John Pashley: "A man of mystery, I was," he wrote, "with a price on my head and a consuming fear in my heart. Lonesome, weary, and hopeless—trying to lose myself in the city of Newark, N.J."[47] Burns quickly found a job selling ads for the *Newark Free Press* but quit the next day after discovering that another ad salesman had once worked for the *Chicago Evening Post* and knew who he was. Burns said he could not risk the salesman identifying him.

"In a few seconds, I was back on the street, jobless again," Burns, once more opening a window into the frenzied mind of a fugitive, wrote in his memoir. "The long arm of coincidence was reaching for me—reaching across thousands of miles and pointing its accusing finger at one out of millions.

CHAPTER 6

"There is the sting, the heartbreaking little things that make it so difficult for a fugitive to go straight and earn an honest living—always the shadow of the past blocking the road of the future, driving him unmercifully from job to job, from place to place."[48]

The act of opening a bank account, so mundane a task for the regular person, caused Burns to worry. He reflected on that incident with another reverie about the mental strains of life on the run.

"Questions and answers," he wrote. "Every answer made by me was a fabrication. The ordeal was over at last. I laid down my money and received my passbook.

"Building a new personality, gathering bit by bit identity cards, a bank book and other things so necessary to prove who you are, and in this case who you are not, the problems of an escaped convict are many and varied if he wants to go straight and take a normal place in the life of the community in which he resides."[49]

Burns worked various jobs as a laborer in Newark; he also wrote the book that made him famous. *I Am a Fugitive from a Georgia Chain Gang!* was published in January 1932. The movie, *I Am a Fugitive from a Chain Gang*, with Paul Muni, fresh from the success of *Scarface*, in the lead role, came out in November 1932, drawing praise from film critics and packed audiences. Burns could have stayed incognito—his true name was on his best-selling book, but he was still living as John Pashley. As the popularity of the book and movie increased, he came out of hiding. He granted interviews to reporters, delivered lectures, attended showings of the movie at theaters in New Jersey, and visited Muni on Broadway.[50] Though he had secretly traveled to Hollywood to consult on the movie while it was in production, by the end of 1932 Burns had become comfortable enough with the situation to let everyone know who he was. With Americans outraged at the conditions of the chain gang and the machinations of the Georgia penal system, both of which the book and movie covered, Burns turned into the rarest kind of fugitive: one who not only comes out of hiding, but all but dares the authorities to capture him. In mid-December 1932, he went so far as to describe his ordeal in a speech he made to employees of the New Jersey State Motor Vehicle Department in Trenton. Burns at the event sat next to Colonel H. Norman Schwarzkopf, the superintendent of the New Jersey State Police; Schwarzkopf had gained nationwide fame in 1932 by leading the New Jersey State Police as they investigated the kidnapping and murder of the Lindbergh baby from the Lindbergh mansion in Princeton, New Jersey, in March of 1932.[51]

With Burns such a public figure, police had no problem finding him. He was arrested on the Georgia warrants on a street in Newark late at night on December 14, 1932. Burns fought extradition to Georgia and had his strongest ally in the governor of New Jersey, A. Harry Moore, who long before Burns's arrest had promised him a fair extradition hearing if Burns were ever captured. A week later, on December 21, 1932, Burns's legend as a fugitive grew: He became one of the few fugitives to defeat an extradition request. After a four-hour extradition hearing before an audience of five hundred people at the State House Assembly Chamber in Trenton, Moore ruled that New Jersey would not return Burns to Georgia. Among the advocates for Burns was the well-known lawyer Clarence Darrow, who wrote a letter on his behalf that was read at the hearing. Even the grocer whose store Burns had helped rob in Atlanta ten years earlier testified that he did not want Burns to return to a chain gang in Georgia.[52] After hearing evidence, among other things, that Burns would likely die if he was returned to the chain gang, Moore granted asylum to Burns and said New Jersey would not extradite him.

"It is the most wonderful Christmas present I ever got," Burns, sobbing, said after the hearing, according to a front-page story in the *New York Times*. "God bless Governor Moore. Let's go at once to thank him."[53]

Moore and Burns shook hands. Moore all but told Burns that he should embrace anonymity once again. "That's all right," Moore told an effusive Burns. "As long as you live the life of a decent citizen in New Jersey, I'll not sign a warrant for your return to Georgia. The best way you can express your thanks to me is by living as a decent citizen. Never mind the publicity stuff."

"I won't exploit this decision for my own benefit," Burns replied.[54]

But Burns did use Moore's decision to his advantage. As the *New York Times* reported in the same article about the extradition hearing, Burns that day made arrangements to speak on the radio the following night. "And before long," according to another report, "he was rehearsing a vaudeville show, complete with black men in chains singing prison songs."[55] Burns was enjoying the publicity as officials in Georgia fumed at Moore's decision, and Burns, in reality, still very much remained a fugitive. He was still wanted in Georgia. He risked getting shipped back there in handcuffs if he ever left New Jersey for another state, and if the governor in that state decided to extradite him. Burns avoided such a fate by staying in New Jersey, where he married, had four children, and made a career as a tax consultant. Including Moore, three New Jersey governors refused to extradite him. But Georgia kept calling, reminding Burns that he still was not completely free.

Burns's fugitive status finally ended on November 1, 1945—twenty-three years after the robbery of the grocery store in Atlanta and fifteen years after Burns's second escape from the chain gang. After two years of negotiations with the reform governor of Georgia, Ellis Arnall, Burns returned to Georgia for a hearing before the state parole board. Arnall had abolished chain gangs, and he spoke up for Burns before the board, telling him that releasing Burns from his sentence would "protect the good name of Georgia."[56] Arnall earlier had asked the board to take action favorable to Burns, but the board refused to take up the case as long as Burns remained a fugitive. Once in Georgia, and before the board, Burns saw his days on the road end. The parole board commuted his sentence to time served, which released him from the custody of Georgia; the board refused a pardon because Burns had pleaded guilty to the robbery.[57] "I am convinced there has never been a fugitive who has so completely rehabilitated himself as this man," Arnall told the parole board.

Robert Elliott Burns died at age sixty-three on June 6, 1955, in East Orange, New Jersey. His legacy includes his book, in which—through a narrative he controlled from start to finish—Burns offered some of the deepest insights into the mental and physical stresses of a life on the lam, stresses made even more severe by the injustice that Burns ran from for so long. "I am a fugitive!" Burns wrote in the foreword to his book. "I am a fugitive from the law—but NOT FROM JUSTICE."[58]

No reasonable person ever had any doubt that Bucky Phillips was a fugitive from justice. For one hundred and fifty-nine days in the spring and summer of 2006, Phillips, a prison escapee, eluded state police in a manhunt that grew to become the largest in the history of the state of New York. The search captivated northwestern New York and ended with Phillips eventually pleading guilty to shooting two troopers, one of them fatally, and getting a life sentence with no parole.

Bucky Phillips—his given name is Ralph J. Phillips—had supporters who helped him and cheered him on far from afar while he was on the lam from April 2, 2006, to September 8, 2006. He became like a folk hero to some around the villages and towns where he grew up in rural Chautauqua County, about an hour and twenty minutes west of Buffalo and just east of the Pennsylvania line. One restaurant served the "Bucky Burger," with the name said to stand for Burger Under Cheese with Ketchup and Yellow mustard, though the sandwich was clearly a nod to the famous fugitive. It was, after all, served only "to go."[59] Messages on T-shirts sold online and in area shops also seemed to back Phillips and taunt the state police, which at one point assigned as many as two hundred troopers to the search.[60] "Where's Bucky?" read one t-shirt design. "Run, Bucky, Run," read another.[61] Both sayings were often uttered, sometimes in jest and sometimes not, throughout the communities near the deep woods where Phillips was thought to be hiding.

Phillips had no regrets. While some fugitives, like Willie Sutton, might express disillusionment and mental exhaustion, and others, like Robert E. Burns, might derive will and energy from the unfairness of the situation, Phillips had a view that was cold-hearted in its pragmatism. He stayed on the lam because he had the backwoods skills to do so. His goals were to stay free as long as he could and to make the state police and his other pursuers look bad, however long that would take. His killing of one trooper and his wounding of two others represented collateral damage in his quest to show how superior he was to those who were chasing him. The manhunt was his way of playing a game with the state police.

"My intentions were to humiliate them," Phillips, then forty-four years old, said at his sentencing in December 2016. "Tie them up with duct tape and call 911."[62]

Months later, in an interview from prison, Phillips said he was sorry for the death of the trooper, Joseph Longobardo, whom Phillips shot with a stolen high-powered rifle. But Phillips showed little remorse otherwise. Like Sutton, Phillips said he got a thrill from the escape. He got an even greater rush from the chase. By the time he was captured, Phillips had achieved the rare distinction of being placed on both the FBI's Ten Most Wanted list (No. 483) and the U.S. Marshal Services Fifteen Most Wanted list. The award for his arrest had risen to $425,000. While on the lam, and with so many people after him, Phillips said, he had fun.

"I enjoyed those few months more than I've enjoyed any other time in my life," he said.[63]

The chase started on April 2, 2006, when Phillips escaped from the Erie County Correctional Facility in Alden, New York. He had been in prison for ninety days for a parole violation, part of a pattern of his being incarcerated most of the time since 1983, including for theft, burglary, and selling drugs. Phillips was never particularly violent, and he was scheduled to be released from prison within four days when he decided to escape. For some reason, he thought his sentence was to last several more years. Either way, by the time he escaped, Phillips seemed resigned to never being able to fit in as a regular person living a crime-free life once he was out of prison. If he wasn't incarcerated, he seemed to be saying, he might as well be a fugitive. He didn't know any other way. "I am just not cut out for the life you folks live," Phillips wrote to his lawyer shortly before he escaped. "I tried it. It didn't work. Oh well."[64] He also said, reflecting on his reasons for fleeing, that, because he believed he was going to stay in prison, "I might as well enjoy myself."[65]

Phillips, according to most news reports at the time, escaped from the Erie County Correctional Facility by using a can opener to cut through the tin ceiling of a warehouse; he shuffled off to freedom through the hole. Phillips later disputed that account, saying that he used a screwdriver and the top of a can of food, but in any case he had displayed an extreme amount of resourcefulness and luck in finding a way to break out of prison.[66] He remained a low-interest fugitive for a time. The authorities looked for him during his first few months on the lam, a period when Phillips said he ate grubs and crayfish in the wild and foraged for food in garbage cans.[67] His profile rose on June 10. Phillips shot and wounded a state trooper, Sean M. Brown, near Elmira, New York, about two and a half hours southeast of Buffalo in New York state's Southern Tier, just north of the Pennsylvania line.

Despite the shooting and the increased manpower, Phillips turned into a folk hero rather than a target of community concern and loathing. The Bucky Burger appeared. So did the Bucky-themed t-shirts. Friends and relatives sheltered Phillips rather than turn him in; in one home where authorities believed Phillips might have been hiding, police recovered a police scanner, another tool for Phillips to stay a step ahead of the law. Police suspected Phillips of breaking into cabins and homes and churches to steal food and supplies. Authorities charged seven people—including Phillips's daughter, her boyfriend, and her mother—with harboring Phillips in Chautauqua County and nearby areas, a region that includes Native American reservations and is filled with hunting cabins and trails and other places where a fugitive, especially a home-grown fugitive like Bucky Phillips, could find refuge. One of the friends was charged with giving Phillips a handgun in late August 2006. Phillips is a Seneca Indian, which bolstered the belief that he had an almost inherent understanding of the woods and how to hide in them, despite the efforts of the state police troopers and, at the end of his flight, the U.S. Marshals Service and the FBI. The elevation of Phillips to a folk hero was shameful and disrespectful to the police, but it was also understandable. After breaking out of prison by using something as pedestrian as a can opener, Bucky Phillips had outsmarted a legion of professionals looking for him. He was a fugitive and a survivalist, whom the state police and their helicopters could not even snare.

"I am sure they set up roadblocks and what not," a retired U.S. marshal said during the search. "But if he's in an area he is familiar with, he can avoid them.

He may know places to hide or he may know people in that area that would be sympathetic, and he may know back roads. He'll know little small dirt roads he can maneuver around, abandoned buildings, abandoned cabins. I mean, the possibilities are endless."[68]

The retired marshal likened Phillips's case to that of Eric Rudolph, the bomber of the 1996 Atlantic Olympics, who was able to stay on the lam for five years because he knew the rural countryside. "It's hard to get somebody in their own backyard, that's the bottom line," the retired marshal, Victor G. Oboyski, told the *New York Times*. "That guy Rudolph, he knew those woods, I mean, they could send A.T.F. and everybody in there, hundreds of agents, but he knew those woods and they couldn't find him. It makes it very difficult for law enforcement when they are dealing with a guy who has intimate knowledge of the area where he is hiding."[69]

Phillips still could have turned himself in. He had no history of serious violence, which suggested he might have sense enough to walk out of the woods and present himself to the police without a fight. He had shot Trooper Brown, who had fortunately survived, and he certainly would get a longer prison sentence for that shooting, but he would still have the chance to get out some day. Perhaps Phillips at that point figured he had nothing to lose by staying on the lam. If he got caught, prison was a sure thing. If he stayed on the run, he was at least free, and who knows if he would ever get caught anyway. With all the help he was getting, along with the goodwill, he might be able to stay on the lam for a long time.

Phillips explained that vengeance—a desire to humiliate his captors—led him to remain on the run. He said a televised remark by the commander of the state police for western New York, Major Michael T. Manning, angered him, but Phillips never elaborated on the offending comment. Yet Phillips said he took personally what Manning said. He set out to get Manning the only way he could—by continuing to evade capture and making the state police red in the face. "What people don't understand: it was all about embarrassing one man," Phillips said after his capture.[70]

The sympathy for Phillips all but disappeared on August 31, 2006, when he used a rifle to shoot and kill Trooper Longobardo and to shoot another trooper, Donald Baker Jr., who survived. Several years earlier, Phillips had once threatened to "splatter pig meat all over Chautauqua County," according to a note he had left behind in prison.[71] Now he seemed intent on carrying out his chilling pledge. Longobardo and Baker had been posted outside of the home of one of Phillips's former companions in a town in Chautauqua County, and they were wearing camouflage uniforms. Phillips told police that he mistook the two troopers for bounty hunters, as if killing a bounty hunter would have been justified. State police believed that Phillips fired at the two first, and that Longobardo fired nine times and Phillips returned fire with eleven rounds. Baker never fired. Phillips said he acted on reflex when he shot. Police said he fired half the shots when he was running away.[72]

The pressure to find Phillips turned immense. On September 6, 2006, the U.S. Marshals Service called him a "suspected cop killer" and named him as the top fugitive on its list of Fifteen Most Wanted fugitives. The marshals added $25,000 to the $225,000 reward it had already offered for Phillips's capture. The director of the U.S. Marshals Service, John Clark, said the service's fugitive task forces would work with local and state police to search for Phillips. Clark did not explain why the marshals got involved so late, but he said the killing of Longobardo had vaulted Phillips to the top of the fifteen most-wanted list. "Ralph 'Bucky' Phillips has placed himself onto the United States Marshals 'Most Wanted Fugitives' list in the most violent way possible. This accused murderer and escapee has shown he is as dangerous as he is desperate," Clark said. "As such, Phillips is a major threat to the safety of communities throughout an entire region."[73]

The FBI put Phillips on its Ten Most Wanted list the next day, on September 7, 2006. Phillips had turned into a rarity: He was on the top most-wanted lists of both the U.S. Marshals Service and the FBI. His status as an escapee put him on the former, and his extreme dangerousness helped land him on the latter. Phillips was the third person on the FBI's Most Wanted list; Osama bin Laden was first. The FBI put out a reward of $100,000 for Phillips, and said the Bureau of Alcohol, Tobacco, Firearms, and Explosives was part of the search as well.[74]

The entire federal government seemed to be looking for Bucky Phillips. He was captured the following day, September 8, 2006, while in Warren County, Pennsylvania, just over the New York state line. At about eight o'clock at night, Phillips surrendered, his hands in the air, as he walked out of the woods. He was no match, in the end, for the troopers and federal agents and helicopters and bloodhounds. "Bucky Phillips, as I told you before, he could run, but he couldn't hide, and he is in custody," declared New York State Police Superintendent Wayne E. Bennett.[75] "Now this miserable creature will suffer for the rest of his life in the New York state prison system," Bennett also said.[76]

Phillips's options had narrowed early that morning, when authorities in Warren County investigated two reports of stolen cars, one at fifty-five minutes after one and the other at twenty-five minutes after two. Police flooded the area and brought out the bloodhounds. They were given Phillips's scent from an item in one of the cars, and they were off. By ten minutes after nine that morning, police spotted Phillips. It was the first of several sightings that day. He was seen with a pistol. Soon Phillips had nowhere to go. The troopers and federal agents and the bloodhounds, all on the ground, joined helicopters overhead in boxing in Phillips in a one-square-mile area filled with tall brush. Phillips had no choice but to give up. If he had waited, he might have found freedom again. Troopers were just getting ready to call off the search for the night due to darkness when Phillips stepped forward.

"He got to the point where there wasn't any place to go," Bennett said. "You get to the point where there's a helicopter over your head and people with high-powered rifles coming toward you. The game is up."[77]

Phillips's capture was shown on live television; his case had caused so much turmoil that residents of western New York were given the opportunity to see the end of the chase unfold in real time. State troopers cheered inside their command tent. As a line of state police cruisers drove away from the area, with Phillips in the back seat of one of them, crowds lined the sides of the road and cheered—for the police. The public infatuation with Bucky Phillips had ended. Residents were as tired of Phillips as he was tired of running. Phillips later scoffed at the public response: "Some people have no life," he said. "They want to say they were part of some big thing."[78]

On the night of his capture, Phillips's time in the spotlight was over. His time was up. His hair long and scraggly, his face dirty, he looked worn out as he sat in the back the police cruiser on his way back to Buffalo. For five months and six days, his resourcefulness and his opportunism had kept him free. And, to a degree, he had succeeded in his aim of humiliating the state police. The troopers had caught him, but only after a seemingly endless pursuit in which one man had proven his wiliness over and over. But such a desire for payback had only gotten him so far. Unlike Robert E. Burns, Phillips could not extend his fight for freedom by arguing, with solid evidence, that he had been treated unfairly and that his flight was one of self-defense and self-preservation rather than an attempt to avoid punishment. Phillips was more like Willie Sutton; caught at last, with no other place to go but back to prison. Whereas Sutton had wit and a sense of introspection about his fugitive status—he expected to get caught sooner or later—Phillips remained steadfast in his defiance even after he was in handcuffs. He was captured, but he never wanted to give up.

"I would have to believe he's somewhat exhausted," Bennett said after Phillips's arrest. "You constantly have to look around. You constantly have to look over your shoulder. I would say he's exhausted. We put a big chase on him today."[79]

The state police were relieved and the residents were relieved, but Phillips seemed worn out only physically. Indeed, months later, in an interview, Phillips told a reporter that he was counting on appeals to get him out of prison.[80] And five years later, in 2011, he was caught in his cell with a prison sweatshirt stuffed with bedding, as if to create a dummy to stand in for him while he tried another prison break. Prison officials described the contraband found in his cell as "escape paraphernalia."[81] He never carried out the plan—at least in reality.[82] But even while in prison once again, serving a life sentence with no parole, Bucky Phillips was thinking about getting out and living like a fugitive.

PART III
THE CHASE GOES ON

7

SETTING THE SNARES

Methods of Pursuit, from the Great Chicken Sting to *America's Most Wanted*

The fugitives were desperate enough to try to stay hidden but not so desperate that they refused to go out, especially with the promise of free tickets to a football game between the Cincinnati Bengals and the hometown Washington Redskins. The date was December 15, 1985, and the fugitives—about one hundred of them—got caught because they succumbed to some of the tricks that many of them had used to stay ahead of the law: disguises and deceit. The fugitives readily participated in the ruse that led to their capture—a ruse that stands as one of the most legendary and effective in the history of the U.S. Marshals Service.

Those who pursue fugitives—marshals, FBI agents, police officers, and bounty hunters—typically focus on individual cases, though police agencies also undertake special operations to cast a wide dragnet for a large number of people. Fugitive hunters must display patience and ingenuity no matter who they are targeting, whether one wily bail jumper or entire group of those on the run—a group like the one that fell for the scheme over the football tickets. In bureaucratic terms, the U.S. Marshal's Service referred to that event as a "unique enforcement operation." In the lore of the service, it is known as "the Great Chicken Sting."[1]

Marshals had long known the fugitives could be susceptible to sting operations, especially if the deceit included the chance that the fugitive would get money, even if the fugitive was due none. One official in the U.S. Marshals Service once marveled at how a fugitive answered his front door when an agent with what is now known as the Bureau of Alcohol, Tobacco, Firearms, and Explosives, disguised as a mail carrier, knocked and said he was delivering an

Internal Revenue Service check. The fugitive came to the front door and was promptly arrested.[2]

The marshals put the scam to work on a much larger scale with the Great Chicken Sting, in which the bait was the free football tickets rather than an IRS refund. In late November 1985, the marshals in the Washington, D.C., area put in motion what was officially known as "Operation Flagship" by sending letters to the last known addresses of three thousand fugitives. The letters were from a made-up group called Flagship International, which operated the new but fictitious Flagship International Sports Television Inc. The acronym for the fake company—F.I.S.T.—was the same acronym for the U.S. Marshals Service's highly successful Fugitive Investigation Strike Teams. But the similarity was lost on the recipients of the letters from Flagship International.

The recipients were likely too excited to be suspicious. The letters invited them to brunch on December 15, 1985, at the Washington Convention Center, where they were to receive tickets to that day's game at RFK Stadium between the Redskins and the Bengals—a contest that had the potential to determine whether either team would go to the playoffs. About one hundred of the fugitives responded to the letters by showing up for the festivities at the convention center. Officers from the marshals service and the local police posed as hosts and guided the fugitives to a registration table, where the hosts verified names and gave out nametags. The guests were served brunch in the main room, where a television played a tape of the 1982 Super Bowl, which the San Francisco 49ers won by defeating the Bengals, the Redskins' hated foe that day. A master of ceremonies, who was in reality an official with the marshals service, pitched the benefits of Flagship International as a TV station. To work up the crowd, one deputy marshal put on a costume for the San Diego Chicken, the ubiquitous professional-sports mascot. The Great Chicken Sting had reached full gear.

And then the party was over.

"You are all under arrest," the master of ceremonies shouted. "Put your hands on top of your heads."[3]

The twenty-five members of the strike force, including members of the District of Columbia police, rushed into the room with shotguns, stun guns, and other weapons to arrest the unlucky attendees. One was an accused murderer. Others had been charged with burglary, rape, and other serious offenses. All the football-mad fugitives in the convention center met the general criteria for fugitives whom the marshals wanted caught more quickly than others: they were accused of jumping bail, escaping from prison, violating parole, or failing to appear in court. The Great Chicken Sting was a double success because so many of the fugitives had been captured at once and in a way that avoided the danger that usually accompanied searches on the street. As the U.S. Marshals Service had found in other instances, brainpower, in the form of a ruse or a sting, often was just as effective as the massive sweeps that involved so much manpower.

"It's a safe, clean and creative way to get these people off the streets," Stanley E. Morris, the director of the U.S. Marshals Service, said after the roundup at the Washington Convention Center. "There's no safer way to make an arrest than away from the home environment."[4]

The sting was so realistic that a representative of an actual cable TV station showed up to complain that Flagship International had not yet been licensed to operate in the District of Columbia.[5] The attention to detail and realistic nature of the gathering at the convention center certainly contributed to its success. But so did the character traits of the fugitives, who, despite knowing that they were wanted, fell for the scheme out of a sense of arrogance and out of greed. The fugitives believed they could outsmart anyone, and at least one of the fugitives remained in a state of disbelief after he was handcuffed and led to the buses idling outside the convention center.

"Can I still have my tickets?" he said.[6]

The Great Chicken Sting was part of one of nine F.I.S.T. operations that the U.S. Marshals Services conducted between 1981 and 1986, and which captured a total of 14,700 fugitives.[7] Another of the more memorable of the F.I.S.T. stings occurred on June 13, 1985, at Miami International Airport. The bait in this case was not free football tickets but free airline tickets. The reverse scam was included in the eighth F.I.S.T. operation. It was based in Miami and had teams there and in five other Florida cities and St. Thomas, in the U.S. Virgin Islands, over eleven weeks in 1985.[8] To create the teams and conduct the sweeps, the U.S. Marshals Service for the first time joined with all thirty-eight police agencies in Florida as well as Canada's Royal Mountain Police and police agencies in eleven other foreign countries, including those in the Caribbean.[9] The eighth F.I.S.T. operation captured 3,816 fugitives at a cost of $3.5 million.[10] Among those captured were forty-eight accused or convicted murders, twenty kidnappers, sixty-one rapists, one hundred and sixty-seven robbers, and five hundred and ninety-three major drug dealers.[11] But none of the fugitives were apprehended in a more unusual fashion than the fourteen who wanted the free airline tickets.

Without even notifying the employees at Miami International Airport, the U.S. Marshals Service set up a bogus airline—Puño Aero Tours, also called Puño Airlines; *puño* is Spanish for "fist." The marshals had no planes for Puño, but they got counter space at the airport, which is all they needed to carry out the sting. Officials with the marshals service mailed letters to the last known addresses of two hundred fugitives, telling them they had won a free weekend trip to the Bahamas on Puño. The round-trip flight was free, according to the letter, and the winners would also get $530 to spend while in the Bahamas. All they had to do was show up at the airport with photo identification, such as a passport or a driver's license. For the recipients of the letter, the request for identification made sense: the airline wanted to be sure the tickets were going to the legitimate winners. For the marshals and other law enforcement agents in on the sting, the photo identification helped them ensure that they would be arresting the right fugitives.[12] "Congratulations!" read the letter from Puño Aero Tours to the two hundred fugitives. "You are a winner of a weekend retreat in the Bahamas. Enclosed please find your Champagne-flight boarding pass. To celebrate the birth of our new airline, we have randomly selected you to join us on our inaugural Champagne flight."[13]

Of the two hundred fugitives who received the letter, fourteen responded and were arrested. Thirteen were taken into custody while in limousines that agents had sent to pick them up, ostensibly to drive them to the airport so they could hop on a Puño plane. The ruse seemed so real to one of those thirteen that, while in the limousine and under arrest, she asked if her arrest could be delayed so she could get to the Bahamas. "Can't we take care of this next week?" the woman said, according to an agent who helped operate the sting. "I've won a free trip, and I want to take that first."[14] The one fugitive arrested at the airport nearly figured out that Puño Aero Tours was a fake. Carrying a tennis racquet and luggage, he got near the ticket counter, where no customers were waiting, and stepped back to look around. An undercover marshal quickly paged a fictitious person to the counter, which assured the fugitive that the airline was operating. The fugitive, wanted on charges that he had stolen a rental car, checked in—and was arrested. "I think he had an idea something was wrong," a marshal said. "After he was arrested, he said, 'I knew it.'"[15] An employee at the airport also had concerns about Puño, but he kept quiet. "Nobody knew anything about the outfit," said the employee, who spoke to one of the agents posing as a ticket agent. "I joked to him that Puño in Spanish is fist," the employee said. "I was ready to contact the police. It was very odd. I almost blew their cover."[16]

The eighth F.I.S.T. operation included other stings, such as marshals in Jacksonville, Florida, flushing fugitives out of hiding by promising them movie screen tests.[17] That scam appealed to the fugitives' vanity. The Puño Aero Tours sting, like the Great Chicken Sting, appealed to something else. "We wanted to be bold about it," one marshal said after the end of the eighth F.I.S.T. operation. "We're trying to figure out how we can feed on people's greed. People want something for nothing, especially crooks."[18] By whatever means it used, the eighth F.I.S.T. operation brought in the most fugitives under F.I.S.T. up to that time, but it had some drawbacks. Its cost, at $3.5 million, also made it the most expensive F.I.S.T. operation, and many of the fugitives were quickly back on the street after they posted bond and got out of what officials in Florida described as prisons too overcrowded to have handled them anyway. "As successful as the F.I.S.T. operation was," one Florida law-enforcement official said, "it serves as a graphic example of how we are digging ourselves a hole. The jail is full, the State Attorney's Office is backlogged, and court dockets are jammed."[19]

The F.I.S.T. operations used on a large scale the techniques and methods that marshals and other government agents have used to hunt fugitives dating back to the Old West and the era of the posse: a focus on the habits and inclinations of the individual fugitives, as agents try to decipher where they might go, who they might see, what incentive—whether based on greed, vanity, desperation—might lure them out of hiding. In the massive eighth F.I.S.T. operation in Florida, agents still used computers and telecommunications devices to help mine swaths of personal data to try to pinpoint the location of a fugitive or someone close to him her or her. The agents also used the most standard tool of the marshal or police officer or FBI agent: the stakeout of a fugitive's home, workplace or favorite bar. In whatever they do, marshals, FBI agents and others try to trace suspects "behavioral patterns. They electronically probe . . . [a] fugitive's friends, past and current arrest records, identification documents, credit card histories, and banking records."[20] As one marshal said after the F.I.S.T. roundups in Florida, "People have to eat to live—and they have to spend money."[21]

At the heart of any fugitive investigation, no matter how massive or small, is the confirmation of the fugitive's name and aliases. From there, whether the pursuer is a U.S. marshal, an FBI agent, a police officer, or a bounty hunter—or a bail enforcement agent, in the more formal description—the goal is to compile as much information as possible on the person from as many sources as possible. One well-known bounty hunter, Bob Burton, referred to a remark from another professional to explain how the search for a fugitive must operate to be successful. The task is obvious but essential: to search for information and search for clues. "All investigations have a life of their own," according to the remark of which Burton is so fond. "You never know what piece is the last piece of the jigsaw puzzle until you are on your fugitive almost in surprise. Thus, all information is important from the start."[22] Burton, who died in 2016 at age seventy-seven, was president of the National Association of Bail Enforcement Agents and, among other things, was technical adviser on *Midnight Run*, the highly regarded 1988 fugitive comedy starring Robert DeNiro and Charles Grodin.[23]

The same tools and tricks that Burton recommended for bounty hunters are those that marshals, FBI agents, and others also use. Once again, the recommendations seem obvious and mundane. But the pursuit of a fugitive, in Burton's telling, is typically not a glamorous affair. It is tedious work, in which the bounty hunter or law enforcement agent must be patient and willing to build a case fact by fact and stakeout by stakeout. "You're sitting in the car in a bad section of town, drinking cold coffee, talking to stupid people, and there's not much romance," Burton, who crisscrossed the United States looking for bail-jumpers and other fugitives, once said. "But, there is adrenaline."[24] To find a fugitive, Burton said, information can be gleaned from neighbors, labor unions, criminal records, civil court records, marriage licenses and property records, city directories, utility records, and postal records.[25] Credit card records and banking records are also key sources for those in law enforcement, which is why cash is the preferred currency for fugitives.

Burton was also quick to encourage the use of everyday people to track a quarry. As in many daily interactions and business ventures, the personal touch strengthens a friendship and seals a deal. Records and documents can only get you so far as you try to locate and capture a fugitive. "[P]rime sources of information," Burton once wrote, include "kids that work in pizza shops and the neighborhood paperboy. Literally dozens of investigations have been solved by telling a paperboy in a suspect's neighborhood that if he wants to make twenty or fifty dollars to call me if he sees such and such a car at 123 Main Street."[26] Even more valuable, Burton also found, is enlisting the help of the fugitive's friend or relative. The FBI and other police agencies rely on informants to gather evidence and find people, and so do bounty hunters. Disgruntled associates and scorned lovers are good sources. So is anyone is who wants to get paid. "Dollars for information are well worth it," Burton advised, "and are a major weapon in the bounty hunter's arsenal."[27]

Using skill and with luck, a bounty hunter or law enforcement agent will find the person who is second in importance to the fugitive—the person who is willing to turn the fugitive in, for whatever reason. In Burton's words, "Ultimately, your search will lead you to the two stars of this trade: the fugitive and the Judas who betrays him. My belief is that we all have a Judas in our lives. When you find him, whether by luck, deduction or detective work, your problems are over."[28] Also from Burton: "My feeling is that out of ten people in anyone's life, three will love him, three will dislike him, and four won't give a damn. The same applies to the fugitive, with perhaps more people in the dislike category."[29]

To find "the Judas," Burton insisted, involves using the telephone to call as many of the fugitive's friends and relatives as possible—a technique that today would extend to contacts via texting and social media, such as Facebook and Twitter. Keep trying, Burton said. Keep trying. "Somewhere among all those numbers you have called is a friend," he once wrote. "That friend will eventually evolve, maybe on the third call, maybe on the tenth, but he or she will surface. And either through trust, the reward, or revenge, that friend will tell you exactly where the fugitive is. Just be patient."[30] Burton once said he worked about two hundred cases a year. Nine times out of ten, he said, he found his fugitive.[31]

In some cases, a fugitive does the work for the bounty hunter or law enforcement agent by him- or herself. The fugitive might slip up and reveal his or her whereabouts by making a phone call or visiting a friend. And sometimes a fugitive might draw attention by not contacting anyone and pursuing a hermetic existence. Such self-imposed isolation, as Willie Sutton noted, can be a signal to outsiders that something is amiss and that maybe a criminal on the run is living, however reluctantly, among them and must be caught. Add to the situation a newspaper photograph of the fugitive, or most-wanted poster, seen in a post office or a gas station, and the popular aura of suspicion is fueled further. By attempting to hide, the fugitive finds no place to hide. That is the reason Sutton had the two apartments and why many fugitives must constantly be on the move.

William Raymond Nesbit, a prison escapee and murderer, learned the danger of trying to hide in a place for too long. He was No. 3 on the FBI's original Ten Most Wanted list but was the first person on the list to be caught, on March 18, 1950, two days after the FBI raised his profile by naming him as one of the nation's most dangerous fugitives. (He was captured about four months before Thomas James Holden, the first No. 1 on the list.) Nesbit was caught while living in a cave in St. Paul, Minnesota. His captors were three teenage boys: James Lewis, who was fourteen years old; James Radeck, who was thirteen; and his brother, Joseph Radeck, sixteen. They were armed with a Buck Rogers "atomic ray" gun, Boy Scout knives, and a slingshot.[32] Their heroics earned them a trip to Washington, D.C., where they met J. Edgar Hoover. Days after Nesbit's capture, Hoover sent a telegram praising the boys like they were young G-Men—the kind of boys that the FBI aimed to influence through the public-relations campaign that Hoover had launched during the 1930s. The portrayals of the FBI agents in movies and in the funny pages had worked. "This is the kind of cooperation that young men and citizens can render law enforcement, which will make their communities safe places in which to live," Hoover wrote.[33]

Even by the standards of the FBI's most-wanted list, Nesbit stood out as a brutal criminal. He was convicted of, among other things, murder and "attempted murder by dynamite," which the FBI said he and his cohorts carried out in "in a scene rivaling the most lurid movie melodrama."[34] The killings originated on New Year's Eve in 1936, when Nesbit and his accomplice stole $37,000 in jewelry from a store in Sioux City, Iowa; the heist was one of the biggest crimes in the city's history and involved, as an accomplice, the proprietor, W. A. Ehlermann, later convicted of "conniving in the robbery of his own store."[35]

The robbery soon turned deadly when the gang reassembled at a powder house five miles away, where they intended to settle an argument over how to divide the stolen jewels.[36] The FBI claimed that some members of the group were trying to kill two others to keep them quiet about the jewelry heist, but other accounts suggest that one of the accomplices, Floyd H. Parker, also known as Harold Baker, was shot to death during the argument over the loot, and that his girlfriend, Helen Sieler, was also shot and wounded.[37] Whatever happened, Nesbit and two others in the gang attempted to get rid of the bodies by blowing them up with the dynamite in the powder house. The explosion, which occurred when Nesbit and the other two gang members had driven off, set off 3,500 pounds of dynamite and 7,000 pounds of black powder. The blast was so intense that it shattered $20,000 worth of glass in windows in Sioux City, five miles away, and was felt up to fifty miles away.[38]

Parker, as the FBI said, "was blown to bits," but Sieler, "true to movie tradition, managed to escape before the explosion."[39] Using her statements and other evidence, prosecutors convicted Nesbit of murder and attempted murder, and he was sentenced to life. The sentence was later reduced to twenty years for good behavior, but Nesbit got out before serving it all. As a trusty at the South Dakota State Penitentiary, Nesbit held a job at the warden's house. He escaped by walking away on September 4, 1946. The FBI said he fled to Sioux City, Los Angeles, or Spokane, Washington.

Nesbit, who was known to work as a butcher and a shoemaker, stayed out of sight of law enforcement until shortly after the FBI placed him on the first Ten Most Wanted list. The FBI announced his inclusion on March 16, 1950, in an article published in newspapers throughout the country. Citing the dynamite incident, the FBI described Nesbit as "one of the most dangerous criminals alive"[40] and the Justice Department characterized him as a fugitive whose time on the run soon would be up. "Now, much of his life already wasted in prison," the department said, "he is the object of an unceasing, relentless search by the FBI. He knows it will continue as long as he lives. He never knows at what moment he will hear the words which will mark the end of his uneasy freedom."[41]

The words did come, from police officers. But they got their man because the group of boys in St. Paul had found Nesbit, then fifty years old, living in an abandoned cave in a bluff near the railroad yards and along the Mississippi River near St. Paul. Nesbit had moved into the cave around Thanksgiving 1949, after he had worked in the apple orchards in Washington state and in the lumber camps in northern Minnesota.[42] Nesbit, known as "Ray," was familiar to some of the boys who helped capture him. They knew he lived in the cave, which was equipped with a cot, stove, and icebox; Nesbit got water from a nearby stream. Some of the boys ran errands for Ray, and they would listen to him tell stories about his adventures.[43] But Nesbit stayed in the cave too long. On March 16, 1950, James Lewis, one of the boys, recognized Ray as the William Ray Nesbit identified in the newspaper story and photograph as the criminal occupying the third spot on the FBI's new Ten Most Wanted list. Lewis showed the newspaper story to his friend James Radeck, who said Ray was too fat to be the same person shown in the article. But the boys examined the photo and became convinced that the man living in the cave down by the Mississippi was one of the most dangerous men in America.

The boys shouted at Nesbit to come out of the cave, but he did not hear them. So the boys, armed with their toy gun and slingshot, threw snowballs and rocks down the chimney of the cave. They wanted to drive out Nesbit, who had also seen the newspaper story and was trying to keep a low profile.[44] The boys' ploy worked. A disturbed Nesbit walked out of his cave long enough for the boys to recognize him, without a doubt, as the infamous fugitive. The boys sprinted to a nearby tavern to telephone the police. Officers arrived at the cave, and William Raymond Nesbit became the first person on the FBI's Ten Most Wanted list to be caught.

"He got smoked out," FBI historian John Fox said of Nesbit's case. "They made a match and went to the local police and he was captured."[45]

In addition to praising the boys who identified Nesbit, J. Edgar Hoover used the occasion of his apprehension to praise American newspaper readers and the newspapers that were now faithfully publishing the stories about the FBI's newly christened top-ten fugitives. Five days after William Raymond Nesbit was caught, another story, reprinted in the Portland *Oregonian*, triggered the arrest of Orba Elmer Jackson on the chicken farm outside Portland on March 23, 1950. Hoover was elated. "Credit must be given to the millions of Americans who read these stories and were alerted to watch for these criminals," Hoover declared on March 27, 1950, in a statement carried in newspapers nationwide. "I urge all citizens interested in the domestic peace and security of the United States to keep noting the photographs and the descriptive data in the series of stories."[46] With so many newspaper readers wanting to help Hoover, no fugitive could risk staying too long in one place—even a cave.

Katherine Ann Power, a student radical in the 1970s, was the rare fugitive who outdistanced the FBI, though in 1993 she eventually turned herself in after twenty-three years of running. Her surrender was not due to a specific investigative technique or long-term surveillance. Guilt drove Power to come out of hiding, and so did the weariness and resignation that so often plagues the long-term fugitive. The FBI played a role as well: though their search for Power waned over the years, agents still knew she was out there. Power risked capture every day. When the constant wariness and the drain of keeping up a double life became overwhelming, Power ended her flight herself to achieve some kind of inner peace "She could not have intimate relations with other people," one of Power's lawyers said when Power appeared in court to answer the charges that had been pending against her for more than two decades. "There were all sorts of questions about how she would raise her son. Who were his grandparents? Who was she? The only way to recreate her life was to own up to who she was and face up to the charges."[47]

Power was the second woman to appear on the FBI's Ten Most Wanted list and one of only ten women to ever make the list; the first woman was Ruth Eisemann Schier, a kidnapper who became No. 293 on December 28, 1968, and was caught on March 5, 1969.[48] Power is also one of the ten fugitives that the FBI removed from the list for reasons not related to death or the dismissal of a case. As a student revolutionary and a bank robber, Power was named No. 315 on October 17, 1970, but removed from the list on June 15, 1984,[49] when the FBI determined that she no longer met the criteria for a top-ten fugitive. The FBI, in other words, determined that, after fourteen years of searching for Power, the leads in the case had dried up, and that increasing the publicity about her by keeping her on the list would not bring agents any closer to apprehending her. By removing Power, the FBI acknowledged that ceding her spot to another fugitive would be more productive for the public and the bureau.

Power most likely was on her way to living on the lam, safely, for the rest of her life until September 15, 1993. At forty-four years old, she surrendered to the authorities and pleaded guilty to charges of bank robbery and manslaughter related to the fatal shooting of a police officer during an armed bank robbery in Boston on September 23, 1970, when Power was twenty-one years old. She then was a senior at Brandeis University and a member of a group of radicals trying to raise money to protest the Vietnam War. During the robbery of the State Street Bank and Trust Company in Brighton, Power and her four associ-

ates, who carried handguns, a shotgun, and a submachine gun, got away with
$26,000. Another radical in the group, William Gilday Jr., killed the police of-
ficer, Walter A. Schroeder, by shooting him in the back.[50]

Power was driving the getaway car; her role made her an accomplice in
the bank robbery and Schroeder's slaying. The crimes, though undeniably
violent, were nonetheless infused with a sense of radical justice that a number
of revolution-minded college students had adopted in the spring of 1970, after
the United States expanded the Vietnam War, which led to protests on college
campuses across the nation. On May 4, 1970, when the Ohio National Guard
fatally shot four students at Kent State University, students like Power were
drawn to more violent actions to oppose the war. At time of the bank robbery,
Power and the others saw their illegal efforts as part of a calling, no matter how
bizarre their plans. Power and her four associates intended to use the $26,000
in stolen bank proceeds to "melt down the wheels of trains that carried military
weapons and to arm the Black Panthers."[51] For the FBI, the reasons behind
the crimes of Power and her cohorts at Brandeis made no difference—she had
broken the law and she was a fugitive. "Power should be considered armed and
extremely dangerous," her FBI most-wanted poster read.[52]

Gilday, the shooter, was caught, with the help of images captured on the
bank's closed-circuit cameras, and he was sentenced to life in prison. Another
of the four, Stanley Bond, was also caught but died in prison in 1972 when a
bomb he was making exploded. Bond was incarcerated while he was awaiting
trial in Schroeder's death. The third man in the group, Robert J. Valeri, was
also caught. H cooperated with the prosecution, was convicted and sentenced
to prison, and later released.[53] The fourth associate and only other woman,
Susan Saxe, went on the run like Power. The FBI made her top-ten fugitive No.
316 on October 17, 1970 (the same date as Power), and Saxe was caught more
than four years later, on a street corner in Philadelphia, on March 27, 1975.[54]
The FBI that day distributed Saxe's photo to police after agents received a tip
that Saxe was in the area. A police officer who saw the photo recognized Saxe
on the street. Saxe had been living in women's communes. Upon her capture
and conviction, Saxe served seven years in prison for manslaughter and bank
robbery.[55] By the time Saxe got out, Katherine Ann Power was still on the run.

But Power was hiding in plain sight. She fled to Oregon—a state, for whatever reason, has attracted fugitives over the years—and in 1977 became known
as Alice Louise Metzinger, a wife and a mother who went on to co-own M's Tea
and Coffee House in Corvallis, in the northwestern part of the state. Power had
used several aliases as a fugitive until she settled on Alice Louise Metzinger,
the name of a baby who had died about the time Power was born. Power got a

Social Security number, birth certificate, and driver's license under that name.[56] Power's husband had long known about her past, but her past was unknown to her son, who was fourteen years old in 1993, or her friends. Power revealed her true identity to her son a month before she turned herself in. She told her friends three days before she turned herself in. Power broke the news at a good-bye party she threw for herself in Oregon.[57] Power made the decision to surrender to authorities in Massachusetts after she saw a therapist for depression. She found that she could no longer live under an assumed name and avoid the consequences of crimes she had committed so long ago. The death of Walter Schroeder, the police officer, had weighed on her, Power said in a statement her lawyer released when she surrendered and pleaded guilty in Superior Court in Boston on September 15, 1993. "His death was shocking to me," Power said, "and I have to examine my conscience and accept any responsibility I have for events that led to it."[58]

Power's lawyers negotiated her surrender, and they negotiated, with the prosecution, her sentence: eight to twelve years in a Massachusetts state prison plus twenty years of probation. The judge, Robert Banks, who sentenced Power on October 6, 1993, was not pleased. He said the sentence should have been harsher, and he rejected arguments that Power deserved leniency because of her depression or the political nature of her crimes.[59] At her plea hearing, Power had sought to put the case against her in a political context even as she said she grieved Schroeder's killing. Power in her statement at the plea hearing said the crimes she committed were "absolutely illegal acts," but "[a]t that time the law was being broken everywhere." She also said of her crimes, "Although at the time those actions seemed the correct course, they were in fact naïve and unthinking."[60] At her sentencing, Power spoke briefly, through tears. She did not attempt to put her crimes in a political context. "I cannot possibly say in words how sorry I am for the death of Officer Schroeder," she said. "My whole adult life has been a continuing act of contrition. . . . I am here today because I also recognize I have a debt to society."[61]

The sentencing hearing focused on the family of Schroeder, who left behind a wife and nine children. His eldest daughter, Clare Schroeder, a police sergeant, detailed her family's loss and said the passage of time had not muted the impact of Power's crimes: "Murdering a policeman in Boston to bring peace to Southeast Asia was utterly senseless then, and it is just as senseless now," Clare Schroeder said.[62] Judge Banks displayed his anger in how he fashioned the sentence. After giving Power eight to twelve years in prison and twenty years of probation, he ordered that Power, while on probation, could make no profits from her crimes, such as through movies or book deals or speaking engagements. "I will not permit profit from the lifeblood of a Boston police officer by someone responsible for his killing," Banks said. "That is repugnant to me."[63]

Power was released from prison in 1999, and her probation expired in 2013. She moved back to Boston and is working on a memoir.[64] Power speaks regularly about her past and how to promote peace. The title of one of her more recent talks in Boston is "A Journey from Guerrilla to Grandmother."[65] Power's twenty-three years as a fugitive continue to define her.

Power's surrender capped an era in the history of the FBI's Ten Most Wanted list. She was among many student activists and antiwar radicals and militants who made the list in the 1960s and 1970s as J. Edgar Hoover widened the scope of the FBI's focus to include subversives as well as bank robbers and kidnappers. Also placed on the list in the 1970s were activists H. Rap Brown (No. 308) and Angela Davis (No. 309), the Weathermen member Bernardine Dohrn (No. 314), and Native American activist Leonard Peltier (No. 335). Their inclusion very much signaled the changing times, but, in many instances, such as in the case of Power, these fugitives had also been accused of dangerous crimes that warranted their capture. And the more traditionally violent and nonpolitical fugitives continues to populate the list. The serial killer Ted Bundy (No. 360) was added on February 10, 1978, and caught five days later.[66] A local police officer in Pensacola, Florida, stopped Bundy for speeding while he was wanted for escaping from prison.

In the case of the subversives and more political fugitives, they were often more difficult to find because they were part of an underground that was more than willing to shelter them and hide them from federal agents or the police. *New York Times* reporter J. Anthony Lukas chronicled the phenomenon in a lengthy piece in December 1970, when he described how political dissenter and radicals—like the wanted person who referred to the Grand Inquisitor in a passage that appeared in Lukas's piece—had become "the new breed of fugitive" who could count fellow radicals to shield them in a network similar to how the Underground Railroad had shuttled fugitive slaves to freedom.[67] Because these fugitives often were not career criminals who were more apt to live peaceful lives, they were able to draw little attention to themselves while on the run—even, in the case of Power, managing a coffee shop in Oregon. And yet these fugitives' self-awareness and sense of guilt also made the susceptible to turning themselves in or slipping up in ways that suggested they might have really wanted, deep down, to get caught.

Such was the case of a lesser-known radical fugitive, Howard Mechanic. He was a twenty-two-year-old senior at Washington University in St. Louis when he was accused of throwing a cherry bomb near firefighters who were putting out a blaze that destroyed the ROTC building on campus May 4, 1970. Mechanic was one of many students who were out that day protesting the deaths of the four students at Kent State. At Washington University, about three thousand protesters, including Mechanic, had assembled to watch the ROTC building burn.[68] He was charged with and convicted of a new federal crime that outlawed interference with a police officer or firefighter who was responding to an incident of civil disorder. The case went to the Supreme Court, which in 1972 upheld Mechanic's conviction by declining to hear his appeal. The time was up for Mechanic to start serving his federal sentence of five years. Then he went on the lam.

Mechanic adopted the name of Gary Tredway and settled in Scottsdale, Arizona, where he raised a family and made a living as a landlord. He was never on the FBI's Ten Most Wanted list, though the FBI repeatedly visited his twin brother in California and took photos of the brother so they could identify Mechanic, someday.[69] Mechanic would have stayed a fugitive and continued to live as Gary Tredway had he not made what turned out to be a poor decision: He ran for Scottsdale City Council in 2000. A newspaper reporter doing a standard candidate profile uncovered Mechanic's past—Mechanic told her all about it—and his cover was blown when the newspaper story appeared. Mechanic, who had continued to embrace left-leaning politics while on the run, went to federal prison to serve his long overdue five-year sentence, which he always maintained was unjust. Whether he acted out of hubris or extreme self-confidence, Howard Mechanic captured himself. "Was I secretly hoping to get caught?" he once said in response to a question from a reporter. "I don't think I was."[70]

Though radical students and would-be revolutionaries flooded the fugitive ranks in the 1960s and 1970s, the FBI remained fixed in the public imagination as the dominant force in tracking down those on the lam. In 1968, the FBI set a record by capturing thirty-three fugitives on the Ten Most Wanted list, with seven of them caught with the public's help.[71] Americans were reminded weekly, on television, of the FBI's efforts and what every citizen could do to assist the apprehension of a fugitive. The 1960s and 1970s marked a period of peak popularity of the FBI on television, and the bureau, again at the direction of the public-relations master J. Edgar Hoover, used the exposure to help find more fugitives. During this era, television became as important a tool for the FBI as the most-wanted poster and the photographs of fugitives circulated among police departments. The advances made during this era, in terms of relying on television to bring more attention to fugitives, would become realized in full decades later with some of the most popular reality-based law enforcement programs in television history, particularly *America's Most Wanted*.

The show that first vaulted the FBI to a higher prominence was *The F.B.I.*, which ran on ABC from 1965 to 1974, totaling two hundred and forty-one episodes, and starred Efrem Zimbalist Jr. as the main character, FBI Inspector Lewis Erskine. The producer of *The F.B.I.*, Quinn Martin, also produced the TV series *The Fugitive* and *The Untouchables* (1959–1963), the TV movie and then TV series that depicted how Eliot Ness (played by Robert Stack) and his unassailable agents brought down public enemies in Prohibition-era Chicago. And Martin produced the 1976 TV series *Most Wanted*, in which Robert Stack played Captain Linc Evers, head of the Los Angeles Police Department's expert fugitive task force.[72] Martin built a career out of dramatizing the battle between fugitives and the authorities, such as the FBI. In each episode of *The F.B.I.*, Zimbalist's Erskine captures Communists, crooks, and fugitives in a plot based on cases out of the FBI's files. At the end of the show, Zimbalist would announce the latest addition to the FBI's Ten Most Wanted list and ask for the public to pitch in to find the person. The underlying message was that Hoover himself would appreciate the cooperation.

The hour-long show, which ran on Sunday nights, turned into a cultural fixture, as its lengthy run proved. Among its many fans were James Earl Ray, the assassin of Martin Luther King Jr. and No. 277 on the Ten Most Wanted list. The feature about the actual fugitives made *The F.B.I.* Ray's favorite television program, and he was said to dream of making the top-ten list, which he considered akin to winning an Academy Award.[73] Ray achieved his goal on April 21, 1968, the day after he was placed on the list and seventeen days after he shot King. *The F.B.I.* featured Ray as the newest top-ten fugitive, and Ray was watching, with glee, in a tavern in Toronto, where he was hiding out. Ray later fled to London, where English authorities captured him about six weeks later.[74]

Other fans included young men (and perhaps women, though *The F.B.I.* had a male lead), who followed the show and aspired to be an FBI agent. That was the case with Louis Freeh, the FBI director from 1993 to 2001, who grew up watching *The F.B.I.* as a boy in Jersey City, New Jersey.[75] The FBI welcomed *The F.B.I.* as a way to boost its image and spur applications from would-be agents at a time when the counterculture viewed the bureau and other government institutions with suspicion. The FBI recognized Zimbalist's role in aiding the bureau by awarding him an honorary special agent badge in 2009. "Efrem's character embodied fidelity, bravery, and integrity," FBI director Robert Mueller said when he presented the honor. "So much so that he inspired a generation of future FBI employees, many of whom pursued a career in the bureau because they watched *The F.B.I.* series as they grew up. In those days, he may well have been the bureau's best and most effective recruiter!"[76]

The FBI made sure that its namesake show met its expectations. The bureau—and, most likely Hoover himself—approved the casting of the four principal actors on the show, including Zimbalist. The check "was in the nature of a routine inquiry to make certain the performers had not indulged in political activities or criminal pursuits that might cause embarrassment for the bureau after the show was on the air."[77] Hoover, who had managed the FBI's image since the days of James Cagney and *G-Men* and the newsreels, strengthened his control in 1954, when Congress, at his request, passed a law that prohibited the commercial use of the bureau's name, initials, and seal without the approval of the FBI director. Hoover was said to be upset over how a radio series had portrayed the bureau.[78] In the case of *The F.B.I.*, the bureau's involvement in the production raised questions about artistic freedom, though others considered the FBI's interest to be reasonable given that the bureau was allowing the series to use its name, among other things.[79]

Whether *The F.B.I.* increased the rate of capture for fugitives is uncertain, though the number of fugitives located was high during the early years of the series: twenty in 1965, sixteen in 1966, seventeen in 1967, the record thirty-three in 1968, eleven in 1969, and five in 1970.[80] Just as important was the FBI's belief that the show reaffirmed to the public that it had the skill and the where-withal to catch the real-life fugitives, just as Zimbalist's character caught them in the fictional episodes. *The F.B.I.* was meant to further a feeling of trust between the FBI and the public; if the public could see that the bureau, as portrayed in *The F.B.I.*, was competent, the public would be more willing to call in with tips to locate the fugitives featured at the end of the program.

Also through the show, the FBI gained a champion in Zimbalist, who used his popularity to defend the FBI's standing; his actions also made sense in that, if the FBI faltered, so would *The F.B.I.* and, quite possibly, Zimbalist's career. Most notably, Zimbalist was the honorary chairman of a nonprofit called the Friends of the FBI, formed in 1971 to raise money to counter what its membership considered unfair criticism of the FBI and Hoover. Zimbalist had gone from a fictional FBI agent whose show prodded the public to help find actual fugitives to the leader of an actual group who said the FBI's naysayers—in Congress and the press—could undermine the bureau's effectiveness, including its ability to find fugitives, and threaten public safety. "The F.B.I. and J. Edgar Hoover are being subjected to the degradation of an attack by self-serving politicians, their supporting media and certain radical elements that ultimately seek the destruction of all law and order in the United States," Zimbalist said in a letter to prospective donors. "We, the Friends of the F.B.I., are determined to counter the campaign against the F.B.I. and Mr. Hoover, which threatens to undermine the whole structure of law and order in the United States."[81] A show that glorified the capture of fugitives had aided the creation of a political shield for the FBI.

Seventeen years later, in 1988, a television show that made its debut quickly turned into a sword for the FBI in its hunt for fugitives. As it had with *The F.B.I.*, the bureau cooperated with *America's Most Wanted*; it was one of only three TV shows in which the FBI played an active role. The other was *Today's F.B.I.*, a fictional program that ran for only eighteen episodes in 1981–1982.[82] With *America's Most Wanted*, the FBI soon came to appreciate the reach and influence of the genre-creating true-crime program, which most famously ran on the Fox network for twenty-three years. During that time, tips from the show helped in the capture of 1,149 fugitives, or an average of one a week.[83] Thomas J. Miles, the law professor who examined the effectiveness of the FBI's Ten Most Wanted list, found, in another study that, unsurprisingly, an appearance on *America's Most Wanted* greatly increased the apprehension hazard in a case, or the chance a fugitive will be caught.[84] "[D]uring the month of broadcast," Miles concluded, "fugitives profiled on *America's Most Wanted* face an average rate of apprehension over seven times that of fugitives who do not appear on the show. While sizable, the estimated impact is not implausible, given that millions typically watch the program. The results indicate that *America's Most Wanted* raises a fugitive's risk of apprehension."[85]

So effective was *America's Most Wanted* in finding those on the lam that the FBI, in its official statistics for its Ten Most Wanted Fugitives program, cites *America's Most Wanted* as responsible for assisting in the capture of seventeen of the fugitives on the Ten Most Wanted list. Only one other television show or other media program is accorded the same honor: *Unsolved Mysteries*, which has aired on a number of networks, including NBC and CBS. The FBI credited that show with two apprehensions.

America's Most Wanted turned into such a cultural force that John Walsh, the show's iconic host, interviewed President Barack Obama in 2010, on the anniversary of the show's one-thousandth episode.[86] And though the FBI appeared wary at the beginning—"We are not in the entertainment business. Our mission is to catch criminals," a bureau spokesman said in 1988, before the premiere of *America's Most Wanted*, glossing over J. Edgar Hoover's image-shaping efforts—law enforcement agencies nationwide were among the show's biggest fans, and the FBI had several agents working as liaisons between the bureau and the show.[87] "A tremendous partner," is how the U.S. Marshals Service described *America's Most Wanted*.[88] A New York City police detective who arrested one fugitive caught with the show's help called *America's Most Wanted* "fantastic." "I wish we could have our own station," he also said. "We could arrest a whole lot of bad guys."[89] In May 1988, as *America's Most Wanted* continued to establish a big audience three months after its launch, the director of the FBI, William Sessions, appeared on the show to announce that the bureau had added three names to its Ten Most Wanted list.[90] The program had expanded the number of eyes watching fugitives by the millions.

In terms of capturing fugitives, the show was a hit for the FBI from the very beginning. Its first episode, which aired for a half hour on Sunday, February 7, 1988, generated the tips that led to the apprehension of David James Roberts, convicted of arson, rape, and murder; he was No. 409 on the FBI's Ten Most Wanted list. The FBI placed him there on April 12, 1987, a year after Roberts escaped from the Indiana State Prison by overpowering his escorts while returning from a medical exam.[91] Roberts was serving multiple life terms for killing four people and raping another.[92] He killed a family of three, including a one-year-old girl, whose house he set on on fire in a dispute over tires in 1974. While out on bail that same year, he killed another child, a six-month-old boy, by leaving him along the side of a road in freezing temperatures after raping the boy's mother in a car and stuffing her in the trunk. The boy died of exposure.[93]

The inaugural episode of *America's Most Wanted* featured Roberts, who, at forty-four years old, now faced even more years of incarceration because of his escape. The *America's Most Wanted* episode aired on stations in the brand-new Fox network in only a few cities, including New York, where it started at 6:30 p.m. But information on Roberts's whereabouts soon flooded the show's hotline; during the first commercial break, as Fox News reported, "the hotline was ringing off the hook"[94] and by the end of the show seventy-five calls had come in identifying Roberts, a native of Perth Amboy, New Jersey.[95] One caller said Roberts looked like "Bob Lord," who was working in a homeless shelter on Staten Island, New York. Another caller said Roberts was her boyfriend, and that he could be found at a hospital where he was receiving medical treatment; Roberts had left by the time the authorities arrived.[96] Using other leads, the FBI arrested Roberts in his apartment in Staten Island on February 11, 1988, four days after his appearance on *America's Most Wanted*. The show and Walsh, the host, had scored their first capture on their first try.

Roberts had some forewarning but he still could not avoid capture. He said he learned several hours before the *America's Most Wanted* broadcast that he was to be featured, and he watched the show.[97] The audience also included Roberts's coworkers at the Carpenter Men's Shelter, the homeless shelter on Staten Island where he worked as a supervisor and was known to be kind and responsible. "The resemblance was striking," a board member of the shelter's parent organization said after Roberts's arrest, "but we were hoping so much it wasn't him."[98] A year later, Walsh, the *America's Most Wanted* host, interviewed Roberts. Walsh asked him what he thought as soon as he learned he was to be featured on *America's Most Wanted*. "Immediately to flee the area," Roberts said.[99] He also confronted Walsh about what he believed was the risk of *America's Most Wanted* targeting innocent people. "I believe that if people are wanted," Walsh replied, "they should be brought back and either proven innocent or guilty."[100]

Though John Walsh's name is all but synonymous with *America's Most Wanted*, he did not create the program. The idea for it came from an aide to the owner of the Fox network, Rupert Murdoch. And the aide got his inspiration from several true-crime shows in Europe, particularly *Crime Watch U.K.*, which the BBC was airing monthly.[101] Fox officials then developed *America's Most Wanted*, where actors would reenact two or three notorious crimes every show. At the end of the segments, photographs and other information on the fugitives accused of the crimes would go up on the screen, along with the hotline number. Workers in the Fox studio would take the calls, with FBI agents, ATF agents and other professionals on hand in case a caller had such a good tip that a federal agent or police detective needed to get on the line. The callers would be promised confidentiality. This was the format for *America's Most Wanted* during its entire run. Walsh was ideal fit as a host during the entire run as well.

The producers of *America's Most Wanted* first wanted to hire a celebrity or a professional actor to host the show. But they hired Walsh, who was forty-two years old in 1988—he "looks like J. Edgar Hoover's dream of a G-man," one reporter wrote[102]—and who had a personal history that had already made him a compelling public figure in the push for victims' rights. Walsh was working as a developer of luxury hotels and living in Florida in 1981 when his six-year-old son, Adam, was kidnapped at a shopping mall and murdered; his severed head was found but never the rest of his body. Intent on finding his son's killer and in helping to locate missing children throughout the United States, Walsh launched a crusade. He appeared on television shows and successfully pressed for child-protection legislation in Congress; the work of him and his wife led to the Missing Children's Act of 1982, which created a national database for missing children,[103] and eventually the Adam Walsh Child Safety and Protection Act of 2006. It created a national sex offender registry and set rules for the registration of sex offenders.

In 1994, John Walsh and his wife founded the National Center for Missing and Exploited Children. His son's murder was the subject of two made-for-television movies, *Adam*, which first aired in 1983, and *Adam: His Song Continues*, which first aired in 1986. In the early 1980s, Walsh's personal experience and his raw energy and passion appealed to the producers of *America's Most Wanted*. Walsh saw the chance to host as an opportunity to find fugitives and criminals and prevent other families from going through a tragedy like that of his son's slaying. Walsh initially aimed his ire at the FBI over the case, but with *America's Most Wanted*, he channeled that anger into a project to ensure, as he once said, "Adam didn't die in vain."[104] The pain of losing his son, he said, was "unbearable." "But you've got to stay focused," he said. "I know that incredible evil walks this planet. That's what I stay focused on."[105]

With his intense stare and his uniform of dark T-shirt and leather jacket, Walsh added to his image as a relentless sentinel for justice who relied on *America's Most Wanted* to spread his uncompromising message. Walsh was also resolute in his pleas for the public to call in; his signature sign-off line was, "And remember, you can make a difference." The tagline for the overall show built on the idea that, if you helped John Walsh and called into *America's Most Wanted*, you were on the side of the good guys in a long struggle against the forces of evil in the United States. The tagline proclaimed, "America Fights Back." J. Edgar Hoover and his boss, Attorney General Homer Cummings, could not have thought of a better line. *America's Most Wanted* obliterated any romanticism that still might have been attached to the fugitive in American culture. The heroes of the show were the FBI agents, the police officers, and the first responders. The emphasis was not on the wiliness of the fugitive but on the perseverance of the cops. Recast on *America's Most Wanted*, Richard Kimble likely would have been portrayed as a devious and cowardly doctor whose flight was another example of his guilt. If your picture appeared on *America's Most Wanted*, you were branded, even more so than if your picture had been displayed in a most-wanted poster stuck to a bulletin board at the post office. *America's Most Wanted* fused two of Americans' passions—television and a desire to see justice done—like never before. With John Walsh advocating for America's victims, *America's Most Wanted* brought the hunting of fugitives into the realm of infotainment.

Critics of the show derided it for what they believed was its disregard for due process, for its implication that all those who were featured on the show had to be guilty of something. Walsh's response, as he first expressed it in his interview with David James Roberts, was that he wanted fugitives apprehended only so that the justice system could go to work on their cases and determine their guilt or innocence. Critics also contended that *America's Most Wanted* spurred the creation of tabloid television and contributed to the spate of true-crime shows that soon would seem to overrun American television. A spin through the TV channels could leave a viewer feeling that criminals had plundered the United States, with only the feds and the police and the likes of John Walsh preventing the nation from sliding into chaos.

But viewers could not get enough of the show for a long time. In its first season, *America's Most Wanted* attracted 25 million viewers a week,[106] and it averaged 9 million viewers a week through most of its run.[107] When the ratings flagged in 1996, Fox pulled *America's Most Wanted* from its schedule for the fall of 1996 but reinstated the show after receiving 85,000 letters and a petition that thirty-four governors signed. True to form, the first fugitive featured on the first episode back was captured.[108] More apprehensions followed, many of them notable on a national scale. In 2003, *America's Most Wanted* helped capture the suspect in the kidnapping of fourteen-year-old Elizabeth Smart from her home in Salt Lake City, Utah, in June 2002; the suspect, Brian D. Mitchell, was later convicted. The show also featured missing children, and Elizabeth Smart was one of those found alive. Between the time that Smart disappeared and Mitchell was arrested, *America's Most Wanted* had broadcast five episodes on the case.

Viewers came to identify with Walsh, and knew how the death of his son drove him. They learned in December of 2008 that, after twenty-seven years, authorities in Hollywood, Florida, finally solved Adam Walsh's murder by accusing a drifter and serial killer, Ottis E. Toole, who confessed to the slaying but recanted before he died in prison in 1996.[109] John Walsh did not get full justice, because Toole was never prosecuted, but he said the resolution of the case at least brought the waiting and uncertainty to a close. "For all the other victims who haven't gotten justice, I say one thing: 'Don't give up hope,'" Walsh said in talking about the end of his son's case.[110]

But time eventually ran out on *America's Most Wanted*. Due to sagging ratings, Fox canceled it in June 2011. Lifetime then took on *America's Most Wanted* but canceled that version in 2013. The true-crime genre that *America's Most Wanted* had pioneered had spawned so many other shows that even the original program could not stay ahead of its progeny. As if to prove, however, that the United States has an insatiable desire to hear about fugitives and criminals, John Walsh in 2014 started hosting *The Hunt with John Walsh* on CNN. A similar show, *In Pursuit with John Walsh*, started to air on the Investigation Discovery channel in early 2019.[111]

The format of those programs is similar to *America's Most Wanted*, which remains a touchstone in the history of fugitives in the United States. At a time, in the 1980s and 1990s, when the country seemed to be more fixated on crime, John Walsh and his show both mirrored and added to the national mood. *America's Most Wanted* acted as a bridge between the paper era, when most-wanted posters were most effective, and the digital era, when the internet forever altered how federal agents and the police would identify and hunt fugitives. When it came along, *America's Most Wanted*, as former top FBI official John Miller once said, "changed the whole business. We could say, 'We want this guy bad.' We could say, 'Let's line it up with *America's Most Wanted*.'"[112]

8

CAUGHT IN THE WORLD WIDE WEB

The Digital Age Catches up to Fugitives, and the Bail System Faces Reforms

The first FBI Ten Most Wanted fugitive to be captured via the internet had a hand in his high-tech undoing. A few weeks before he was nabbed in Guatemala, in the spring of 1996, a handyman known as Bill Young—or "Uncle Bill" to many people in the town of Antigua—helped set up a computer for a friend's fourteen-year-old boy. The state-run telephone company for Guatemala had started internet service about four months earlier, so the family of Young's friend was eager to tap into the great unknown that was the World Wide Web.[1] While exploring on the internet, the boy came across the website for the FBI and its Ten Most Wanted list; the FBI had established the FBI.gov website on June 30, 1995, a date the agency marks with pride.[2] The boy quickly noticed the photo of one of the fugitives, a serial bank robber and prison escapee named Leslie Ibsen Rogge[3] (No. 430 on the top-ten list). He had been on the lam from prosecution in the United States after breaking out of a prison in Idaho eleven years earlier. Leslie Ibsen Rogge, the boy realized, looked a lot like Uncle Bill. Within weeks, Rogge was in the custody of the FBI; he surrendered on May 18, 1996, at the U.S. Embassy in Guatemala City. Rogge had become the first fugitive that the bureau found with the help of the internet. "This represents the end of the romantic notion that you can run south of the border and disappear," one resident of Antigua, where Rogge had lived unnoticed for so many years, said after his arrest.[4]

Since Rogge's capture, the FBI has nabbed three more fugitives with tips generated through publicity on the internet, including two caught with information disseminated on the FBI's website.[5] The four cyber-captures represent a fraction of the 486 fugitives that have been captured or located from the 561 people who have appeared on the FBI's Ten Most Wanted list since 1950. And the four represent a fraction of the 162 fugitives the FBI said were caught as the result of citizen cooperation. *America's Most Wanted*, with the seventeen captures to its credit, has far outpaced the internet as a fugitive-catching platform. When Rogge was caught, a prediction accompanied his arrest: that the internet was about to become a "powerful new tool," especially in tracking international fugitives.[6] The number of cyber-captures would appear to belie this notion, at least in terms of the FBI's statistics. As the *Washington Post* noted in an editorial published after Rogge's capture (the internet-related angle made his story noteworthy),"It's also worth keeping in mind that, other than the romance of technology, it [the use of the World Wide Web] doesn't represent that great an advance on current global media that have made celebrities or fugitives' faces familiar to a vast public—just ask Salman Rushdie. The Rogge nabbing is the first that the FBI credits to its home pages specifically, but TV's *America's Most Wanted* has scored similar coups."[7] The editorial also noted, rightly, that the internet could be used for good or ill, that the Mafia or an authoritarian government could easily use go online to hunt an enemy just as easily as the FBI could go online to seek help capturing a runaway murderer. The advent of the digitally created "global village," the *Post* wrote, again using the Rogge case as a starting point, "is reassuring and unnerving in about equal proportion."[8]

The pursuit of fugitives via the internet is nonetheless vital to the criminal justice system in the twenty-first century. "It's the next step in technology," a police official and expert on fugitives said of the internet days after Rogge's arrest. "If the internet is the future, that's where we want to be to stay a step ahead of the criminals."[9] The *New York Times*, in a 1997 article that also held up the Rogge arrest as an example of police embarking on a new frontier in law enforcement, had this to say about the possibilities of the web: "The authorities say that no fugitive is ever really safe in an age when the next-door neighbor or the kid down the block can be the kind of vigilant citizen who regularly checks out the Justice Department's wanted list on the World Wide Web."[10] A top official in the U.S. Marshals Service told the paper that tracking down fugitives "is getting a little bit easier using these sophisticated programs."[11] The service also has a strong presence on the web.

Changes related to fugitives have not stopped with the digital transformation of the methods of both the pursuer and the pursued. The basic system that helps define fugitives appears to be headed for far-reaching changes as well. The bail system, grounded in Anglo-Saxon law and derived from the frankpledge and other ancient practices meant to safeguard the community and ensure the appearance of the accused, has become subject to increased criticism that it discriminates against the poor and disenfranchised. The reforms are focused on the criminal justice system and how it sets bail, and the bail-bond industry and how it helps finance pretrial freedom for those the justice system believes are flight risks. The proposals likely will have little effect on the number of high-profile fugitives, many of whom are escapees and suspects who are running from the law before they have been arrested and even considered for bail. But a review of the push for bail reform is relevant in the context of fugitives. The bail system for centuries has been society's primary apparatus to prevent criminal defendants from becoming fugitives while allowing the defendants—still presumed to be innocent until conviction—to remain free while awaiting prosecution. The bail system, in its own way, tries to answer a question that has become no less complicated since the adoption of the Eighth Amendment: who among the accused is at risk for turning into a fugitive? It is a critical question in any era, including the digital one.

With virtually any topic searchable on the internet, the placement of information about fugitives online was an obvious fit. The use of the internet nonetheless signaled, yet again, how law enforcement adapted to the prevailing media tools of the day—posters stuck in post offices, the movies, television, the web—to hunt for those on the run. From internet sites to electronic billboards, the FBI, U.S. Marshals Service, and scores of other police agencies have shown little hesitation in using the innovations of the digital age to age to shrink the world of the fugitive to such a degree that anonymity is nearly impossible to achieve.

At the same time as this cyber revolution has been taking place in law enforcement, the types of fugitives have been changing as well. Bank robbers, the bane of the nation for decades starting in the 1930s, are becoming less represented on the most-wanted lists than fugitives wanted for what have become the more high-profile crimes of the age: domestic and international terrorism. In response to the terrorist attacks of September 11, 2001, the FBI on October 10, 2001, released its Most Wanted Terrorists list, and on January 17, 2002, released its FBI Seeking Information—Terrorism list, which the bureau uses to solicit information to prevent future terrorist attacks. The Seeking Information category has expanded to include a site that focuses on unidentified bank robbers: the web page displays surveillance photos of bank robbers and details about the heists in the hope that someone will recognize a thief and call in a tip. The two terrorism-related lists and the top-ten most wanted fugitives list remain the bureau's three major most wanted lists, and the two newer lists use the original top-ten fugitive list as a blueprint. And that list, more than ever, reflects the times. The 1960s saw the FBI focus on fugitives, such as Katherine

Ann Power, wanted for radical violence. The 1970s witnessed the list expand to include more members of organized crime, the breakup of which became an FBI initiative. And as drug trafficking became more prevalent in the 1980s and 1990s, large-scale drug dealers appeared on the FBI's list more often.

Today, fugitives wanted for cyber-related crimes, such as bank fraud, and other offenses carried out with newer technology, such as production of child pornography and its online dissemination, have also come to populate the most-wanted lists more frequently. After putting its Ten Most Wanted list on its web site in 1996, the FBI broadened the scope of the types of fugitives it was seeking. The bureau kept the main top-ten list but created ancillary online most-wanted lists with web pages that are themed: fugitives wanted for murder, for example, and bank robbery, white-collar crimes, cybercrimes, criminal-enterprise investigations, human trafficking, counterintelligence, and crimes against children. Many of the fugitives on the niche lists, especially those accused of hacking or other cybercrimes, are foreign nationals. Getting fugitives on these lists requires less stringent steps than putting a fugitive on Ten Most Wanted list, a process that still involves FBI headquarters soliciting suggestions from its field offices nationwide: "Any FBI agent can request that a fugitive be added to one of the crime-specific pages."[12] But the smaller, specialized lists allowed the FBI to highlight more than just the fugitives on what are the major three lists: the Ten Most Wanted Fugitives list and the two terrorism-related lists. And the fugitives featured on the niche lists are still worth hunting for, in terms of potential financial gain. Rewards of $50,000 or more are not uncommon.

The U.S. Marshals Service has taken a similar approach on the web. Its Fifteen Most Wanted fugitives lists is still its major list, but it also has lists of fugitives online in other categories, such as fugitives wanted in major cases and fugitives wanted as part of local investigations. The Bureau of Alcohol, Tobacco, Firearms, and Explosives and the Drug Enforcement Administration maintain online lists as well. Anyone who desires to help find a federal fugitive, no matter what the crime or the agency involved, only has to go to the Department of Justice's web page for most-wanted fugitives. The site features links to all the agencies' most wanted lists. With a click, the hunting can begin.

Fugitives accused of crimes on the niche lists still can go straight to the top of FBI's Ten Most Wanted list. In a particularly telling example, after Osama bin Laden was killed in May 2011 and Whitey Bulger was captured in June 2011, two spots opened at the top of the FBI's Ten Most Wanted list. The FBI in 2012 filled one of the slots with the case of Eric J. Toth (No. 495), a teacher at an affluent private elementary school in Washington, D.C., and camp counselor in Wisconsin accused of producing child pornography, including videos.[13]

Among the evidence against him was a media card for a camera that investigators said was loaded with images that would be "any parent's nightmare."[14]

Toth was on the lam for five years, including a time when he faked his suicide, until he was captured in Nicaragua in 2013. He pleaded guilty and was sentenced in 2014 to twenty-five years in federal prison, putting an end to his days as "among the vilest of predators on the FBI's Most Wanted list."[15] The FBI was so concerned about Toth that he was featured on *America's Most Wanted*, and the FBI had his face displayed on bus stops and billboards around Washington, D.C., and across the nation, including such well-traveled spots as New York's Times Square.[16] An alert tourist in Nicaragua tipped off the authorities after recognizing Toth,[17] whose image had become ubiquitous due to the FBI's efforts to publicize his case both online and through more traditional means.

The capture of Leslie Ibsen Rogge, while the first of its kind, showed how the FBI continues to use a combination of techniques to find fugitives, even with the introduction of the internet and, later, platforms such as Twitter and Facebook. Before he was a captured in Guatemala in the spring of 1996, Rogge had been featured five times on *America's Most Wanted* since 1990. The FBI placed the captured Rogge under two categories: fugitives caught with help of the internet, and fugitives caught with the help of *America's Most Wanted*.[18] Rogge, who had also appeared on *Unsolved Mysteries*, told FBI agents after his arrest that he had watched the *America's Most Wanted* episodes that had featured him and afterward moved each time to avoid suspicion.[19] The television show helped keep the trail for Rogge hot, though the internet is finally what did him in, even as he tried to build a new life for himself in Central America. "A lot of people thought using the internet would never fly in Central and South America," the head of the FBI's Miami office, which covers Latin America, said after Rogge's arrest. "But it did, because people are so hungry for news from the States."[20]

Rogge's notoriety was well deserved. An ex-sailor in the Navy, he was fifty-six years old when he was captured in Guatemala in May 1996, and was a veteran of the criminal justice system who, by his own accounts, had robbed $2 million from as many as thirty banks over the previous two decades.[21] Rogge had been on the run for ten years and eight months when he was caught, and he had been on the FBI's ten most-wanted list for six years and four months, since January 24, 1990.[22] Rogge, who the FBI said was born in Seattle, stole his first car when he was thirteen years old[23] and first went to federal prison in Leavenworth, Kansas, in the 1970s for convictions that included car theft. Once out, he robbed a bank in Key Largo, Florida, in 1984; authorities captured him on a forty-two-foot-sloop he had been sailing off the coast of the Bahamas.[24] His stint in the Navy had made Rogge a skilled sailor, making escape on a boat always a possibility. Rogge was convicted of the Key Largo bank robbery and was sentenced to twenty-five years in prison. While in custody, he is said to have told the FBI that he had robbed as many as twenty-five banks.[25]

Whether or not that number was accurate, Rogge had been accused of robbing a bank in Post Falls, Idaho, and was transferred there to stand trial. He was convicted and sentenced to another twenty-five years in federal prison in September 1985. Four days later, while awaiting a transfer to federal prison, Rogge escaped from the Latah County Jail, in Moscow, Idaho. Rogge got away with the help of the county jailer, who unlocked a door to the prison's recreation room so Rogge could walk out. The jailer was convicted of giving Rogge a map; the jailer said two men had threatened to kill him and his family unless he helped Rogge, so the jailer aided in the escape.[26] The breakout sent Rogge on his long flight from justice that did not end until he was caught in Guatemala. After fleeing Idaho, he was believed to have settled in Rockville, South Carolina, where he repaired marine engines while living on a boat moored at the Botany Bay Marina; the FBI seized the boat in 1989, but still could not find Rogge.[27] He had become elusive, even as he continued to leave a trail by breaking the law.

While on the lam, Rogge was accused of robbing three banks: one each in Arkansas, North Carolina, and Missouri.[28] He fancied himself "a gentleman bank robber,"[29] who traveled with a police scanner and who once said the ideal way to rob a bank was to be polite, much like Willie Sutton, and show up in a three-piece suit carrying an empty briefcase. Ask the bank manager to fill the briefcase with cash, Rogge said, and run out of the bank if the manager refused.[30] Rogge's smooth ways benefited him in Guatemala, where he fit in with the locals after arriving in the early 1990s. Rogge and his wife, Judy Kay Wilson, held themselves out as Bill and Anna Young; he worked as a handyman known as "Mr. Fix-It" after he detailed his services in an ad he placed in a magazine in Antigua in 1992. He set up computers and fixed cars, appliances, and marine motors. Ever the sailor, Rogge ended up opening a boat-repair shop on the Guatemalan coast, where he had moved with his wife.[31]

By that time, the area around Antigua was filled with speculation that Bill Young might be the same man—Leslie Ibsen Rogge—whose story had been featured on *America's Most Wanted*. And then the fourteen-year-old son of Rogge's friend started browsing the internet, and Rogge's chances to stay free dwindled. The boy identified "Uncle Bill," as Rogge, the FBI flooded Guatemala City after getting the tip, and Rogge, fearing that Guatemalan authorities might kill him, walked into the U.S. embassy and turned himself in.[32] The FBI had no problem identifying Rogge: as his most-wanted poster made clear, he had several tattoos, including one of a seahorse on his right shoulder and one of a devil on his right forearm. "Les," the devil tattoo also read.[33]

Rogge was sentenced to sixty-five years in federal prison after being convicted of a series of bank robberies; he also had to continue the sentence that he ended prematurely by walking out of the prison in Moscow, Idaho, in September 1995.[34] Rogge, displaying the chutzpah that served him well as bank robber and fugitive, characterized his departure from the prison as an "erroneous release"[35] rather than an escape, but his efforts to minimize his crimes have gone nowhere. Leslie Ibsen Rogge, done in by the internet, is incarcerated at the Bureau of Prison's Federal Medical Center in Butner, North Carolina, north of Raleigh. He is all but certain to die in prison. The release date for Rogge, who is seventy-eight years old, is October 26, 2045. By then, he will be one hundred and five—and the World Wide Web will undoubtedly become even wider.

As was apparent in Rogge's case, in which *America's Most Wanted* also contributed to his capture, the internet has supplemented rather than replaced more traditional techniques for catching fugitives, such as the publication of most-wanted features in newspapers. Most of these fugitives are of the local kind, wanted by the county sheriff or the local police department for jumping bail or skipping out on child-support payments. But the features, though set down in newsprint rather than online, still are effective. Eager readers are known to scan the most-wanted sections as soon as they appear on the designated week and call in with tips soon after the newspaper arrives on their doorsteps. Getting a reward is an incentive, but so is, in many cases, a desire to see a two-timing boyfriend or a deadbeat dad rounded up and thrown in prison.[36]

Sometimes a most-wanted feature can make a newspaper more noteworthy than it might have been otherwise. Such was the case with the *Washington Examiner*, a local media outlet in Washington, D.C., that published a weekly most-wanted story from 2008 until 2013, when the *Examiner* halted publication of its daily print edition and became a weekly magazine with a larger presence on the web. In the years that the most-wanted features ran, they were among the *Examiner*'s most popular articles; the U.S. Marshals Service said in 2010 that it was catching a fugitive a month in the area of Washington, D.C., due to information from *Examiner* readers.[37] Tips came from readers disgruntled with the fugitives. Tips came from readers who felt guilty that they had been withholding information about a fugitive. And sometimes the fugitives turned themselves in, afraid of the increased exposure after their mug shot appeared in the *Examiner*. "They panic," an official with the U.S. Marshals Service said of those fugitives covered in the *Examiner*. "That flushes them out of their hiding places."[38]

The FBI has also flushed out fugitives by using an outsized and digitized version of the typical newspaper most-wanted feature. In 2007, the bureau started using electronic billboards to advertise for most-wanted fugitives, and now, through partnerships with outdoor-advertising companies, which donate space, the bureau has access to 7,300 billboards in forty-six states.[39] The project originated in Philadelphia, upon the suggestion of an executive with Clear Channel, the media company. In a scenario that would have pleased J. Edgar Hoover, the executive graduated from a local FBI Citizens Academy, part of a community outreach program in which the bureau teaches residents how it operates. The executive then offered to let the FBI use billboards to help catch fugitives and spread information about missing children.

In September of 2007, the FBI launched its Digital Billboard Initiative by posting information on eleven fugitives on eight billboards throughout Philadelphia.[40] By December of 2007, the FBI had expanded the program to 150 digital billboards in twenty cities nationwide, such as Atlanta, Cleveland, Indianapolis, and Newark, all locales where Clear Channel operated billboards along heavily traveled roads.[41] The focus of the advertisements, the FBI said, would continue to be "very violent, dangerous fugitives."[42] As of late 2017, the FBI had captured fifty-seven fugitives with tips received as a result of electronic billboards nationwide.[43] The FBI relies on its field offices and fugitive task forces to suggest which fugitives should be featured. The electronic billboards allow the information to go up quickly and interchangeably and in specific locations where investigators believe a fugitive is roaming. As soon as one fugitive is caught, another can take his or her place.

The FBI's most-wanted messages usually appear for ten seconds, which often is enough time for a photo to make an impression on a passing motorist. Some of the more notable fugitives that the electronic billboards helped capture, according to the FBI, include a man wanted for shooting at police officers in New Jersey in 2013, and who was found in Florida in 2014 after someone saw him on a billboard; an accused drug trafficker from Buffalo who had been on the run for about a year but who turned himself in four days after he was featured on an electronic billboard in Buffalo; a suspect with ties to drug trafficking and money laundering turned himself in at the prodding of friends and relatives three weeks after he was featured on an electronic billboards around Norfolk, Virginia, in 2013.[44] The FBI and other agencies use the billboards for other public-safety purposes, such as to alert the public to dangers or to encourage motorists to contact the FBI with information on certain crimes in general, such as human trafficking and identity theft.

Driving into a town and seeing a fugitive's face and name flashed on a billboard can be an unsettling experience, especially if the person is wanted for a rape, murder, or another violent crime. The billboards that feature fugitives risk portraying a community as unsafe; they are meant, however, to make a community safer by helping the FBI and other agencies catch criminals with greater speed. Plus electronic billboards and similar forms of digital messaging are just as ubiquitous in American society in the 2010s as smartphones. The FBI intensified the search for Eric J. Toth, the child pornographer, by using the electronic billboards in New York's Times Square, and the FBI has advertised for information using smaller digital billboards, such as those at bus stops and newsstands.[45]

As advertisers do, the FBI and other police agencies want their information visible in the most-trafficked spots in a town, such as along a highway, or in a city, such as in the middle of Times Square. "When you talk about Times Square, you are really talking about the crossroads of the United States, maybe even the crossroads of the world," an FBI special agent in New York once explained. "We have tens of thousands of New Yorkers that are in there every day, but we also have millions of visitors from all around the world that go through Times Square on a yearly basis. So this opens up a whole new set of eyes for us. Well, the goal is to have these people look up and see this billboard, right in the middle of Times Square, see one of these bad guys, pick up the telephone, and call the FBI."[46]

The FBI's foray into electronic billboards coincided with a boom in the industry overall, as rock stars and tech-friendly companies, such as Snapchat, gravitated to them even as Facebook and Twitter and similar platforms allow for the broadcasting of messages on what can be considered a more personal scale.[47] The FBI and other agencies also use those platforms to publicize fugitives. But one theory is that electronic billboards and similar digital media have become attractive because, in the age of so many distractions, such as smartphones, the billboards demand attention. They are so large and placed in spots such as along the highway or in Times Square where you cannot look away, especially when the electronic billboards are advertising a killer or a rapist who is on the loose. The audience is captive and—the FBI hopes—captivated.

On a smaller scale—the scale of the smartphone screen and the computer terminal—the digital age has benefited the FBI, U.S. Marshals Service, and other police agencies in another major way. In looking for fugitives, the agencies have often found clues on such platforms as Facebook, with the fugitives themselves leaving the trail. Routine practice for investigators these days is to go online and try to find fugitives based on electronic information they leave behind. One survey of 1,200 members of law enforcement from 2012 found that four out of the five respondents reported that they used social media platforms such as Facebook and YouTube as part of investigations. Of the respondents, 67 percent reported that they found that using social media helps solve crimes more quickly.[48] Commenting on the survey and other findings, one report noted that Facebook postings have provided evidence of crimes, such as stolen merchandise, and the report said that "Facebook has even been used to pinpoint fugitives' locations, leading to their capture. These people might 'check in' at a specific place or post photos that could give clues as to where they are."[49]

The police's tracking of Facebook "friends" is another tool that has worked in finding fugitives. In his book, the bounty hunter Bob Burton stressed that contacting friends of a fugitive would help lead eventually to the fugitive him- or herself. Burton was talking about real-life friends. Facebook has provided even more opportunities to identify, from afar and in cyberspace, a fugitive's friends and associates. The method worked in 2014, when police in Los Angeles turned to Facebook to locate one of its most-wanted fugitives, Eduardo "Limpy" Rodriguez. The thirty-five-year-old gang leader had been on the run for eleven years, avoiding prosecution on charges that he killed four people, including three in what was described as execution-style slayings.[50] He was also charged with two counts of attempted murder when he disappeared in 2003. Even featuring Rodriguez on *America's Most Wanted* proved fruitless.

Los Angeles police believed Rodriguez, also known as Juan Carlos Campos Gamino, had fled to Mexico. Stymied for years, members of the Los Angeles force had police officers in nearby Glendale take a look at the case. A Glendale officer started running the names of Rodriguez's friends and relatives through the internet. The officer came across a Facebook page for a woman with posted photos of a man that looked like Rodriguez. The search revealed more Facebook photos: there was Rodriguez in Las Vegas, there was Rodriguez at the Griffith Observatory in Los Angeles. One of the women on Facebook turned out to be Rodriguez's fiancée. Police located the woman's residence in Riverdale, and investigators, including those with the U.S. Marshals Service, staged a stakeout. In November of 2014, the officers caught Rodriguez shortly after he left the house to go to work. Authorities said his fiancée had no idea that her boyfriend, a carpenter, was living under an assumed name and was really Eduardo Rodriguez, the second-in-command of the Toonerville Mexican street gang who was wanted for four counts of murder.[51] The case, as the *Los Angeles Times* reported, "left officials marveling at how a search of Facebook did what years of 'wanted' bulletins and even a segment on *America's Most Wanted* could not."[52]

The leader of the Toonerville gang was also a notorious fugitive. But that person was caught through more conventional means. The crime boss, Timothy McGhee, went on the lam in the fall of 2002 to avoid prosecution on charges that he killed three people and tried to kill four others in gang-related violence; investigators in Los Angeles said he was a suspect in as many as twelve murders, either as the killer or the person who supervised the killings. Police once called McGhee a "monster" and a "thrill killer" who oversaw about two hundred gang members and directed their operations with military precision.[53]

The U.S. Marshals Service put McGhee on its Fifteen Most Wanted Fugitives list, and he became one of the most sought-after fugitives in the United States. As many as sixty local and federal investigators were part of the chase.[54] He was caught in February 2003 in Bullhead City, Arizona, in the northwestern part of the state near the borders of California and Nevada. Authorities said the big tip came from a newspaper reader in the nearby Mojave Desert; the reader recognized McGhee from a photograph and story about him and told police McGhee was living in Bullhead City. He was found at a mobile home. A U.S. Marshals fugitive task force captured him along with the Los Angeles Police Department's fugitive warrants section and the Bullhead City police SWAT team.[55]

McGhee, who was twenty-nine when he was arrested, was as brazen on the run as he was when he was leading the Toonerville gang. He smiled at spectators during his arrest, and police said they later seized one of his t-shirts: "Fugitive. Can't see me," it read.[56] McGhee's adventures as a criminal are scheduled to end in his execution. In January of 2009, he was sentenced to death for his conviction for the three murders; as of late 2018, he remained on death row at San Quentin State Prison.[57]

In the case of Eduardo Rodriguez and the online sleuthing, investigators were able to review Facebook accounts by public means. But law enforcement agencies can also get search warrants and court orders to obtain data from Facebook in cases in which the user allows only his or her friends, rather than the public, to view information. And sometimes law enforcement does not need to get a warrant to access what the Facebook user—and fugitive or criminal—designed to be private information. A Facebook user's friend can provide police access to the user's private account without the police needing a warrant.

That was the core finding in a notable court decision regarding privacy, Facebook, and law enforcement. A federal district judge in New York issued the decision in August of 2012, in the case of Melvin Colon, a gang member who was arrested in New York on murder charges. Police got a warrant for Colon's Facebook account. But they established the probable cause for the warrant by first viewing Colon's Facebook profile after his Facebook friend allowed investigators access to the profile through the friend's Facebook account; the friend was a cooperating witness. On Colon's profile, according to the judge, William H. Pauley III, investigators found that "Colon posted messages regarding prior acts of violence, threatened new violence to rival gang members, and sought to maintain the loyalties of other alleged members of Colon's gang."[58]

Pauley, in the key element of is ruling, found that the government did not violate Colon's Fourth Amendment rights against unlawful searches and seizures when his Facebook friend allowed the police to view Colon's private Facebook profile. Pauley wrote, "Colon's legitimate expectation of privacy ended when he disseminated posts to his 'friends' because those 'friends' were free to use the information however they wanted—including sharing it with the Government. . . . When Colon posted to his Facebook profile and then shared those posts with his 'friends,' he did so at his peril."[59] The ruling's lesson for fugitives and other criminals who use Facebook: be careful who your "friends" are.

As the internet was altering the pursuit of fugitives in the 2000s, another kind of revolution started to take shape in the long-established industry that was created as a check to those who might want to go on the lam. The bail-bond system came under increased scrutiny from judicial reformers who considered the system as biased against the poor and members of racial minorities. From the time of its earliest iterations under Anglo-Saxon law, the Anglo-American bail-bond system was designed to ensure the court appearances of defendants through the use of bail as a surety. But, reformers said, instead of providing a way for defendants to stay out of prison, the bail-bond system in many respects was providing the mechanism to keep defendants in prison before their trials, even if they were not a flight risk or a danger to their communities. A defendant who could not afford bail could not get out of prison. The lack of financial resources had turned into a punishment of its own.

The push for changes to the bail-bond system represented a third wave of reforms or attempted reforms to the system. The first wave—based on the Federal Bail Reform Act of 1966—triggered the establishment of percentage bonds and pre-release mechanisms, such as electronic monitoring, to reduce the number of inmates being held because they could not make bond. The second wave—based on the Bail Reform Act of 1984—allowed federal judges to weigh whether a defendant was a danger to the community when considering the setting of bond. The third wave of reform is taking aim at the entire bail-bond system and whether monetary bail in and of itself was fair and constitutional. Under the administration of President Barak Obama, the system came under criticism from Attorney General Eric Holder, among others.

For the third-wave reformers, the Eighth Amendment's guarantee against the setting of "excessive" bail took on new meaning when, for a poor defendant, any amount of bail was unaffordable and therefore excessive. "Poverty is not a crime, and hundreds of thousands of Americans, convicted of nothing, should not be in jail today because they cannot afford cash bail," U.S. Sen. Bernie Sanders, of Vermont, the erstwhile presidential candidate, said in July of 2018. "In the year 2018, in the United States, we should not continue having a 'debtor prison' system. Our destructive and unjust cash bail process is part of our broken criminal justice system—and must be ended."[60]

Sanders, an independent who caucuses with senators in the Democratic Party, proposed on July 25, 2018, the No Money Bail Act, which would apply most directly only to federal criminal defendants but would encourage states to shift away from monetary bail as well. The bill would end the use in the federal courts of secured bonds—bonds in which defendants must post money or property as collateral for their release. No federal courts, according to the bill, "may use payment of money as a condition of pretrial release in any criminal case,"[61] though defendants could still be held without bond if found to be too much of a flight risk or a community threat. The bill would provide grants to states to expand or develop pretrial release programs to reduce the number of inmates being held on bond before trial. Under Sanders's proposal, the federal government would withhold certain grants from states that continue to use money bail systems, and the proposal would require a study, after three years, to make sure the alternative bail systems were not leading to the incarceration of disparate classes of defendants, such as those who are women or African-American.[62] "It has always been clear that we have separate criminal justice systems in this country for the poor and for the rich," Sanders's office said in summarizing the bill. "A wealthy person charged with a serious crime may get an ankle monitor and told not to leave the country; a poor person charged with a misdemeanor may sit in a jail cell. And this disproportionately affects minorities—fifty percent of all pretrial detainees are Black or Latinx."[63]

Sanders's bill went to the Senate Judiciary Committee, where it sat with no action through the rest of 2018. Passage immediately appeared unlikely. Some proponents of eliminating cash bail argue that the bill did not go far enough.[64] On the other side are more conservative observers who consider the elimination of cash bail in the federal system unconstitutional under the Eighth Amendment, though they leave open the possibility that legislatures can make changes. "The Framers' primary concern in drafting the Eighth Amendment's Bail Clause was to ensure that bail not be set unreasonably high—which was not to say that bail must be affordable, or even available, to all defendants," an extensive Heritage Foundation report on bail found in 2017.[65] The studied continued: "The Supreme Court has repeatedly rejected constitutional challenges to the use of money bail in the United States. To the extent that arguments can be made against its use today, they are ordinarily policy questions, not legal or constitutional issues. . . . Rather than contort the text of the Constitution to achieve their policy goals, advocates for bail reform should make their arguments to legislators and the public, the proper venues for this discussion."[66]

The bail-bond industry has also opposed legislation that would eliminate money bail, arguing that the current system is constitutional and that other issues, rather than bail, contribute to overcrowding at jails and prisons.[67] But as the federal legislation has flagged, a number of states have proceeded with bail reform, following the lead of Washington, D.C., which eliminated cash bail in 1992. The courts in the District of Columbia use a risk-assessment evaluation to determine the likelihood of a defendant returning for hearings or turning into a fugitive. In 2017, the District of Columbia courts released 95 percent of defendants without requiring cash bail, and 84 percent returned for all their court appearances. Of those who were released while awaiting prosecution, 2 percent were charged with violent crimes.[68] A tax on poor people is how one judge in the District of Columbia characterized cash bail, and she said the risks associated with releasing someone before trial are risks inherent in the American justice system: "That's the price of our ordered system of liberty and justice. The only way to get a complete assurance of safety is, of course, to incarcerate everyone, which is not the American way."[69]

Over the past several years, several states, such as Kentucky, New Jersey, and New Mexico, have followed the lead of the District of Columbia and limited the use of cash bail. But California went the furthest. On August 28, 2018, Governor Jerry Brown signed into law Senate Bill 10, which fully eliminated cash bail—the object of the appeal in the case of Kenneth Humphrey, the San Francisco robbery defendant who could not make bail of $350,000. The passage of the law could render the California Supreme Court's pending review of Humphrey's case moot. California Senate Bill 10, effective in October of 2019, institutes a system similar to the arrangement in the District of Columbia in that it allows judges to employ risk assessments to determine whether defendants are too dangerous to be released. With the passage of the law, Brown said, "California reforms its bail system so that rich and poor alike are treated fairly."[70] California's chief justice, Tani Cantil-Sakauye, whose support of the bill helped it clear the California State Assembly, called the signing of the law "a transformative day for our justice system. Our old system of bail money was outdated, unsafe, and unfair."[71] California had dismantled the industry that was born amid corruption in the state in 1898, with the McDonough Brothers Bail Bond Brokers in San Francisco.

The California law had among its detractors, groups that typically would not be aligned. The American Bail Association opposed the law as unnecessary and the American Civil Liberties Union (ACLU) attacked it as unfair. The ACLU's California branch said the use of risk assessments gave too much discretion to judges, leaving open the possibility that racial bias could still come into play as judges decided whom to release and whom to keep in prison. The law left the California Judicial Council to work through the details of the pretrial risk assessments, but the law gave more direction on what factors must exist for a judge to detain a defendant before trial at the request of the prosecution: "if there is a substantial likelihood that no condition or combination of conditions of pretrial supervision will reasonably assure public safety or the appearance of a person in court."[72] The California branch of the ACLU, which originally co-sponsored Senate Bill 10, withdrew its support over such language. "We oppose the bill because it seeks to replace the current deeply-flawed system with an overly broad presumption of preventative detention," the ACLU of California said. "This falls short of critical bail reform goals and compromises our fundamental values of due process and racial justice."[73]

In the end, even lawmakers who shared the ACLU's qualms voted for the bill, reasoning that the bail reform law as proposed was better than no bail reform law at all.[74] The debate over the law touched on longstanding issues that reveal the tensions of living in a free society—tensions that, as the California Court of Appeal noted in the Humphrey case, Alexis de Tocqueville raised in 1835. A defendant is presumed innocent until found guilty and is thus not subject to automatic incarceration. At the same time, how does society ensure that a defendant, released before trial, will not harm the community? How can a free society determine who, when given the chance, will choose to become a fugitive?

No matter how the bail system changes, fugitives will always be with us, especially those who never jumped bail because they fled before they could be arrested. Two of the most recent additions to the FBI's Ten Most Wanted list in 2018 show the range of fugitives that federal agents and others must continue try to find on a daily basis. The list is not getting smaller, and the fugitives are not getting any less dangerous.

The FBI on April 12, 2008, added to the list Rafael Caro Quintero, also known as Rafael Caro-Quintero, the subject of the $20 million reward—the highest reward in the history of the FBI, with the money coming from the State Department's Narcotics Rewards Program.[75] The main crime for which Caro Quintero is wanted is the 1985 kidnapping, murder, and torture of undercover DEA Special Agent Enrique "Kiki" Camarena, a murder that sparked tensions between the United States and Mexico. The killing remains one of the DEA's biggest tragedies; *Time* magazine put Camarena's face on the cover on November 7, 1988, for a story about his death.[76]

Known as "a godfather of Mexican drug trafficking"[77] and the "prince" of Mexican drug traffickers,[78] Caro Quintero, or RCQ, is also accused of being a key supplier of heroin, cocaine, and marijuana to the United States in the late 1970s. The FBI announced his addition to the Ten Most Wanted list (No. 518 overall) with the DEA, the U.S. Marshals Service, and the Department of State, all of which are assisting in the hunt. The authorities said Caro Quintero is believed to be hiding in Mexico, and that the huge reward was meant to flush him out and rattle those closest to him. "The reward in this case represents a serious amount of money," FBI Special Agent Mike Rollins, one of the investigators, said in announcing Caro Quintero's addition to the list at a news conference held at DEA headquarters near Washington, D.C.—another indication of the importance of the case.[79]

The Caro Quintero case is both old and new. It stems from a murder that occurred in 1985 but has gained renewed interest due to a court decision in Mexico in 2013. Caro Quintero, who is believed to be in his sixties, was not placed on the Ten Most Wanted list in 1985 when Camarena was killed while working undercover in Mexico as a DEA agent. The FBI said Caro Quintero was upset because he believed Camarena was responsible for a 1984 raid that the Mexican government carried out on Caro Quintero's marijuana plantation. Camarena, the FBI said, was closing in on exposing another large drug operation when he was kidnapped in 1985. Four months later, he was found dead, the result of what the FBI said was a hit that Caro Quintero ordered.[80] A federal grand jury in Los Angeles indicted Caro Quintero in 1988 in Camarena's murder and on drug-trafficking charges, but Caro Quintero also faced arrest in Mexico for the killing.[81]

President Ronald Reagan retaliated for the murder by shutting down most business along the U.S.-Mexican border. Mexican authorities vowed to prosecute Caro Quintero.[82] He was initially on the lam in 1985, with the help of a Mexican federal police officer, but was finally captured in Costa Rica and then convicted in 1989 and sentenced to forty years in prison. But a Mexican judge released Caro Quintero on August 9, 2013, saying that he should have been tried in state court rather than federal court.[83] Caro Quintero disappeared once he left prison, though authorities said he eventually took over control of the Sinaloa drug cartel, an association Caro Quintero denied in an interview with a Mexican news site in April 2018.[84] The Sinaloa cartel's leader had been Joaquin "El Chapo" Guzman, another infamous fugitive who was convicted in federal court in New York in early 2019 on charges that he ran one of the biggest drug operations in the world.[85]

Caro Quintero's release in 2013 infuriated the Obama administration, which on August 14, 2013, five days after Caro Quintero's got out of prison, formally asked Mexico to rearrest him. The request, which had Mexico's approval, triggered another international search for Caro Quintero. But a debate loomed over whether he could ever be extradited to the United States to be prosecuted for Camarena's murder under the 1988 indictment. Some contended that Caro Quintero was protected under double jeopardy, because he had already been convicted of the murder in Mexico, while others said the Mexican judge's ruling that released Caro Quintero also invalidated his conviction, allowing him to be tried in the United States.[86] The United States could also seek to charge Caro Quintero with offenses, such as those related to drug trafficking, for which he had not been convicted in Mexico.

The government would have to untangle those issues once Caro Quintero was captured. By putting his name on the Ten Most Wanted list on April 12, 2018, the FBI, Drug Enforcement Agency, and the State Department clearly hoped that the pressure and publicity—plus a $20 million reward—would generate the kinds of tips that had benefited the FBI in so many cases before. The arrest of Caro Quintero would also offer recompense to the DEA, whose agents continue to mourn Camarena's death and deal with its aftermath; the murder has been credited with jump-starting the "war on drugs" under the Reagan administration.[87] "Caro Quintero had tremendous power three decades ago, and he still has power today," Russ Ellersick, another FBI special agent working the Caro Quintero case, said at the new conference on the case in April 2018.[88] And as the likes of drones and helicopters now chase Caro Quintero,[89] the FBI is also relying on a tool that did not exist in 2013—social media. One of the many ways the FBI announced Caro Quintero's inclusion on the Ten Most Wanted list on April 12, 2018, was through a post on its @FBIMostWanted account on Twitter.[90] The post linked to a YouTube video of the news conference.

Six months later, the FBI, also using Twitter, announced that it had added another person to the Ten Most Wanted list: Lamont Stephenson, wanted on charges that he strangled his fiancée and killed her dog in their apartment in Newark, New Jersey, on October 17, 2014. Police in New Jersey charged him with homicide in November 2014, and, after he disappeared, the FBI in September 2017 charged him in federal court with unlawful flight to avoid prosecution—a UFAP case. And as Stephenson remained on the lam, the FBI on October 11, 2018, named him to the Ten Most Wanted list and announced a reward of $100,000 for information leading to his capture; the notification went out on Twitter as well.[91] As of November 2018, Stephenson, who is forty-three years old, was the most recent fugitive added to the Ten Most Wanted list and the 521st fugitive to be on the list overall.

The FBI's role in Stephenson's case reflects one of the missions that J. Edgar Hoover established so many years ago: That the bureau, through the use of UFAP warrants, would aid local and state police in hunting down fugitives throughout the United States, especially the fugitives who represented the greatest threat—those on the Ten Most Wanted list. The FBI listed Stephenson as "armed and dangerous" in placing him on the list.[92]

The FBI emphasized Stephenson's volatility and unpredictability. Agents and others said he had been engaged to the victim, forty-year-old Olga DeJesus, shortly before her death, and that he had moved in her with her after the two had been in an intense but short courtship after they reconnected at their twentieth high school reunion in June 2017.[93] DeJesus was found dead in her bed—the dog was found dead near the apartment door[94]—and the FBI said Stephenson was known to be possessive and controlling of DeJesus. "To strangle someone to death is an act of rage," said Christopher Smith, a detective in Essex County, New Jersey, where Stephenson was charged with homicide. "God forbid he is living with another woman and he's that possessive. He could do this to someone else."[95] After leaving DeJesus's apartment, Stephenson was seen on surveillance cameras at Newark's Penn Station. His demeanor, the FBI said, was concerning. "He wasn't in a panic at all," said FBI Special Agent Carl Priddy, the lead investigator on the case in the FBI's Newark office. "For him to be calm and collected after he had just strangled his fiancée shows a certain coldness and calculation. He is definitely capable of doing this again."[96]

The violent nature of the crime and Stephenson's behavior afterward led the FBI to consider him dangerous enough to place on the Ten Most Wanted list. The FBI also said publicity would likely assist in Stephenson's capture, which made his case meet the other main criteria for a fugitive to earn a top-ten ranking. After the killing, the FBI said, he took a cab to Newark Penn Station and then fled by bus or train to another area of the country, such as Virginia or the Carolinas, where he was known to have relatives. But finding Stephenson had proved particularly difficult because of the lack of ways to track him. Since the day of DeJesus's murder, Priddy said in announcing Stephenson's addition to the Ten Most Wanted list, Stephenson "has been completely off the radar. Compared to a lot of other subjects we go after, Stephenson has been difficult to find because he had no criminal history. Apart from his picture, law enforcement does not have even a set of fingerprints to help identify him."[97]

By placing Stephenson on the Ten Most Wanted list, the FBI hoped to make him feel as if all was closing in on him. His face was on posters, on the internet, on social media. Stephenson had become a member of a notorious category of criminal, the kind that the FBI and the U.S. Marshals Service and the police viewed as the worst fugitives of them all. The case of Lamont Stephenson represented yet another link to the public enemies lists of the 1930s, to the FBI's original identification orders, to the laws that resulted in the UFAP warrant and other measures that defined the powers of the FBI and U.S. Marshals Service in hunting down those on the lam. Stephenson, like the 560 men and women before him, had gone on the Ten Most Wanted list because he needed to be caught more than nearly every other fugitive. "You have now joined the notorious ranks of the top 10 fugitives in the world," the FBI special agent in charge of the Newark office, Gregory W. Ehrie, said in announcing the elevation of Stephenson's case. "We will find you. I suggest you turn yourself in at the first available opportunity."[98]

AFTERWORD

In all the documents, books, and other publications written about fugitives in the United States, one stands out: the transcript of the hearing on fugitives that the Senate Subcommittee on Criminal Justice Oversight held on June 22, 2000. The title of the hearing captures the theme of the hearing on that day as well as the theme of studies and reports on fugitives throughout the history of the United States: *Fugitives: The Chronic Threat to Safety, Law, and Order.* Not only are fugitives always present, but the threat they present is everlasting. To search for a fugitive is to embark on a task that can be repeated over and over again with an endless supply of quarry, from a fugitive thief running through the marshes of New Jersey in 1901 to a drug lord hiding out in Mexico in 2018 to escape extradition to the United States and avoid prosecution on charges that he orchestrated the murder of an undercover special agent with the DEA in 2015.

Excerpts from the hearing, including statements from Senator Strom Thurmond, the chairman of the subcommittee, and John W. Marshall, director of the U.S. Marshals Service, have appeared throughout this account of fugitives in America. But the hearing bears revisiting for another look at what the participants said about fugitives in urgent but often elegant words. The hearing proved historic in that it helped expand the creation of fugitive task forces through the passage of the Presidential Threat and Protection Act in December 2000. Marshall, in remarks at the hearing, explained the difficulties in finding fugitives. "Since these fugitives know they are wanted, they are continually on the run," he said. "Fugitive investigations are fluid and time is of the essence when gathering information and executing investigative leads. A fugitive may literally be 'here today and gone in an hour.'"[1]

Edward T. Norris, the police commissioner in Baltimore, testified about murders that fugitives had committed, and how task forces and added teamwork would help in their capture. Norris characterized fugitives as heartless. "Wanted offenders who were deft at avoiding detection and thrive in the cracks of our criminal justice system perpetuate the carnage that haunts our urban areas," Norris testified. "The implementation of a forceful fugitive apprehension program as proposed by the U.S. Marshals Service will seal these cracks and end this unnecessary violence. The criminal community in any city is a close-knit, small, and identifiable group. Career criminals don't stop offending because they have a warrant out for their arrest. Fugitives are a bold and lethal breed, unfazed by the flaccid threat that a warrant alone represents."[2]

In comments he made in the Senate on December 6, 2000, Senator Patrick Leahy of Vermont summarized the work of the Subcommittee on Criminal Justice Oversight. Citing the most current figures available at the time, Leahy expounded on why fugitives had become a deep threat to the country. "According to the FBI, nearly 550,000 people are currently fugitives from justice on federal, state, and local felony charges combined," Leahy said. "This means that there are almost as many fugitive felons as there are citizens residing in my home state of Vermont. The fact that we have more than one half million fugitives from justice, a significant portion of whom are convicted felons in violation of probation or parole, who have been able to flaunt court order and avoid arrest, breeds disrespect for our laws and poses undeniable risks to the safety of our citizens."[3]

Eighteen years later, the threat still exists, as shown by the nearly 2.5 million outstanding warrants on file with the National Crime Information Center as of late 2018. But to address a problem that will never vanish, the FBI and U.S. Marshals Service in particular have taken the approach that makes the most sense: go after the most violent, most dangerous fugitives first, and work your way down from there. The strategy—the strategy of posses, most-wanted posters, identification orders, public enemies lists, top-ten fugitives lists, and top-fifteen fugitive lists—has led to the apprehension of countless fugitives. The strategy has also helped burnish the reputations of the FBI and the U.S. Marshals Service and made the figure of the fugitive an icon of American culture. Every fugitive—every person featured on one of those lists—has a story. And in a nation that rebels founded to escape an oppressive regime, the tale of the fugitive continues to resonate—especially in the rare instance when the fugitive is innocent.

Lawmakers most likely will continue to act, as Congress did in 2000, at the urging of the likes of Strom Thurmond, and John W. Marshall, and Edward T.

Norris. The FBI and the U.S. Marshals Service will continue to populate their most-wanted lists and spread the word about fugitives from justice on Facebook and Twitter and YouTube. And the fugitives, they will continue to run as we Americans, enamored with *The Fugitive*, the TV show and the movie, as well as reality programs like *America's Most Wanted*, will continue to watch the chase from afar, rooting mostly for the pursuers but sometimes for the pursued.

As Oscar Wilde said, reflecting on Jesse James, America often makes heroes of its criminals. And as Robert Elliot Burns wrote in *I Am a Fugitive from a Georgia Chain Gang!*, still one of the most stunning memoirs of its kind, the fugitive can become "a man of mystery" who tries to lose himself in every city he visits, in every town he passes through. But as was so clear from the testimony before the Senate Subcommittee on Criminal Justice Oversight, the heroes in the fight against fugitives are usually the FBI agents and the U.S. marshals and the police officers and the deputy sheriffs. Those on the lam far outnumber those with badges. But those with badges accept the challenge. They know the game and its terms. They know that legs of the fugitive can be fast. They also know that the gaze of the law can be unblinking.

NOTES

1. Ernest Hemingway, "On the Blue Water: A Gulf Stream Letter," *Esquire*, April 1, 1936, 25.

2. Mark Giuliano, interview by John Maynard, "Inside Media: The FBI's Ten Most Wanted: The Story Behind the List," Newseum, Washington, D.C., March 21, 2015, http://www.newseum.org/event/inside-media-the-fbis-ten-most-wanted-the-story-behind-the-list.

INTRODUCTION

1. Jerry Clark, recollections and personal notes.

2. U.S. Marshals Service, Office of Public Affairs, Fact *Sheet, Fugitive Operations 2018*, https://www.usmarshals.gov/duties/factsheets/facts.pdf.

3. J. Anthony Lukas, "On the Lam in America," *New York Times Magazine*, December 13, 1970, 31.

4. Merriam-Webster Dictionary, s.v., "lamster," https://www.merriam-webster.com/dictionary/lamster.

5. William Safire, "On Language: On the Lam, Who Made Thee?" *New York Times Magazine*, March 1, 1998.

6. Safire, "On Language," 1998.

7. Merriam-Webster Dictionary, s.v., "lamster."

8. "Vice Ring 'Seizure' is Laid to Lucania," *New York Times*, May 14, 1936. Lucky Luciano's given name was Charles Lucania.

9. Meyer Berger, "Sutton, Bank Thief, Captured in Street by Brooklyn Police," *New York Times*, February 19, 1952.

CHAPTER ONE

1. "Wanted on Burglary Charge," *Brooklyn Daily Eagle*, April 29, 1901, 20. See also "Charged with 2 Burglaries," *Brooklyn Daily Eagle*, March 7, 1901, 1.

2. "Fox Hunters Chase a Man," *New York Times*, April 30, 1901, 8.

3. "They Think They Have the Thief," *Brooklyn Daily Eagle*, March 9, 1901, 1. See also "Wanted on Burglary Charge," *Brooklyn Daily Eagle*, April 29, 1901, 1.

4. Evie Lotze, John Clark, D. Alan Henry, and Jolanta Juszkiewicz, *The Pretrial Services Reference Book* (Washington, DC: Pretrial Services Resource Center, 1999), 1.

5. Brief Amicus Curiae of the Cato Institute Supporting Plaintiff-Appellee, November 17, 2017, *Maurice Walker v. City of Calhoun, GA*, United States Court of Appeals for the 11th Circuit, No. 17-13139, 2.

6. Lotze et al., *The Pretrial Services Reference Book*, 2n3.

7. Thomas J. Miles, "Estimating the Effect of *America's Most Wanted*: A Duration Analysis of Wanted Fugitives," *Journal of Law & Economics*, 48, no. 1 (2005), 281.

8. *Fugitives: The Chronic Threat to Safety, Law, and Order: Hearing Before the Subcommittee on Criminal Justice Oversight of Sen. Judiciary Comm.*, 106th Cong. 33-34 (9) (statement of John W. Marshall, director of the U.S. Marshals Service).

9. *Fugitives*, 9–10.

10. Elsa De Haas, *Antiquities of Bail* (New York: AMS Press, 1966), 128.

11. Timothy R. Schnacke, Michael R. Jones, and Claire M. B. Brooker, *The History of Bail and Pretrial Release* (Rockville, MD: Pretrial Justice Institute, 2010), 1, https://cdpsdocs.state.co.us/ccjj/Committees/BailSub/Handouts/HistoryofBail-Pre-TrialRelease-PJI_2010.pdf.

12. De Haas, *Antiquities of Bail*, 4.

13. Schnacke et al., *The History of Bail and Pretrial Release*, 2.

14. Schnacke et al., *The History of Bail and Pretrial Release*, 2.

15. De Haas, *Antiquities of Bail*, 11.

16. Anthony Musson, "Wergeld: Crime and the Compensation Culture in Medieval England," (lecture, Museum of London, London, October 5, 2009), https://www.gresham.ac.uk/lectures-and-events/wergeld-crime-and-the-compensation-culture-in-medieval-england.

17. De Haas, *Antiquities of Bail*, 26.

18. De Haas, *Antiquities of Bail*, 26.

19. Schnacke et al., *The History of Bail and Pretrial Release*, 2.

20. De Haas, *Antiquities of Bail*, 5.

21. Schnacke et al., *The History of Bail and Pretrial Release*, 2.

22. June Carbone, "Seeing through the Emperor's New Clothes: Rediscovery of Basic Principles in Administration of Bail," *Syracuse Law Review*, 34 (1983): 520 n16.

23. John Michael Seibler and Jason Snead, "Legal Memorandum: The History of Cash Bail," Heritage Foundation, Washington, D.C., no. 213, August 25, 2017, 2, https://www.heritage.org/sites/default/files/2017-08/LM-213.pdf.

24. Schnacke et al., *The History of Bail and Pretrial Release*, 2.

25. Carbone, "Seeing through the Emperor's New Clothes," 522.

26. De Haas, *Antiquities of Bail*, 91

27. Brief Amicus Curiae of the Cato Institute Supporting Plaintiff-Appellee, November 17, 2017, *Maurice Walker v. City of Calhoun, GA*, 5.

28. Carbone, "Seeing through the Emperor's New Clothes," 524n 38.

29. Carbone, "Seeing through the Emperor's New Clothes," 524n 38.

30. Carbone, "Seeing through the Emperor's New Clothes," footnote, 524–25n38.

31. Carbone, "Seeing through the Emperor's New Clothes," 526–27.

32. Carbone, "Seeing through the Emperor's New Clothes," 527.

33. Carbone, "Seeing through the Emperor's New Clothes," 523n35.

34. Schnacke et al., *The History of Bail and Pretrial Release*, 3.

35. Brief Amicus Curiae of the Cato Institute Supporting Plaintiff-Appellee, November 17, 2017, *Maurice Walker v. City of Calhoun, GA*, 9.

36. Carbone, "Seeing through the Emperor's New Clothes," 530.

37. Brief Amicus Curiae of the Cato Institute Supporting Plaintiff-Appellee, November 17, 2017, *Maurice Walker v. City of Calhoun, GA*, 9. See also *Stack v. Boyle*, 342 U.S. 1, 4 (1951).

38. Schnacke et al., *The History of Bail and Pretrial Release*, 8–9.

39. Schnacke et al., *The History of Bail and Pretrial Release*, 10n38.

40. Schnacke et al., *The History of Bail and Pretrial Release*, 17.

41. Stuart Taylor Jr., "Court Backs Law Letting U.S. Widen Pretrial Jail," *New York Times*, May 27, 1987.

42. *United States v. Salerno*, 481 U.S. 739, 744 (1987).

43. *United States v. Salerno*, 481 U.S., 755 (1987).

44. *United States v. Salerno*, 481 U.S., 767 (1987).

45. Adam Liptak, "Illegal Globally, Bail for Profit Remains in U.S.," *New York Times*, January 29, 2008.

46. Liptak, "Illegal Globally, Bail for Profit Remains in U.S."

47. *Taylor v. Taintor*, 83 U.S. 366, 371 (1872).

48. Schnacke et al., *The History of Bail and Pretrial Release*, 7.

49. Merritt Barnes, "'Fountainhead of Corruption': Peter P. McDonough, Boss of San Francisco's Underworld," *California History*, 58, no. 2 (1979): 146.

50. Barnes, "Fountainhead of Corruption," 147.

51. Barnes, "Fountainhead of Corruption," 152.

52. Barnes, "Fountainhead of Corruption," 152.

53. Bob Egelko, "Court Ruling Could Change State's Approach to Bail," *San Francisco Chronicle*, January 25, 2018, https://www.sfchronicle.com/bayarea/article/Court-ruling-could-change-state-s-approach-to-12526554.php.

54. Opinion and Order, January 25, 2018, *In re Kenneth Humphrey, on Habeas Corpus*, Court of Appeal, First District, Division 2, California, Case No. A152056, 30.

55. Opinion and Order, January 25, 2018, *In re Kenneth Humphrey, on Habeas Corpus*, 35.

56. Opinion and Order, January 25, 2018, *In re Kenneth Humphrey, on Habeas Corpus*, 3.

57. Evan Sernoffsky, "SF Inmate in Landmark Battle Over Bail Wins Release," *San Francisco Chronicle*, May 3, 2018, https://www.sfchronicle.com/news/article/Judge-orders-defendant-in-legal-bail-battle-to-be-12885426.php.

58. Sernoffsky, "SF Inmate in Landmark Battle Over Bail Wins Release."

59. Bob Egelko and Evan Sernoffsky, "State Supreme Court to Review Landmark Case on Money Bail System," *San Francisco Chronicle*, May 23, 2018, https://www.sfchronicle.com/news/article/State-Supreme-Court-to-review-landmark-case-on-12938615.php.

60. Opinion and Order, January 25, 2018, *In re Kenneth Humphrey, on Habeas Corpus*.

61. Opinion and Order, January 25, 2018, *In re Kenneth Humphrey, on Habeas Corpus*, 45.

62. Alexis de Tocqueville, *Democracy in America* (1835; repr., Mineola, NY: Dover Thrift Editions, 2017), 56, quoted in Opinion and Order, January 25, 2018, *In re Kenneth Humphrey, on Habeas Corpus*, 45n29.

63. Opinion and Order, January 25, 2018, *In re Kenneth Humphrey, on Habeas Corpus*.

64. Opinion and Order, January 25, 2018, *In re Kenneth Humphrey, on Habeas Corpus*, 2.

65. Alexis de Tocqueville, *Democracy in America*, trans. Henry Reeve (Boston: John Allyn Publishers, 1876), 55.

66. Tocqueville, *Democracy in America*, 56.

67. Tocqueville, *Democracy in America*, 56.

CHAPTER TWO

1. Secretary of State Timothy Pickering to Thomas Nelson, U.S. district attorney of Virginia, 11 September, 1797, Timothy Pickering Papers, Massachusetts Historical Society, microfilm, Reel 37, 24. See also Frederick S. Calhoun, *The Lawmen: United States Marshals and Their Deputies, 1789–1989* (Washington, D.C.: Smithsonian Institute Press, 1989), 16.

2. Timothy Pickering to David Meade Randolph, U.S. marshal of Virginia, 11 February, 1797, Timothy Pickering Papers, Massachusetts Historical Society, microfilm, Reel 37, 25.

3. Timothy Pickering to Charles Lee, U.S. attorney, 7 March, 1797, Timothy Pickering Papers, Massachusetts Historical Society, microfilm, Reel 37, 63.

4. Timothy Pickering to Charles Lee, U.S. attorney, 7 March, 1797, Timothy Pickering Papers, Massachusetts Historical Society, microfilm, Reel 37, 63.

5. Timothy Pickering to Thomas and Peter Mackie, of Philadelphia, 7 March, 1797, Timothy Pickering Papers, Massachusetts Historical Society, microfilm, Reel 37, 64.

6. Timothy Pickering to Cyrus Griffin, U.S. district judge in Virginia, 17 August, 1797, Timothy Pickering Papers, Massachusetts Historical Society, microfilm, Reel 7, 88.

7. "U.S. Marshals to get F.B.I.'s Responsibility for Finding Escapees," *New York Times*, September 30, 1979.

8. The Federal Bureau of Investigation and the U.S. Marshals Service are not limited to the United States in pursuing and transporting fugitives. In another example of their joint fugitive-related roles, the FBI is empowered to seek fugitives from the United States in other countries while the U.S. Marshals Service is responsible for transporting the fugitives, once caught, to the United States. Both agencies are authorized to seek American fugitives in foreign countries. See *Fugitives: The Chronic Threat to Safety, Law, and Order: Hearing Before the Subcommittee on Criminal Justice Oversight of Sen. Judiciary Comm.*, 106th Cong. 33–34 (2000) (statement of Andreas Stephens on behalf of the FBI); and Katherine Unterman, *Uncle Sam's Policemen: The Pursuit of Fugitives Across Borders* (Cambridge MA: Harvard University Press, 2015).

9. Judiciary Act of Sept. 24, 1789, 1 Stat. 73 (1789).

10. Calhoun, *The Lawmen*, 13. See also David S. Turk, *Forging the Star: The Official Modern History of the United States Marshals Service* (Denton TX: University of North Texas Press, 2016), 2.

11. Unterman, *Uncle Sam's Policemen*, 131.

12. Unterman, *Uncle Sam's Policemen*, 131.

13. Calhoun, *The Lawmen*, 3.

14. Office of the Comptroller General of the United States, *U.S. Marshals Dilemma: Serving Two Branches of Government*, U.S. General Accounting Office, April 19, 1982, 1.

15. Calhoun, *The Lawmen*, 3.

16. Unterman, *Uncle Sam's Policemen*, 131.

17. Andrew Glass, "Congress Enacts First Fugitive Slave Law, Feb. 12, 1793," *Politico*, February 12, 2014, https://www.politico.com/story/2014/02/this-day-in-politics-congress-enacts-first-fugitive-slave-law-feb-12-1793-103375.

18. Glass, "Congress Enacts First Fugitive Slave Law."

19. Fugitive Slave Act of 1850, September 18, 1850.

20. Fugitive Slave Act of 1850.

21. James Oakes, "The Power of Running Away," *New York Review of Books*, December 6, 2018, 46.

22. Calhoun, *The Lawmen*, 91.

23. Calhoun, *The Lawmen*, 91.

24. Calhoun, *The Lawmen*, 93.

25. U.S. Marshals Service—"History," https://www.usmarshals.gov/history/cards/index.html. See also Ryan M. McDermott, "U.S. Marshals Service Honors Work of Douglass with Wreath Laying," *Washington Times*, March 1, 2017.

26. Turk, *Forging the Star*, 3.

27. Turk, *Forging the Star*, 2.

28. Office of the Comptroller General of the United States, *U.S. Marshals Dilemma: Serving Two Branches of Government*, 2.

29. Jerry Clark and Ed Palattella, *A History of Heists: Bank Robbery in America* (Lanham, MD: Rowman & Littlefield, 2015), 40.

30. Clark and Palattella, *A History of Heists*, 48.

31. Clark and Palattella, *A History of Heists*, 49.

32. Clark and Palattella, *A History of Heists*, 50.

33. "Dalton Band Exterminated," *New York Times*, April 20, 1894

34. "Dalton Band Exterminated."

35. Clark and Palattella, *A History of Heists*, 50

36. Seth Ferranti, "The History of the Most Wanted Poster," *Huffington Post*, December 14, 2016, https://www.huffingtonpost.com/entry/the-history-of-the-most-wanted-poster_us_5851ba70e4b0865ab9d4e8d7.

37. David S. Turk, email correspondence with Ed Palattella, July 25, 2018.

38. Jeremy Agnew, *Crime, Justice and Retribution in the American West, 1850–1900* (Jefferson, NC: McFarland & Company, 2017), 7.

39. Agnew, *Crime, Justice and Retribution in the American West.*

40. Turk, *Forging the Star*, 4.

41. Though popular culture depicted criminals as keeping the United States under siege, "Statistics now show that there was no crime wave," writes Richard Gid Powers, a historian of the FBI. See Richard Gid Powers, *G-Men: The FBI in American Popular Culture* (Carbondale, IL: Southern Illinois University Press, 1983), xii, xiii.

42. Clark and Palattella, *A History of Heists*, 76.

43. Clark and Palattella, *A History of Heists*, 76.

44. Powers, *G-Men*, 40.

45. Powers, *G-Men*, 41.

46. Clark and Palattella, *A History of Heists*, 69.

47. Federal Bureau of Investigation, "A Brief History: The Nation Calls, 1908–1923," https://www.fbi.gov/history/brief-history/the-nation-calls.

48. Federal Bureau of Investigation, "A Brief History."

49. Federal Bureau of Investigation, "A Brief History."

50. Federal Bureau of Investigation, "A Brief History."

51. Federal Bureau of Investigation, "A Brief History."

52. Clark and Palattella, *A History of Heists*, 74.

53. Clark and Palattella, *A History of Heists*, 80.

54. Powers, *G-Men*, 38.

55. Powers, *G-Men*, 38.

56. Powers, *G-Men*, 22.

57. Clark and Palattella, *A History of Heists*, 80.

58. Clark and Palattella, *A History of Heists*, 68.

59. Associated Press, "It Is 'F.B.I' Not 'G-men,'" *New York Times*, June 30, 1935.

60. "Crime War School Will Open July 29," *New York Times*, July 5, 1935.

61. "'G Men' Stationed in Jersey," *New York Times*, July 2, 1935.

62. Leland Tracy, "Favorable Representations of the Fugitive in American Popular Culture: The Story of Bonnie and Clyde," in *Authority and Displacement in the English-Speaking World (Volume II: Exploring American Shores)*, Florence Labaune-Demeule, ed. (Newcastle upon Tyne, UK: Cambridge Scholars Publishing, 2015), 23.

63. Erin E. White, "Fresh Pursuit: A Survey of Law among States with Large Land Based Tribes," *American Indian Law Journal*, vol. 3., no. 1, 2014, 227.

64. Tracy, "Favorable Representations of the Fugitive in American Popular Culture," 23.

65. See, for example, the Pennsylvania Consolidated Statutes, Title 42, Section 8953, on "Statewide municipal police jurisdiction." It states that a police officer is authorized to cross municipal boundaries in cases in which, among other things, the officer "is in hot pursuit of any person for any offense which was committed, or which he has probable cause to believe was committed, within his primary jurisdiction and for which offense the officer continues in fresh pursuit of the person after the commission of the offense."

66. Turk, *Forging the Star*, 10.

67. Turk, *Forging the Star*, 10.

68. Turk, *Forging the Star*, 3.

69. Turk, *Forging the Star*, 11.

70. Turk, *Forging the Star*, 5.

71. Office of the Comptroller General of the United States, *U.S. Marshals Dilemma: Serving Two Branches of Government*, 3.

72. Office of the Comptroller General of the United States, *U.S. Marshals Dilemma*, 3.

73. U.S. Marshals Service, "Factsheet," https://www.usmarshals.gov/duties/fact sheets/facts.pdf.

74. FBI "FY 2019 Budget Request at a Glance," https://www.justice.gov/jmd/page/file/1033146/download.

75. Turk, *Forging the Star*, 167.

76. U.S. General Accounting Office, *Briefing Report to the Chairman, Subcommittee on Security and Terrorism, Committee on the Judiciary, United States Senate, Criminal Justice: Who Should Be Responsible for State Fugitives—the FBI or U.S. Marshals?* September 1986, 10.

77. Calhoun, *The Lawmen*, 306.

78. "U.S. Marshals to Get F.B.I.'s Responsibility for Finding Escapees," *New York Times*, September 30, 1979.

79. "U.S. Marshals to Get F.B.I.'s Responsibility for Finding Escapees."

80. Calhoun, *The Lawmen*, 307.

81. Calhoun, *The Lawmen*, 307.

82. Turk, *Forging the Star*, 216.

83. U.S. Code, Title 28, Part II, Chapter 7 § 566.

84. Richard L. Shiffrin, deputy assistant attorney general, *Authority of FBI Agents, Serving as Special Deputy United States Marshals, to Pursue Non-Federal Fugitives, Memorandum for Howard M. Shapiro, General Counsel, Federal Bureau of Investigation*, February 21, 1995, https://biotech.law.lsu.edu/blaw/olc/fistopcc.htm.

85. Presidential Threat Protection Act of 2000, December 19, 2000, Pub. L. No. 106-544, 114 Stat. 2715 (2000).

86. Turk, *Forging the Star*, 368.

87. Shiffrin, *Authority of FBI Agents*.

88. Clark and Palattella, *A History of Heists*, 79. See also Powers, *G-Men*, 45.

89. "Fugitive Felon Act: Its Function and Purpose," *Washington University Law Review* no. 3 (1964): 355–56.

90. "Fugitive Felon Act: Its Function and Purpose, 355–356."

91. "Fugitive Felon Act: Its Function and Purpose, 356.

92. "Fugitive Felon Act: Its Function and Purpose, 356.

93 *Fugitives: The Chronic Threat to Safety, Law, and Order: Hearing Before the Subcommittee on Criminal Justice Oversight of Sen. Judiciary Comm.*, 106th Cong. 33-34 (200) (statement of Andreas Stephens on behalf of the FBI).

94. Shiffrin, *Authority of FBI Agents*.

95. Shiffrin, *Authority of FBI Agents*.

96. Shiffrin, *Authority of FBI Agents*.

97. U.S. General Accounting Office, *Briefing Report to the Chairman, Subcommittee on Security and Terrorism*, 12.

98. U.S. General Accounting Office, *Briefing Report to the Chairman, Subcommittee on Security and Terrorism*, 12.

99. U.S. General Accounting Office, *Briefing Report to the Chairman, Subcommittee on Security and Terrorism*, 12.

100. *Fugitives: The Chronic Threat to Safety, Law, and Order: Hearing Before the Subcommittee on Criminal Justice Oversight of Sen. Judiciary Comm.*, 106th Cong. 33-34 (200) (statement of Andreas Stephens on behalf of the FBI) .
Shiffrin, *Authority of FBI Agents*.

101. "Fugitive Felon Act: Its Function and Purpose," 365.

102. "Fugitive Felon Act: Its Function and Purpose," 366.

103. "Cummings Tells Anti-Crime Plans," *New York Times*, May 13, 1934.

104. Associated Press, "$30,000 Raid Is Laid to Dillinger Gang," *New York Times*, May 19, 1934.

105. Clark and Palattella, *A History of Heists*, 205.

106. Associated Press, "$30,000 Raid Is Laid to Dillinger Gang."

107. U.S. General Accounting Office, *Briefing Report to the Chairman, Subcommittee on Security and Terrorism, Committee on the Judiciary, United States Senate, Criminal Justice: Who Should Be Responsible for State Fugitives—the FBI or U.S. Marshals?*

108. Shiffrin, *Authority of FBI Agents.*

CHAPTER THREE

1. Richard Gid Powers, *G-Men: Hoover's FBI in American Popular Culture* (Carbondale, IL: Southern Illinois University Press, 1983), 21n45.

2. Powers, *G-Men*, 21.

3. Powers, *G-Men*, 21.

4. "Urges National Thug List," *New York Times*, October 8, 1933.

5. Curt Gentry, *J. Edgar Hoover: The Man and The Secrets* (New York: W. W. Norton & Co., 1991), 172.

6 Laurence Bergreen, *Capone: The Man and the Era* (New York: Simon & Schuster, 1994), 366.

7. Powers, *G-Men*, 23.

8. Bergreen, *Capone*, 86.

9. Powers, *G-Men*, 23.

10. Associated Press, "Asserts Two Gangs Monopolize Crimes," *New York Times*, September 15, 1931.

11. Associated Press, "Asserts Two Gangs Monopolize Crimes."

12. "Anti-Gang League to War on Rackets," *New York Times*, December 19, 1930.

13. Powers, *G-Men*, 20.

14. Powers, *G-Men*, 20.

15. "Urges National Thug List."

16. Powers, *G-Men*, 16.

17. Powers, *G-Men*, 13.

18. G. Russell Girardin and William J. Helmer, prepared with assistance of Rick Mattix, *Dillinger: The Untold Story, Anniversary Edition* (Bloomington, IN: Indiana University Press, 2009), 110.

19. Girardin et al., *Dillinger: The Untold Story.*

20. "Cummings Offers Kidnapping Advice," *New York Times*, July 14, 1933.

21. From this point forward in this chapter and beyond, the term *FBI* will be used also to refer to its predecessor agencies, the Bureau of Investigation (1909–1933) and the Division of Investigation (1933–1935). Using *FBI* interchangeably with the other titles is meant to reduce undue confusion, as the predecessor agencies eventually became the FBI, on July 1, 1935.

22. Gentry, *J. Edgar Hoover*, 172.

23. Federal Bureau of Investigation, "Some of the FBI's Famous Identification Orders," https://archives.fbi.gov/archives/news/stories/2006/december/historic-identi fication-orders.

24. Federal Bureau of Investigation, "Ten Most Wanted Fugitives FAQ," https://www.fbi.gov/wanted/topten/ten-most-wanted-fugitives-faq.

25. Chicago Crime Commission official history, http://www.chicagocrimecommis sion.org.

26. Powers, *G-Men*, 60.

27. Franklin D. Roosevelt, Inaugural Address (speech, Washington, D.C., March 4, 1933), http://www.fdrlibrary.marist.edu/_resources/images/msf/msf00628.

28. Homer C. Cummings, address at the Banquet of the Federal Bar Association (speech, Washington, D.C., June 25, 1934), https://www.justice.gov/sites/default/files/ag/legacy/2011/09/16/06-25-1934.pdf.

29. Cummings, "The Law and the Prophets" (radio address, July 9, 1934), https://www.justice.gov/sites/default/files/ag/legacy/2011/09/16/07-09-1934.pdf.

30. Powers, *G-Men*, 43.

31. Some believe professional hit men connected to a syndicated and working with Verne Miller killed Frank Nash to keep him quiet, and that Richetti and Floyd were never involved in the Kansas City Massacre. See Gentry, *J. Edgar Hoover*, 168–69.

32. Associated Press, "Cummings Details Men to Hunt," *New York Times*, June 18, 1933.

33. Associated Press, "Cummings Details Men to Hunt."

34. Associated Press, "Cummings Details Men to Hunt."

35. Gentry, *J. Edgar Hoover*, 171.

36. "Dillinger Eludes Man-Hunt by 5,000," *New York Times*, April 25, 1934.

37. Powers, *G-Men*, 121.

38. Powers, *G-Men*, 121.

39. Elliott J. Gorn, *Dillinger's Wild Ride: The Year that Made America's Public Enemy Number One* (Oxford: Oxford University Press, 2009), 81.

40. Gorn, *Dillinger's Wild Ride*, 81.

41. Gorn, *Dillinger's Wild Ride*, 123.

42. Act of June 6, 1934, Pub. L No. 73-295, 48 Stat. 910 (1934).

43. Gorn, *Dillinger's Wild Ride*, 122.

44. "U.S. Offers $10,000 To Get Dillinger," *New York Times*, June 24, 1934.

45. "U.S. Offers $10,000 To Get Dillinger."

46. Ford, Charles E. (director). 1936. *"You Can't Get Away With It!,"* copy of film short available online from the National Archives and Records Administration, https://archive.org/details/gov.archives.arc.12074.

47. "U.S. Offers $10,000 To Get Dillinger."

48. "U.S. Offers $10,000 To Get Dillinger."

49. Gentry, *J. Edgar Hoover*, 172. Gentry's biography of Hoover is among the most extensive and comprehensive of its kind, though even Gentry does not provide

the means, such as a speech, by which Hoover labeled John Dillinger "Public Enemy Number One." See also Giradin et al., *Dillinger*, 288–89n14.

50. "U.S. Offers $10,000 To Get Dillinger."

51. Gorn, *Dillinger's Wild Ride*, 123.

52. John Toland, *The Dillinger Days* (New York: Random House, 1963), 13–15 on the robbery case; 14–34 for an account of what Dillinger learned in prison.

53. Jerry Clark and Ed Palattella, *A History of Heists: Bank Robbery in America* (Lanham, MD: Rowman & Littlefield, 2012), 22. See also Richard Maxwell Brown, "Western Violence: Structure, Values, Myth," *Western Historical Quarterly* 24, no. 1 (1993), 8.

54. Powers, *G-men*, 115. See also Gorn, *Dillinger's Wild Ride*, for a photo of the target.

55. Bergreen, *Capone*, 367.

56. Gorn, *Dillinger's Wild Ride*, 133.

57. Toland, *The Dillinger Days*, 303.

58. Associated Press, "Rhodes Scholar Mistaken for Dillinger in England," *New York Times*, June 20, 1934.

59. "On the Block: Dillinger a Downtown Visitor," *South Bend* (IN) *Tribune*, April 13, 2015, https://www.southbendtribune.com/news/local/on-the-block-dillinger-a-downtown-visitor/article_bbd6b2bd-a75e-5932-aa91-cba8bf4e06b3.html. See also Girardin et al., *Dillinger*, 199–200.

60. Gentry, *J. Edgar Hoover*, 173.

61. Girardin et al., *Dillinger*, 217, 245.

62. Girardin et al., *Dillinger*, 245.

63. Gorn, *Dillinger's Wild Ride*, 145.

64. "Dillinger Slain in Chicago; Shot Dead by Federal Men in Front of Movie Theatre," *New York Times*, July 23, 1934.

65. Gentry, *J. Edgar Hoover*, 174.

66. Andrew Tully, *The FBI's Most Famous Cases* (New York: William Morrow, 1965), 97. J. Edgar Hoover wrote the book's introduction and provided commentary, such as his remarks on Dillinger.

67. Powers, *J. Edgar Hoover*, 114.

68. Powers, *J. Edgar Hoover*, 114.

69. Russell Owen, "Men Who Track Down the 'Public Enemy,'" *New York Times*, October 28, 1934.

70. Owen, "Men Who Track Down the 'Public Enemy.'" The account does not match the official findings of the autopsy, which found that Dillinger was shot in the neck and left side, but not in the head.

71. Owen, "Men Who Track Down the 'Public Enemy.'"

72. Owen, "Men Who Track Down the 'Public Enemy.'"

73. Maurice Carroll, "F.B.I. Computers Rush Data to Police: New York First City to Be Hooked Up to Information 'Bank,'" *New York Times*, January 28, 1967.

74. For more discussion on the double standard of the Production Code, see Girardin et al., *Dillinger*, 110.

75. For a particularly insightful analysis of how the *G-Men* movie changed the image of the FBI, see Powers, *G-Men*, 50–64.

76. Powers, *G-Men*, 103.

77. Powers, *G-Men*, 104.

78. Ford, *"You Can't Get Away With It!"*

79. Ford, *"You Can't Get Away With It!"*

80. Ford, *"You Can't Get Away With It!"*

81. Ford, *"You Can't Get Away With It!"*

82. Ford, *"You Can't Get Away With It!"*

83. Daarel Burnette II, "From Al Capone to Today's 'Most Wanted': Chicago Crime Commission Releases Its 1st List Since 1937," *Chicago Tribune*, July 13, 2010, http://articles.chicagotribune.com/2010-07-13/news/ct-met-most-wanted-list-20100713_1_most-wanted-al-capone-list.

84. Bryan Burrough, *Public Enemies: America's Greatest Crime Wave and the Birth of the FBI*, 1933–34 (New York: The Penguin Press, 2004), 547.

85. Federal Bureau of Investigation "Wall of Honor Factsheet," Nelson B. Klein, https://www.fbi.gov/history/wall-of-honor/nelson-b-klein.

86. Federal Bureau of Investigation "Wall of Honor Factsheet," https://www.fbi.gov/history/wall-of-honor.

87. Ford, *"You Can't Get Away With It!"*

88. Powers, *G-Men*, 142.

CHAPTER FOUR

1. Virginia Groark, "FBI List Marks 50 Years of Finding 'Most Wanted,'" *Chicago Tribune*, March 15, 2000.

2. Donna J. Dove and Jeffrey M. Maynard, *FBI's Ten Most Wanted Fugitives Program: 50th Anniversary, 1950–2000* (Lisbon, MD: K & D Limited, 2000), article reproduced on back cover.

3. Dove and Maynard, *FBI's Ten Most Wanted Fugitives Program*. See also James F. Donovan, United Press, "FBI's Most-Wanted Fugitives Named," *Washington* (D.C.) *Daily News*, February 7, 1949. Also, Donovan, "FBI Reveals 10 Most-Wanted U.S. Criminals," Jamestown (NY) *Post-Journal*, February 10, 1949.

4. John Fox, interview by John Maynard, "Inside Media: The FBI's Ten Most Wanted: The Story Behind the List," Newseum, Washington, D.C., March 21, 2015, http://www.newseum.org/event/inside-media-the-fbis-ten-most-wanted-the-story-behind-the-list.

5. David Stout, "The Nation: Poster Boys of Crime," *New York Times*, March 19, 2000.

6. Curt Gentry, *J. Edgar Hoover, The Man and The Secrets* (New York: W.W. Norton & Co., 1991), 172.

7. Fox, Newseum interview.

8. Stout, "The Nation: Poster Boys of Crime."

9. Barbara Fifer and Martin Kidston, *Wanted! Wanted Posters of the Old West* (Helena, MT: Farcountry Press, 2003), 5.

10. Federal Bureau of Investigation, "Ten Most Wanted Fugitives FAQ," https://www.fbi.gov/wanted/topten/ten-most-wanted-fugitives-faq, accessed November 21, 2018.

11. Federal Bureau of Investigation, "Ten Most Wanted Fugitives FAQ."

12. Federal Bureau of Investigation, "Ten Most Wanted Fugitives FAQ."

13. Dove, *FBI's Ten Most Wanted Fugitives Program*, 4.

14. "The U.S. Has Announced a $20 Million Reward for a Fugitive Mexican Drug Lord," *Time*, April 24, 2018, http://time.com/5238903/mexican-drug-lord-reward-caro-quintero.

15. FBI, "Ten Most Wanted Fugitives FAQ."

16. FBI, "Ten Most Wanted Fugitives FAQ."

17. Mark Giuliano, interview by John Maynard, "Inside Media: The FBI's Ten Most Wanted: The Story Behind the List," Newseum, Washington, D.C., March 21, 2015, http://www.newseum.org/event/inside-media-the-fbis-ten-most-wanted-the-story-behind-the-list.

18. Dashiell Bennett, "Happy 500th Fugitive the FBI 'Ten Most Wanted' List," *The Atlantic*, June 18, 2003, https://www.theatlantic.com/national/archive/2013/06/fbi-most-wanted-500th-fugitive/314149/.

19. FBI, "New Top Ten Fugitive: 'Family Annihilator' William Bradford Bishop, Jr. Wanted for 1976 Murders," https://www.fbi.gov/news/stories/new-top-ten-fugitive-1.

20. FBI, "New Top Ten Fugitive: 'Family Annihilator' William Bradford Bishop, Jr."

21. FBI, "New Top Ten Fugitive: 'Family Annihilator' William Bradford Bishop, Jr."

22. Del Quentin Wilber, "FBI Removes Accused Killer of His Family from Ten Most Wanted List," *Wall Street Journal*, June 28, 2018.

23. FBI, "Ten Most Wanted Fugitives FAQ."

24. FBI, "Ten Most Wanted Fugitives FAQ."

25. FBI, "Ten Most Wanted Fugitives FAQ."

26. FBI, "Ten Most Wanted Fugitives FAQ."

27. Michael and Judy Ann Newtown, *The FBI Most Wanted: An Encyclopedia* (New York: Garland Publishing, 1989), 214–15.

28. Federal Inmate Locator, https://www.bop.gov/inmateloc.

29. FBI, "Ten Most Wanted Fugitives FAQ."

30. Michael A. Fuoco, "Fugitive Sets Record on FBI's Top 10 List," *Pittsburgh Post-Gazette*, September 4, 1999.

31. Andy Castillo, "FBI Renews Effort in Massachusetts to Find 1980 Police Chief Killer," 22 News, WWLP.com, March 16, 2106, https://www.wwlp.com/news/massachusetts/fbi-renews-efforts-in-massachusetts-to-find-1980-police-chief-killer/1043766053.

32. FBI, "Former Ten Most Wanted Fugitive Donald Eugene Webb Located," news release, July 14, 2017, https://www.fbi.gov/contact-us/field-offices/boston/news/press-releases/former-ten-most-wanted-fugitive-donald-eugene-webb-located.

33 Travis Anderson, "Fugitive Told Wife to Bury Him in Backyard When He Died," *Boston Globe*, July 19, 2017.

34. Kyle Swenson, "How a Secret Room Led the FBI to Solve the Mystery of a Police Chief's Murder after 27 Years," (London) *Independent*, July 18, 2017.

35. Duane Swierczynski, *The Encyclopedia of the FBI's Ten Most Wanted List* (New York: Facts on File, 2004), 220.

36. Swierczynski, *The Encyclopedia of the FBI's Ten Most Wanted List*, 219.

37. Mark Sabljak and Martin H. Greenberg, *Most Wanted: A History of the FBI's Ten Most Wanted List* (New York: Bonanza Books, 1990), 26.

38. James Lee, International News Service, "FBI Admits Triple Killer Wily Prey, Lists Description, Habits of Criminal," (Portland) *Oregonian*, June 20, 1951.

39. Lee, International News Service, "FBI Admits Triple Killer Wily Prey, Lists Description, Habits of Criminal."

40. Jerry Clark and Ed Palattella, *A History of Heists: Bank Robbery in America* (Lanham, MD: Rowman & Littlefield, 2015), 86.

41. Clark and Palattella, *A History of Heists*.

42. Clark and Palattella, *A History of Heists*.

43 Swierczynski, *The Encyclopedia of the FBI's Ten Most Wanted List*, 4.

44. David Ward with Gene Kassebaum, *Alcatraz: The Gangster Years* (Berkeley: University of California Press, 2009),438–39.

45. Ward, *Alcatraz: The Gangster Years*, 69.

46. Ward, *Alcatra: The Gangster Years*, 49.

47. Ward, *Alcatraz: The Gangster Years*, 438–39.

48. Ward, *Alcatraz: The Gangster Years*, 438–39.

49. James Stuart, "Fugitive Nabbed Near Beaverton," *Oregonian*, June 24, 1951.

50. James Lee, "FBI Admits Triple Killer Wily Prey, Lists Description, Habits of Criminal." See also Ward, *Alcatraz: The Gangster Years*, 438–39.

51. Ward, *Alcatraz: The Gangster Years*, 438–39. See also Sabljak, *Most Wanted*, 26.

52. Dove, *FBI's Ten Most Wanted Fugitives Program*, 6.

53. Keith Hansen, "Employer, Landlady, Neighbor Praise Character of Fugitive Arrested by the FBI," *Oregonian*, June 24, 1951. See also Lee, "FBI Admits Triple Killer Wily Prey, Lists Description, Habits of Criminal," and Stuart, "Fugitive Nabbed Near Beaverton."

54. Stuart, "Fugitive Nabbed Near Beaverton."

55. Lee, "FBI Admits Triple Killer Wily Prey, Lists Description, Habits of Criminal." See also Finn J.D. John, "FBI's Most Wanted Gangster Was Busted in Beaverton," *Offbeat Oregon* blog, May 31, 2015, https://offbeatoregon.com/1505e.holden-fbi-most-wanted-caught-341.html.

56. Lee, "FBI Admits Triple Killer Wily Prey, Lists Description, Habits of Criminal."

57. Lee, "FBI Admits Triple Killer Wily Prey, Lists Description, Habits of Criminal."

58. John, "FBI's Most Wanted Gangster Was Busted in Beaverton."

59. Lee, "FBI Admits Triple Killer Wily Prey, Lists Description, Habits of Criminal."

60. Hansen, "Employer, Landlady, Neighbor Praise Character of Fugitive Arrested By the FBI."

61. Hansen, "Employer, Landlady, Neighbor Praise Character of Fugitive Arrested By the FBI."

62. Hansen, "Employer, Landlady, Neighbor Praise Character of Fugitive Arrested By the FBI."

63. Stuart, "Fugitive Nabbed Near Beaverton."

64. Stuart, "Fugitive Nabbed Near Beaverton."

65. Stuart, "Fugitive Nabbed Near Beaverton."

66. Stuart, "Fugitive Nabbed Near Beaverton."

67. Herb Penny, "Holden Arrest 2d From List," *Oregonian*, June 24, 1951.

68. Penny, "Holden Arrest 2d From List"; Newtown, *The FBI Most Wanted: An Encyclopedia*.

69. Donovan, United Press, "FBI's Most-Wanted Fugitives Named."

70. Martinazzi, "1950: No. 7 on the F.B.I.'s Most Wanted List," *Tualatin* (Oregon) *Life*, September 2014, 10, http://tualatinlife.com/new/wp-content/uploads/2014/09/56-Tu-History-.50.pdf.

71. Penny, "Holden Arrest 2d From List." See also FBI, *FBI's Ten Most Wanted Fugitives Program*.

72. Martinazzi, "1950: No. 7 on the F.B.I.'s Most Wanted List."

73. "Oregon Poor Hideout," *Oregonian*, June 28, 1951.

74. "Oregon Poor Hideout."

75. FBI, "Ten Most Wanted Fugitives FAQ."

76. FBI, "Ten Most Wanted Fugitives FAQ."

77. Dove, *FBI's Ten Most Wanted Fugitives Program*, 6.

78. Sabljak, *Most Wanted: A History of the FBI's Ten Most Wanted*, 6.

79. David S. Turk, David S. Turk, *Forging the Star: The Official Modern History of the United States Marshals Service* (Denton TX: University of North Texas Press, 2016), 219.

80. U.S. Marshals Service, "Fact Sheet: Fugitive Apprehension, 2018," fiscal 2017 data, April 13, 2008, https://www.usmarshals.gov/duties/factsheets/fugitive_ops.pdf.

81. David S. Turk, email correspondence with Ed Palattella, July 25, 2018.

82. Seth Ferranti, "The History of the Most Wanted Poster," *Huffington Post*, December 14, 2016, https://www.huffingtonpost.com/entry/the-history-of-the-most-wanted-poster_us_5851ba70e4b0865ab9d4e8d7.

83. Turk, email correspondence with Palattella, July 26, 2018.

84. Turk, *Forging the Star*, 220.

85. U.S. Marshals Service, "Fugitive Investigations," https://www.usmarshals.gov/investigations/index.html.

86. U.S. Marshals Service, "Fact Sheet: Fugitive Apprehension, 2018."

87. U.S. Marshals Service, "Fact Sheet: Fugitive Apprehension, 2018."

88. Thomas J. Miles, "An Empirical Analysis of the FBI's Ten Most Wanted," *Journal of Empirical Legal Studies*, 5, no. 2, (2008), 276.

89. Dove, *FBI's Ten Most Wanted Fugitives Program*, back page.

90. Groark, "FBI List Marks 50 Years of Finding 'Most Wanted.'"

91. Miles, "An Empirical Analysis of the FBI's Ten Most Wanted," 279.

92. Miles, "An Empirical Analysis of the FBI's Ten Most Wanted," 276.

93. Miles, "An Empirical Analysis of the FBI's Ten Most Wanted," 305.

94. Brad Heath, "For a Million Fugitives, Freedom Starts at County Line, *USA Today*, August 6, 2014, https://www.usatoday.com/story/news/nation/2014/08/06/fugitives-las-vegas-wont-pick-up/13607595/.

95. Holly C. Morris, FBI public affairs specialist, Criminal Justice Information Service, email to Jerry Clark, November 20, 2018.

96. *Fugitives: The Chronic Threat to Safety, Law, and Order: Hearing Before the Subcommittee on Criminal Justice Oversight of Sen. Judiciary Comm.*, 106th Cong. 33-34, June 22, 2000, (1) (statement of Sen. Strom Thurmond).

CHAPTER FIVE

1. Oscar Wilde to Norman Forbes-Robertson, April 19, 1882, cited in 112–113, included in *The Letters of Oscar Wilde*, edited by Rupert Hart-Davis (New York: Harcourt, Brace & World, 1962), 112–113.

2. Wilde to unknown correspondent, April 19, 1882, *The Letters of Oscar Wilde*, 113.

3. William Beverly, *On the Lam: Narratives of Flight in J. Edgar Hoover's America* (Jackson, MS: University Press of Mississippi, 2003), xi.

4. Beverly, *On the Lam*, 4.

5. Richard Maxwell Brown, "Western Violence: Structure, Values, Myth," *Western Historical Quarterly* 24, no. 1 (1993): 8.

6. Leland Tracy, "Favorable Representations of the Fugitive in American Popular Culture: The Story of Bonnie and Clyde," in *Authority and Displacement in the English-*

Speaking World (Volume II: Exploring American Shores), Florence Labaune-Demeule, ed. (Newcastle upon Tyne, UK: Cambridge Scholars Publishing, 2015), 17.

7. Tracy, "Favorable Representations of the Fugitive in American Popular Culture," 19.

8. Tracy, "Favorable Representations of the Fugitive in American Popular Culture," 19.

9. Tracy, "Favorable Representations of the Fugitive in American Popular Culture," 19–20.

10. Wayne Gard, *Frontier Justice* (Norman, OK: University of Oklahoma Press, 1949), 190.

11. Jerry Clark and Ed Palattella, *A History of Heists: Bank Robbery in America* (Lanham, MD: Rowman & Littlefield, 2015), 20.

12. T. J. Stiles, *Jesse James: Last Rebel of the Civil War* (New York: Alfred A. Knopf, 2002), 367.

13. Stiles, *Jesse James*, 367. See also Ted P. Yeatman, *Frank and Jesse James: The Story behind the Legend* (New York: Fall River Press, 2000), 252.

14. Stiles, *Jesse James*, 365.

15. Yeatman, *Frank and Jesse James*, 252.

16. Yeatman, *Frank and Jesse James*, 252.

17. Stiles, *Jesse James*, 363.

18. Stiles, *Jesse James*, page 7 in second photo gallery.

19. Stiles, *Jesse James*, 373.

20. Stiles, *Jesse James*, 374.

21. Yeatman, *Frank and Jesse James*, 269.

22. Yeatman, *Frank and Jesse James*, 269.

23. "Jesse James Murderers: The Ford Brothers Indicted, Plead Guilty, Sentenced to Be Hanged, and Pardoned All in One Day," *New York Times*, April 18, 1882.

24. William A. Settle, Jr., "The James Boys and Missouri Politics," *Missouri Historical Review* 36, no. 4 (1942): 419.

25. Yeatman, *Frank and Jesse James*, 271.

26. Yeatman, *Frank and Jesse James*, 271.

27. Stiles, *Jesse James*, 377.

28. "Fears of Frank James's Revenge," *New York Times*, April 9, 1882.

29. Stiles, *Jesse James*, 378.

30. Settle, "The James Boys and Missouri Politics," 419.

31. Settle, "The James Boys and Missouri Politics," 419.

32. Editorial from the *Daily Register* (NY), April 20, 1882, quoted in Charles E. Grinnell, "Review of the Month, General Notes," *American Law Review*, May 1882, 400.

33. "Review of the Month, General Notes," 404.

34. "Review of the Month, General Notes," 402.

35. William A. Settle, Jr., *Jesse James Was His Name: Or, Fact and Fiction Concerning the Careers of the Notorious James Brothers of Missouri* (Columbia, MO: University of Missouri Press, 1966), 173–74.

36. Jeff Guinn, *Go Down Together: The True, Untold Story of Bonnie and Clyde* (New York: Simon & Schuster, 2009) 313.

37. Elliott J. Gorn, *Dillinger's Wild Ride: The Year That Made America's Public Enemy Number One* (Oxford: Oxford University Press, 2009), xviii.

38. John Toland, *The Dillinger Days* (New York: Random House, 1963), 78.

39. Tracy, "Favorable Representations of the Fugitive in American Popular Culture," 39.

40. Guinn, *Go Down Together*, 174.

41. Guinn, *Go Down Together*, 176.

42. Guinn, *Go Down Together*, 276.

43. Clark and Palattella, *A History of Heists*, 108.

44. Tracy, "Favorable Representations of the Fugitive in American Popular Culture," 27–28.

45. Jan I. Fortune, ed., with Nell Barrow and Emma Parker, *Fugitives: The Story of Clyde Barrow and Bonnie Parker* (Dallas: The Ranger Press, 1934), iii–iv.

46. Steve Cocheo, "The Bank Robber, the Quote, and the Final Irony," *ABA Banking Journal* 89, no. 3 (1997): 71–72.

47. L. R. Kirchner, *Robbing Banks: An American History*, 1831–1999 (Rockville Centre, NY: Sarpedon, 2000), 107.

48. Federal Bureau of Investigation, "Famous Cases and Criminals: Willie Sutton," http://www.fbi.gov/history/famous-cases/willie-sutton.

49. Duane Swierczynski, *The Encyclopedia of the FBI's Ten Most Wanted List* (New York: Facts on File, 2004), 10. See also Clark and Palattella, *A History of Heists*, 121.

50. Willie Sutton with Edward Linn, *Where the Money Was* (1976; repr. New York: Broadway Books, 2004), 311.

51. Lorena Mongelli, "Former Cop Recalls NYPD Arrest of Willie Sutton 60 Yrs. Later," *New York Post*, February 18, 2012. See also Meyer Berger, "Sutton, Bank Thief, Captured in Street by Brooklyn Police," *New York Times*, February 19, 1952.

52. Berger, "Sutton, Bank Thief." See also Sutton with Linn, *Where the Money Was*, 315–16.

53. Swierczynski, *The Encyclopedia of the FBI's Ten Most Wanted List*, 13–16.

54. Sutton with Linn, *Where the Money Was*, 323–24.

55. The advertisement can be seen at https://www.youtube.com/watch?v=VLN 1p6nP7pY.

56. "An F.B.I. Hunt, Then Capture," *New York Times*, from online timeline of Whitey Bulger case, "Whitey Bulger: Capture of a Legend," https://archive.nytimes.

com/www.nytimes.com/interactive/us/bulger-timeline.html#/%23time256_7543#t ime256_7547.

57. Robert D. McFadden, "Whitey Bulger Is Dead in Prison at 89; Long-Hunted Boston Mob Boss," *New York Times*, October 30, 2018.

58. McFadden, "Whitey Bulger Is Dead in Prison at 89."

59. Adam Nagourney and Abby Goodnough, "Long Elusive, Mob Legend Ended Up a Recluse," *New York Times*, June 23, 2011.

60. Nagourney and Goodnough, "Long Elusive, Mob Legend Ended Up a Recluse."

61. Nagourney and Goodnough, "Long Elusive, Mob Legend Ended Up a Recluse."

62. Katherine Q. Seelye, "Crime Boss Bulger Gets 2 Life Terms and Is Assailed by Judge for His 'Depravity,'" *New York Times*, November 14, 2013.

63. Seelye, "Crime Boss Bulger Gets 2 Life Terms."

64. Matt Rocheleau, "Here Are the Key Unanswered Questions about James 'Whitey" Bulger's Killing," *Boston Globe*, October 31, 2018.

65. Tracy, "Favorable Representations of the Fugitive in American Popular Culture," 30.

66. Tise Vahimagi, "The Fugitive," in *Encyclopedia of Television, Second Edition*," ed., Horace Newcomb (New York: Fitzroy Dearborn, 2004), 946.

67. Vahimagi, "The Fugitive," 946.

68. Vahimagi, "The Fugitive," 945.

69 Soraya Roberts, "Hollywood Doesn't Make Movies Like *The Fugitive* Anymore," *The Atlantic*, August 6, 2018, https://www.theatlantic.com/entertainment/archive/2018/08/the-fugitive-harrison-ford-25-years-later/566729/.

70. *The Fugitive* (Warner Bros.), 1993. See also, http://www.moviequotedb.com/movies/fugitive-the/quote_8959.html.

71 Internet Movie Database, "The Fugitive," https://www.imdb.com/title/tt0106977/.

72. Vahimagi, "The Fugitive," 945. See also Stephen Battaglio, "50 Years Before Peak TV, 'The Fugitive' Set Precedent for Big Series Finales," *Los Angeles Times*, August 26, 2017, http://www.latimes.com/business/hollywood/la-et-st-fugitive-fiftieth-anniversary-20170828-story.html; and "Who Shot J.R.? She Did. On 'Dallas.' 35 Years Ago." *Los Angeles Daily News*, November 18, 2015, https://www.dailynews.com/2015/11/18/who-shot-jr-she-did-on-dallas-35-years-ago/.

73. Donald Liebenson, "How *The Fugitive*'s Heart-Pumping Finale Changed TV Forever," *Vanity Fair*, August 29, 2017, https://www.vanityfair.com/hollywood/2017/08/the-fugitive-tv-show-series-finale-judgment-anniversary-kimble-one-armed-man. See also Donald Liebenson, "Top Secret," Chicago Tribune, April 19, 1994.

74. Stanley Fish, *The Fugitive in Flight* (Philadelphia: University of Pennsylvania Press, 2011), 17.

CHAPTER SIX

1. J. Anthony Lukas, "On the Lam in America," *New York Times Magazine*, December 13, 1970, 74. In this brilliant piece of reporting, Lukas does not name this fugitive nor identify the fugitive's gender. The male pronoun is used here for convenience.

2. Lukas, "On the Lam in America," 74.

3. Lukas, "On the Lam in America," 74.

4. J. Reid Meloy and Jessica Yakely, "Antisocial Personality Disorder," in *Gabbard's Treatments of Psychiatric Disorders*, ed. Glen O. Gabbard (Washington, D.C: American Psychiatric Association Publishing, 2014), 1,016.

5. H. J. Eysenck, *Crime and Personality* (London: Routledge & Kegan Paul, 1977), 58.

6. Meyer Berger, "Sutton, Bank Thief, Captured in Street by Brooklyn Police," *New York Times*, February 19, 1952.

7. Willie Sutton with Edward Linn, *Where the Money Was* (1976; repr., New York: Broadway Books, 2004), 299.

8. Berger, "Sutton, Bank Thief, Captured in Street by Brooklyn Police."

9. Sutton with Edward Linn, *Where the Money Was*, 161.

10. Sutton with Edward Linn, *Where the Money Was*, 161.

11. Berger, "Sutton, Bank Thief, Captured in Street by Brooklyn Police."

12. Berger, "Sutton, Bank Thief, Captured in Street by Brooklyn Police."

13. Berger, "Sutton, Bank Thief, Captured in Street by Brooklyn Police."

14. Sutton with Edward Linn, *Where the Money Was*, 298–99.

15. Berger, "Sutton, Bank Thief, Captured in Street by Brooklyn Police."

16. Berger, "Sutton, Bank Thief, Captured in Street by Brooklyn Police."

17. Sutton with Edward Linn, *Where the Money Was*, 299.

18. Sutton with Edward Linn, *Where the Money Was*, 300.

19. Berger, "Sutton, Bank Thief, Captured in Street by Brooklyn Police."

20. Berger, "Sutton, Bank Thief, Captured in Street by Brooklyn Police."

21. Berger, "Sutton, Bank Thief, Captured in Street by Brooklyn Police."

22. The Rev. Vincent G. Burns, introduction to *I Am a Fugitive from a Georgia Chain Gang!* by Robert E. Burns (1932; repr., Athens, GA: University of Georgia Press, 1997), 11.

23. Burns, *I Am a Fugitive from a Georgia Chain Gang!*, 44.

24. Burns, *I Am a Fugitive from a Georgia Chain Gang!*, 58

25. Burns, *I Am a Fugitive from a Georgia Chain Gang!*, 65.

26. Burns, *I Am a Fugitive from a Georgia Chain Gang!*, 67.

27. William Beverly, *On the Lam: Narratives of Flight in J. Edgar Hoover's America* (Jackson, MS: University Press of Mississippi, 2003), 4.

28. Matthew J. Mancini, foreword to *I Am a Fugitive from a Georgia Chain Gang!*, xi.

29. Mancini, foreword to *I Am a Fugitive from a Georgia Chain Gang!*, xxi. Mancini in this passage also maintains that, while *I am Fugitive from a Georgia Chain Gang!*, represents Robert E. Burns's "thoughts and experiences" and that he "approved every sentence," the true author of the book was Burns's brother, the Rev. Vincent G. Burns, a Unitarian minister, and one of Robert E. Burns's most steadfast advocates.

30. Burns, *I Am a Fugitive from a Georgia Chain Gang!*, 71.

31. Burns, *I Am a Fugitive from a Georgia Chain Gang!*, 71.

32. Burns, *I Am a Fugitive from a Georgia Chain Gang!*, 71.

33. Burns, *I Am a Fugitive from a Georgia Chain Gang!*, 71–72.

34. Burns, *I Am a Fugitive from a Georgia Chain Gang!*, 93.

35. Burns, *I Am a Fugitive from a Georgia Chain Gang!*, 93.

36. Burns, *I Am a Fugitive from a Georgia Chain Gang!*, 87.

37. Burns, *I Am a Fugitive from a Georgia Chain Gang!*, 91.

38. Mancini, foreword to *I Am a Fugitive from a Georgia Chain Gang!*, vii.

39. Shane Bauer, "The Origins of Prison Slavery: How Southern Whites Found Replacements for Their Emancipated Slaves in the Prison System," *Slate*, October 2, 2018, https://slate.com/news-and-politics/2018/10/origin-prison-slavery-shane-bauer-american-prison-excerpt.html.

40. "Georgia Penitentiary at Midgeville," *New Georgia Encyclopedia*, https://www.georgiaencyclopedia.org/articles/history-archaeology/georgia-penitentiary-milledgeville. See also Mancini, foreword to *I Am a Fugitive from a Georgia Chain Gang!*, vii.

41. "A Fugitive from Georgia's Prison System," *New York Times*, January 31, 1932.

42. Burns, *I Am a Fugitive from a Georgia Chain Gang!*, 118.

43. "Burns's Wife Opposes His Clemency Plea," *New York Times*, July 22, 1929.

44. Beverly, *On the Lam*, 3.

45. Burns, *I Am a Fugitive from a Georgia Chain Gang!*, 133.

46. Burns, *I Am a Fugitive from a Georgia Chain Gang!*, 202.

47. Burns, *I Am a Fugitive from a Georgia Chain Gang!*, 244.

48. Burns, *I Am a Fugitive from a Georgia Chain Gang!*, 245.

49. Burns, *I Am a Fugitive from a Georgia Chain Gang!*, 245.

50. Marc Mappen, "Jerseyana," *New York Times*, January 12, 1992.

51. "Chain-Gang Convict Fights Extradition," *New York Times*, December 16, 1932.

52. Mappen, "Jerseyana."

53. "Burns Extradition Refused by Moore," *New York Times*, December 22, 1932.

54. "Burns Extradition Refused by Moore."

55. Mappen, "Jerseyana."

56. "Georgia Frees Burns, 'Fugitive from Chain Gang,' After 23 Years," *New York Times*, November, 2, 1945.

57. "Georgia Frees Burns, 'Fugitive from Chain Gang,' After 23 Years."

58. Burns, *I Am a Fugitive from a Georgia Chain Gang!*, 5.

59. Michael Wilson, "Dragnet Yields Whimsy and Dread Upstate," *New York Times*, July 15, 2006.

60. Michael Wilson, "On Back Roads and in Deep Woods, Fugitive Has Edge Over Pursuers," *New York Times*, September 3, 2006.

61. Wilson, "Dragnet Yields Whimsy and Dread Upstate."

62. Carolyn Thompson, Associated Press, "Escapee Gets Life in Trooper's Death," *Washington Post*, December 19, 2006.

63. Michael Wilson, "Fugitive Tells of Life on the Run and of a Killing," *New York Times*, April 7, 2006.

64. Michael Wilson, "After Years Behind Bars, Now a Life on the Run," *New York Times*, September 8, 2006.

65. Wilson, "Fugitive Tells of Life on the Run and of a Killing."

66. Wilson, "Fugitive Tells of Life on the Run and of a Killing."

67. Wilson, "Fugitive Tells of Life on the Run and of a Killing."

68. Wilson, "On Back Roads and in Deep Woods, Fugitive Has Edge Over Pursuers."

69. Wilson, "On Back Roads and in Deep Woods, Fugitive Has Edge Over Pursuers."

70. Wilson, "Fugitive Tells of Life on the Run and of a Killing."

71. Carolyn Thompson, Associated Press, "Convict Caught in N.Y. Trooper Shooting," *Washington Post*, September 9, 2006.

72. Thompson, "Convict Caught in N.Y. Trooper Shooting."

73. U.S. Marshals Service, "Suspected Cop Killer Makes Marshals' '15 Most Wanted,'" news release release, September 6, 2006, https://www.usmarshals.gov/investigations/most_wanted/phillips/phillips-090606.htm.

74. Federal Bureau of Investigation, "Ralph B. [*sic*] Phillips Added to FBI Top Ten List," news release, September 7, 2006, https://archives.fbi.gov/archives/news/pressrel/press-releases/ralph-b.-phillips-added-to-fbi-top-ten-list.

75. Michael Wilson and David Staba, "Fugitive Wanted in Shootings of 3 Troopers Surrenders," *New York Times*, September 9, 2006.

76. Thompson, "Convict Caught in N.Y. Trooper Shooting."

77. Thompson, "Convict Caught in N.Y. Trooper Shooting."

78. Wilson, "Fugitive Tells of Life on the Run and of a Killing."

79. Wilson and Staba, "Fugitive Wanted in Shootings of 3 Troopers Surrenders."

80. Wilson and Staba, "Fugitive Wanted in Shootings of 3 Troopers Surrenders."

81. Associated Press, "'Bucky' Phillips Loses Prison Privileges," Albany (NY) *Times-Union*, November 8, 2011.

82. Wilson, "Ex-Fugitive Is Suspected of New Plot," *New York Times*, November 8, 2011.

CHAPTER SEVEN

1. David S. Turk, *Forging the Star: The Official Modern History of the United States Marshals Service* (Denton TX: University of North Texas Press, 2016), 244.

2. Turk, *Forging the Star*, 244–45.

3. Ronald J. Ostrow, "Free Football Party Lures Fugitives into Arms of the Law," *Los Angeles Times*, December 16, 1985.

4. Ostrow, "Free Football Party Lures Fugitives into Arms of the Law."

5. Ostrow, "Free Football Party Lures Fugitives into Arms of the Law."

6. Turk, *Forging the Star*, 246.

7. U.S. Marshals Service, "History—Fugitive Investigative Strike Teams (FIST): Fugitive Investigations—Creative Stings: 'Puno Airlines,'" https://www.usmarshals.gov/history/fist/airlines.htm.

8. U.S. Marshals Service, "History—Fugitive Investigative Strike Teams (FIST)," https://www.usmarshals.gov/history/fist/index.html.

9. U.S. Marshals Service, "History—Fugitive Investigative Strike Teams (FIST)." See also "Tampa-Based Probe Flushes Out Fugitives," *Tampa* (FL) *Tribune*, June 17, 1985.

10. KiKi Bochi, "Killer, Fugitive for 30 years, Swept Up by FIST of the Law," *Fort Lauderdale* (FL) *News*, June 20, 1985.

11. U.S. Marshals Service, "History—Fugitive Investigative Strike Teams (FIST)," https://www.usmarshals.gov/history/fist/index.html.

12. "Tampa-Based Probe Flushes Out Fugitives."

13. "Tampa-Based Probe Flushes Out Fugitives."

14. "Tampa-Based Probe Flushes Out Fugitives."

15. "Tampa-Based Probe Flushes Out Fugitives."

16. "Tampa-Based Probe Flushes Out Fugitives."

17. Jeff Leen, *Miami Herald*, "Airline Scam Lands Wanted Man in Jail," *Tallahassee* (FL) *Democrat*, June 17, 1985.

18. Leen, "Airline Scam Lands Wanted Man in Jail."

19. Bochi, "Killer, Fugitive for 30 years, Swept Up by FIST of the Law."

20. "Tampa-Based Probe Flushes Out Fugitives."

21. "Tampa-Based Probe Flushes Out Fugitives."

22. Bob Burton, *Bail Enforcer: The Advanced Bounty Hunter*, (Boulder, CO: Paladin Press, 1990), 23.

23. Arthur H. Rotstein, Associated Press, "Arizona Bounty Hunter Sees His Job as Boredom Mixed with Terror," *Los Angeles Times*, February 12, 1995, http://articles.latimes.com/1995-02-12/local/me-31062_1_bounty-hunter-bounty-hunting-bob-burton.

24. Rotstein, "Arizona Bounty Hunter Sees His Job as Boredom Mixed with Terror."

25. Burton, *Bail Enforcer*, 26–28.

26. Burton, *Bail Enforcer*, 28.

27. Burton, *Bail Enforcer*, 34.

28. Burton, *Bail Enforcer*, 31.

29. Burton, *Bail Enforcer*, 31.

30. Burton, *Bail Enforcer*, 35.

31. Rotstein, "Arizona Bounty Hunter Sees His Job as Boredom Mixed with Terror."

32. "Fugitive Cornered in Cave," Minneapolis *Star Tribune*, March 19, 1950.

33. "3 Boys Win Praise of FBI," Minneapolis *Star Tribune*, March 19, 1950.

34. James Lee, International News Service, "Vicious Killer Tried 'Murder by Dynamite," *Lebanon* (PA) *Daily News*, March 16, 1950.

35. "Fugitive Cornered in Cave," Minneapolis *Star Tribune*, March 19, 1950.

36. "Fugitive Cornered in Cave," and Duane Swierczynski, *The Encyclopedia of the FBI's Ten Most Wanted List* (New York: Facts on File, 2004), 5.

37. Swierczynski, *The Encyclopedia of the FBI's Ten Most Wanted List*, and "Fugitive Cornered in Cave."

38. Swierczynski, *The Encyclopedia of the FBI's Ten Most Wanted List*, and "Fugitive Cornered in Cave."

39. Lee, "Vicious Killer Tried 'Murder by Dynamite.'"

40. Lee, "Vicious Killer Tried 'Murder by Dynamite.'"

41. Lee, "Vicious Killer Tried 'Murder by Dynamite.'"

42. "Fugitive Cornered in Cave."

43. Swierczynski, *The Encyclopedia of the FBI's Ten Most Wanted List*, 5.

44. "Fugitive Cornered in Cave."

45. John Fox, interview by John Maynard, "Inside Media: The FBI's Ten Most Wanted: The Story Behind the List," Newseum, Washington, D.C., March 21, 2015, http://www.newseum.org/event/inside-media-the-fbis-ten-most-wanted-the-story-be hind-the-list.

46. "FBI Chief Lauds Newspapers in Capture of Two," *Greensburg* (IN) *Daily News*, March 27, 1950.

47. Sara Rimer, "60's Radical, Linked to a Killing, Surrenders after Hiding 23 Years," *New York Times*, September 16, 1993.

48. Swierczynski, *The Encyclopedia of the FBI's Ten Most Wanted List*, 163–64.

49. Swierczynski, *The Encyclopedia of the FBI's Ten Most Wanted List*, 178.

50. Rimer, "60's Radical, Linked to a Killing, Surrenders after Hiding 23 Years."

51. Rimer, "60's Radical, Linked to a Killing, Surrenders after Hiding 23 Years."

52. Federal Bureau of Investigation most-wanted poster, http://fbimostwanted.us/zc/index.php/?main_page=wordpress&p=33.

53. Sara Rimer, "Ex-Radical Gets 8 to 12 Years in Killing, and a Rebuke," *New York Times*, October 7, 1993.

54. Swierczynski, *The Encyclopedia of the FBI's Ten Most Wanted List*, 178–79.

55. Rimer, "Ex-Radical Gets 8 to 12 Years in Killing, and a Rebuke."

56. Canda Fuqua, "Former Fugitive Katherine Ann Power to Speak in Corvallis," *Corvallis* (OR) *Gazette-Times*, October 30, 2013.

57. Rimer, "60's Radical, Linked to a Killing, Surrenders after Hiding 23 Years."

58. Rimer, "60's Radical, Linked to a Killing, Surrenders after Hiding 23 Years."

59. Rimer, "Ex-Radical Gets 8 to 12 Years in Killing, and a Rebuke."

60. Rimer, "60's Radical, Linked to a Killing, Surrenders After Hiding 23 Years."

61. Christopher B. Daley, "Ex-Fugitive Katherine Power Sentenced 8–12 Years for 1970 Robbery," *Washington Post*, October 7, 1993.

62. Rimer, "Ex-Radical Gets 8 to 12 Years in Killing, and a Rebuke."

63. Rimer, "Ex-Radical Gets 8 to 12 Years in Killing, and a Rebuke," and Daley, "Ex-Fugitive Katherine Power Sentenced 8–12 Years for 1970 Robbery."

64. Katherine Ann Power, email message to Ed Palattella, October 22, 2018.

65. Katherine Ann Power, email message to Ed Palattella, October 22, 2018; and "Writings and Talks by Katherine Ann Power," Practical Peace (blog), accessed on October 21, 2018, http://www.practicalpeace.com/writings-talks/prison-years/73/my -ten-books.html.

66. Swierczynski, *The Encyclopedia of the FBI's Ten Most Wanted List*, 203.

67 J. Anthony Lukas, "On the Lam in America," *New York Times Magazine*, December 13, 1970, 56.

68. Lisa Belkin, "Doesn't Anybody Know How to Be a Fugitive Anymore?" *New York Times Magazine*, April 30, 2000, 62–63.

69. Belkin, "Doesn't Anybody Know How to Be a Fugitive Anymore?," 62.

70. Belkin, "Doesn't Anybody Know How to Be a Fugitive Anymore?," 62.

71. Swierczynski, *The Encyclopedia of the FBI's Ten Most Wanted List*, 85.

72. Penelope McMillan, "Quinn Martin, Producer of Hit Television Series, Dies," *Los Angeles Times*, September 7, 1987.

73. Lukas, "On the Lam in America," 59.

74. Swierczynski, *The Encyclopedia of the FBI's Ten Most Wanted List*, 157.

75. Bruce Porter," Running the FBI," *New York Times Magazine*, November 2, 1997, 45.

76. Mike Barnes and Duane Byrge, "Actor Efrem Zimbalist Jr. Dies at 95," *Hollywood Reporter*, May 2, 2014, https://www.hollywoodreporter.com/news/efrem -zimbalist-jr-dead-star-700983.

77. Jack Gould, "Actors 'Cleared' For F.B.I. Series," *New York Times*, June 2, 1965.

78. Gould, "Actors 'Cleared' For F.B.I. Series."

79. Gould, "Actors 'Cleared' For F.B.I. Series."

80. FBI, "Ten Most Wanted Fugitives FAQ," https://www.fbi.gov/wanted/topten/ ten-most-wanted-fugitives-faq.

81. Robert M. Smith, "Friends of F.B.I. in a Fund Appeal," *New York Times*, July 21, 1971.

82. Frank J. Prial, "Freeze! You're on TV," *New York Times Magazine*, September 25, 1988, 63.

83. Brian Stetler, "Considering Next Steps for 'Wanted,'" *New York Times*, May 17, 2011.

84. Thomas J. Miles, "Estimating the Effect of *America's Most Wanted*: A Duration Analysis of Wanted Fugitives," *Journal of Law & Economics*, 48, no. 1 (2005), 281.

85. Miles, "Estimating the Effect of *America's Most Wanted*," 295.

86 Stetler, "Considering Next Steps for 'Wanted,'"

87. Prial, "Freeze! You're on TV," 63.

88. Stetler, "Considering Next Steps for 'Wanted.'"

89. Robert D. McFadden, "Man Wanted as the Killer of 6 Is Caught Because of TV Show," *New York Times*, April 11, 1988.

90. Prial, "Freeze! You're on TV," 63.

91. Swierczynski, *The Encyclopedia of the FBI's Ten Most Wanted List*, 217, 244–45.

92. Valerie J. Phillips, "Escaped Murderer Hunted in Indiana," *Chicago Tribune*, October 25, 1986.

93. Phillips, "Escaped Murderer Hunted in Indiana," and Swierczynski, *The Encyclopedia of the FBI's Ten Most Wanted List*, 244–45.

94. Fox News, "Top 10 Captures by *America's Most Wanted*," https://www.foxnews.com/us/top-10-captures-by-americas-most-wanted.

95. William K. Rashbaum, United Press International, "TV Show Leads to Capture of Fugitive Killer," February 12, 1988, https://www.upi.com/Archives/1988/02/12/TV-show-leads-to-capture-of-fugitive-killer/3106571640400/.

96. Claire Suddath, "Top 10 *America's Most Wanted* Captures," *Time*, January 5, 2010, http://content.time.com/time/specials/packages/article/0,28804,1951726_1951715_1951695,00.html.

97. Swierczynski, *The Encyclopedia of the FBI's Ten Most Wanted List*, 244–45. See also FBI, "Most Wanted: 409. David James Roberts," https://www.fbi.gov/wanted/topten/topten-history/hires_images/FBI-409-DavidJamesRoberts.jpg/view.

98. Stacey Okun, "Double Life of a Murderer Shocks S.I.," *New York Times*, February 13, 1998.

99. Swierczynski, *The Encyclopedia of the FBI's Ten Most Wanted List*, 244–45.

100. Swierczynski, *The Encyclopedia of the FBI's Ten Most Wanted List*, 244–45.

101. Prial, "Freeze! You're on TV," 58.

102. Steve Erlanger, "Television: Manhunting, In an Armchair," *New York Times*, February 7, 1988.

103. Olivia B. Waxman, "The U.S. Is Still Dealing with the Murder of Adam Walsh," *Time*, August 10, 2006.

104. Russell Shorto, "A Life of Crime," *New York Times Magazine*, August 25, 2002, 31.

105. Shorto, "A Life of Crime," 30.

106. Phil McCombs, "John Walsh's Pursuit," *Washington Post*, April 25, 1989.

107. Barbara Whitaker, "End of an Abduction: TV's Role: 'America's Most Wanted' Enlists Public," *New York Times*, March 14, 2003.

108. Associated Press, "Show Returns; Viewer Helps Nab Fugitive" *Deseret News* (Salt Lake City, UT), November 12, 1996.

109. Yolanne Almanzar, "27 Years Later, Case Is Closed in Slaying of Abducted Child," *New York Times*, December 16, 2008.

110. Almanzar, "27 Years Later, Case Is Closed in Slaying of Abducted Child."

111. Denise Petski, "John Walsh Investigation Series Set at ID; Discovery Green-lights 'Undercover Billionaire,'" *Deadline Hollywood*, April 10, 2018, https://dead line.com/2018/04/john-walsh-investigation-series-id-discovery-undercover-billionaire -1202361744/.

112. Amanda Cochran, 'America's Most Wanted' Host John Walsh on Cancellation: Show Needs to Be on TV," CBS News, May 7, 2013, https://www.cbsnews.com/news/ americas-most-wanted-host-john-walsh-on-cancellation-show-needs-to-be-on-tv/.

CHAPTER EIGHT

1. Federal Bureau of Investigation, "The FBI Website at 20: Two Decades of Fighting Crime and Terrorism," https://www.fbi.gov/news/stories/the-fbi-website-at-20-2.

2. Federal Bureau of Investigation, "The FBI Website at 20."

3. The FBI on its most-wanted poster and in other reference spells Rogge's middle name as "Isben." The correct spelling is "Ibsen." See Dane Batty, *Wanted: Gentleman Bank Robber: The True Story of Leslie Ibsen Rogge, One of the FBI's Most Elusive Criminals* (Hillsboro, OR: Nish Publishing Co., 2010). Batty is Rogge's nephew.

4. Molly Moore, "You Can Run, But Not Hide, From the Net," *Washington Post*, June 6, 1996.

5. FBI, "Ten Most Wanted Fugitives FAQ," https://www.fbi.gov/wanted/topten/ten-most-wanted-fugitives-faq.

6. Moore, "You Can Run, But Not Hide, From the Net."

7. "Global Village Cops?" editorial, *Washington Post*, June 10, 1996, https://www. washingtonpost.com/archive/opinions/1996/06/10/global-village-cops/172951da-802d-48db-a825-613956c9d62e/?utm_term=.3a57db976314.

8. "Global Village Cops?"

9. Raoul V. Mowatt, Knight-Ridder Tribune, "Police Hope to Nab Criminals in Their World Wide Web," *Chicago Tribune*, May 29, 1996.

10. Peter Truell, "Authorities Can Track Fugitive Financiers, But They Can't Bring Them In," *New York Times*, January 16, 1997.

11. Truell, "Authorities Can Track Fugitive Financiers, But They Can't Bring Them In."

12. Kaveh Waddel, "The FBI's Most-Wanted Cybercriminals: The Agency's List Is Growing as Foreign Hackers Continue to Attack the U.S.," The Atlantic, April 27, 2016, https://www.theatlantic.com/technology/archive/2016/04/the-fbis-most-wanted-cybercriminals/480036/.

13. Michael S. Schmidt, "To Replace Bin Laden on Most Wanted List, a Teacher in a Pornography Case," *New York Times*, April 10, 2012. Also FBI, "Ten Most Wanted," https://www.fbi.gov/wanted/topten/topten-history/hires_images/fbi-495-eric-justin-toth/view.

14. Allison Klein and Justin Jouvenal, "Tourist in Nicaragua Recognized Ex-Beauvoir Teacher on FBI List," *Washington Post*, April 23, 2013.

15. Justin Jouvenal, "Former Beauvoir Teacher Eric Toth Sentenced for Producing Child Pornography," *Washington Post*, March 11, 2014.

16. Allison Klein, "Ex-Beauvoir Teacher Eric Toth, Wanted on Child Pornography Charges, Is Found Abroad," *Washington Post*, April 22, 2013.

17. Klein and Jouvenal, "Tourist in Nicaragua Recognized ex-Beauvoir Teacher on FBI List."

18. FBI, "Ten Most Wanted Fugitives FAQ."

19. Moore, "You Can Run, But Not Hide, From the Net."

20. Moore, "You Can Run, But Not Hide, From the Net."

21. Jesse Kornbluth, "So He Stole $2 Million from 30 Banks—Leslie Rogge's Book Is as Much Fun as 'Butch Cassidy,'" *Huffington Post*, September 20, 2010; updated May 25, 2011, https://www.huffingtonpost.com/jesse-kornbluth/so-he-stole-2-million-fro_b_731519.html.

22. United Press International, "Fugitive Surrenders to FBI," UPI Archives, May 19, 1996, https://www.upi.com/Archives/1996/05/19/Fugitive-surrenders-to-FBI/7184832478400/.

23. Kornbluth, "So He Stole $2 Million from 30 Banks – Leslie Rogge's Book Is as Much Fun as 'Butch Cassidy.'"

24. Moore, "You Can Run, But Not Hide, From the Net."

25. Moore, "You Can Run, But Not Hide, From the Net."

26. Associated Press and *Lewiston* (ID) *Tribune*, "FBI Finds Man in Guatemala who Escaped from Latah Jail in 1985," *Lewiston Tribune*, May 20, 1996.

27. "FBI Finds Man in Guatemala who Escaped from Latah Jail in 1985."

28. UPI, "Fugitive Surrenders to FBI."

29. Kornbluth, "So He Stole $2 Million from 30 Banks—Leslie Rogge's Book Is as Much Fun as 'Butch Cassidy.'"

30. Samantha Malott, "He's Willing to Speak for the Accused: Lifelong Defense Attorney Discusses Working with 'Less than Deluxe,'" *Moscow-Pullman* (ID) *Daily News*, March 5, 2015.

31. Moore, "You Can Run, But Not Hide, From the Net."

32. Moore, "You Can Run, But Not Hide, From the Net."

33. FBI most-wanted poster for Leslie Ibsen Rogge, www.crimemagazine.com/wanted-gentleman-bank-robber.

34. Opinion and Order, May 27, 2016, *Leslie Ibsen Rogge v. Marion Feather*, United States District Court for the District of Oregon, Case No. 3:15-CV-01732-HZ, 5.

35. Opinion and Order, *Leslie Ibsen Rogge v. Marion Feather*.

36. At the *Erie Times-News*, in Erie, Pennsylvania, where author Ed Palattella works, the most-wanted feature runs on Thursday. The sheriff has reported that his office's hotline gets calls in the early morning most Thursdays, or as soon as the newspaper hits the stands and the streets.

37. Jeremy Peters, "Media Decoder: Now in Print: To Catch a Fugitive," *New York Times*, December 13, 2010.

38. Peters, "Media Decoder."

39. FBI, "10 Years of Digital Billboards: Partnership Brings Safety Messages Directly to the Public," December 7, 2017, http://fbi.gov, https://www.fbi.gov/news/stories/10-years-of-digital-billboards.

40. FBI, "Digital Billboard Initiative: Catching Fugitives in the Information Age," December 24, 2014, http://fbi.gov, https://www.fbi.gov/news/stories/digital-billboard-initiative.

41. Associated Press, "Digital Billboards to Show Fugitives," *New York Times*, December 28, 2007.

42. Associated Press, "Digital Billboards to Show Fugitives."

43. FBI, "10 Years of Digital Billboards."

44. FBI, "Digital Billboard Initiative."

45. FBI, "10 Years of Digital Billboards."

46. FBI Special Agent Rick Kolko, interview with *Inside the FBI* podcast, "Fugitives on a Times Square Billboard," January 5, 2010, https://www.fbi.gov/audio-repository/news-podcasts-inside-fugitives-on-a-times-square-billboard.mp3/view.

47. Janet Morrisey, "Look Up: In the Digital Age, Billboards Are Far from Dead," *New York Times*, September 4, 2016.

48. LexisNexis, "Role of Social Media in Law Enforcement Significant and Growing," July 18, 2012, LexisNexis.com, https://www.lexisnexis.com/en-us/about-us/media/press-release.page?id=1342623085481181.

49. "Can the Police Use Facebook to Investigate Crimes?" *Government Technology*, March 5, 2017, http://www.govtech.com/public-safety/can-the-police-use-facebook-to-investigate-crimes.html.

50. Joseph Serna, "LAPD 'Most Wanted' Fugitive Found through Facebook," *Los Angeles Times*, November 14, 2014.

51. City News Service, "Facebook Helps Arrest One of LAPD's—and America's—Most Wanted Fugitives in Riverside," *Los Angeles Daily News*, November 14, 2014.

52. Serna, "LAPD 'Most Wanted' Fugitive Found through Facebook."

53. Greg Krikorian, "Jury Convicts L.A. Gang Leader of Three Murders," *Los Angeles Times*, October 26, 2007.

54. Andrew Blankstein and Richard Winton, "Gang Leader Held in Arizona," *Los Angeles Times*, February 3, 2003.

55. Blankstein and Winton, "Gang Leader Held in Arizona."

56. Krikorian, "Jury Convicts L.A. Gang Leader of Three Murders."

57. Jack Leonard, "Gang Leader Timothy Joseph McGhee Convicted of 3 Murders," *Los Angeles Times*, January 10, 2009.

58. Opinion and Order, August 10, 2012, United *States of America v. Joshua Meregildo et al.*, United States District Court for the Southern District of New York, Case No. 11-CR-576 (WHP), 3.

59. Opinion and Order, United *States of America v. Joshua Meregildo et al.*, 4.

60. Office of U.S. Sen. Bernie Sanders, "Sanders Introduces Bill to End Money Bail," news release, July 25, 2018, https://www.sanders.senate.gov/newsroom/press-releases/sanders-introduces-bill-to-end-money-bail.

61. No Money Bail Act of 2018, S. 3271, 115th Cong. (2018).

62. Office of U.S. Sen. Bernie Sanders, "Sanders Introduces Bill to End Money Bail," news release.

63. Office of U.S. Sen. Bernie Sanders, "Sanders Introduces Bill to End Money Bail," bill summary attached to news release.

64. Sarah Lazare, "Bernie Sanders and Kamala Harris Both Fall Short on Abolishing Money Bail," *In These Times*, November 13, 2018, http://inthesetimes.com/article/21575/bernie-sanders-and-kamala-harris-both-fall-short-on-bail-abolition.

65. John Michael Seibler and Jason Snead, "Legal Memorandum: The History of Cash Bail," Heritage Foundation, Washington, D.C., no. 213, August 25, 2017, 1, https://www.heritage.org/sites/default/files/2017-08/LM-213.pdf.

66. Seibler and Snead, "Legal Memorandum: The History of Cash Bail."

67. For a full range of arguments from the American Bail Coalition, see http://www.americanbailcoalition.org/criminal-justice/.

68. Truman Morrison, senior judge on the Superior Court in Washington, D.C, interview by Melissa Block, *Weekend Edition Sunday*, National Public Radio, September 2, 2018, https://www.npr.org/2018/09/02/644085158/what-changed-after-d-c-ended-cash-bail.

69. Morrison, interview by Melissa Block, *Weekend Edition Sunday*.

70. Thomas Fuller, "California Is the First State to Scrap Cash Bail," *New York Times*, August 28, 2018.

71. Fuller, "California Is the First State to Scrap Cash Bail."

72. Fuller, "California Is the First State to Scrap Cash Bail."

73. ACLU of California, "ACLU of California Changes Position to Oppose Bail Reform Legislation," news release, August 20, 2018, https://www.aclunc.org/news/aclu-california-changes-position-oppose-bail-reform-legislation.

74. Alexei Koseff, "Bill to Eliminate Bail Advances despite ACLU Defection," the *Sacramento Bee*, August 20, 2018, https://www.sacbee.com/news/politics-government/capitol-alert/article217031860.html.

75. U.S. Department of State, Narcotics Rewards Program, "Wanted: Rafael Caro-Quintero," https://www.state.gov/j/inl/narc/rewards/275634.htm.

76. "Death of Narc," cover of *Time* magazine, November 7, 1988.

77. FBI, "New Top Ten Fugitive: Help Us Catch a Killer," news release on Rafael Caro-Quintero, April 12, 2018, https://www.fbi.gov/news/stories/new-top-ten-fugitive-rafael-caro-quintero-041218.

78. Patrick J. McDonnell, "U.S. Offers $20-million Reward for Fugitive Caro Quintero, 'Prince' of Mexican Narcos," *Los Angeles Times*, April 13, 2018.

79. FBI, "New Top Ten Fugitive: Help Us Catch a Killer."

80. FBI, "New Top Ten Fugitive: Help Us Catch a Killer."

81. Peter Baker and Randal C. Archibold, "U.S. Seeks Arrest of Mexican Kingpin Who Was Freed in American's Murder," *New York Times*, August 14, 2013.

82. McDonnell, "U.S. Offers $20-million Reward for Fugitive Caro Quintero, 'Prince' of Mexican Narcos."

83. Ali Watkins, "U.S. Puts New Pressure on Mexico in Decades-Old Murder of D.E.A. Agent," *New York Times*, April 12, 2018.

84. McDonnell, "U.S. Offers $20-million Reward for Fugitive Caro Quintero, 'Prince' of Mexican Narcos."

85. McDonnell, "U.S. Offers $20-million Reward for Fugitive Caro Quintero."

86. Baker and Archibold, "U.S. Seeks Arrest of Mexican Kingpin Who Was Freed in American's Murder."

87. Watkins, "U.S. Puts New Pressure on Mexico in Decades-Old Murder of D.E.A. Agent."

88. FBI, "New Top Ten Fugitive: Help Us Catch a Killer."

89. McDonnell, "U.S. Offers $20-million Reward for Fugitive Caro Quintero, 'Prince' of Mexican Narcos."

90. FBI (@FBIMostWanted), "The #FBI names Rafael Caro-Quintero as the 518th addition to its 'Ten Most Wanted Fugitives' List," Twitter, April 12, 2018, 2:53 p.m., https://twitter.com/FBIMostWanted/status/984504824501682176.

91. FBI (@FBIMostWanted), "The #FBI has named Lamont Stephenson to Its Ten Most Wanted Fugitives list," Twitter, October 11, 2018, 10:20 a.m., https://twitter.com/FBIMostWanted/status/1050435988856557569.

92. FBI, "New Top Ten Fugitive: Help Us Catch a Murderer: Lamont Stephenson," news release, October 11, 2018, https://www.fbi.gov/news/stories/new-top-ten-fugitive-lamont-stephenson-101118.

93. Dan Ivers, "Warrant Issued for Fiancé in Strangling Death of Newark Woman," November 5, 2018, NJ.com, https://www.nj.com/essex/index.ssf/2014/11/warrant_issued_for_fianc_in_strangling_death_of_newark_woman.html.

94. "Police Searching for Killer of Newark Woman, Found Dead Along with Family Dog," Eyewitness News, August 7, 2105, http://abc7ny.com/news/police-searching-for-killer-of-newark-woman-found-dead-along-with-family-dog/911915/.

95. FBI, "New Top Ten Fugitive: Help Us Catch a Murderer."

96. FBI, "New Top Ten Fugitive: Help Us Catch a Murderer."
97. FBI, "New Top Ten Fugitive: Help Us Catch a Murderer."
98. Andrew Ford, "FBI Most Wanted: NJ Fugitive Hunted, Accused of Killing Fiancée and Dog," *Asbury* (NJ) *Park Press*, October 11, 2018.

AFTERWORD

1. *Fugitives: The Chronic Threat to Safety, Law, and Order: Hearing Before the Subcommittee on Criminal Justice Oversight of Sen. Judiciary Comm.*, 106th Cong. 33-34, June 22, 2000, (11) (statement of John W. Marshall).
2. *Fugitives: The Chronic Threat to Safety, Law, and Order*, (18) (statement of Edward T. Norris).
3. 146 Cong. Rec. S11652-11653 (statement of Sen. Leahy).

SELECTED
BIBLIOGRAPHY

Agnew, Jeremy. *Crime, Justice and Retribution in the American West, 1850–1900.* Jefferson, NC: McFarland & Company, 2017.

Armstrong, Joshua, with Anthony Bruno. *The Seekers: A Bounty Hunter's Story.* New York: Harper Collins, 2000.

Barnes, Merritt. "'Fountainhead of Corruption': Peter P. McDonough, Boss of San Francisco's Underworld," *California History*, 58, no. 2 (1979): 142–53.

Bergreen, Laurence. *Capone: The Man and the Era.* New York: Simon & Schuster, 1994.

Berkin, Carol. *A Brilliant Solution: Inventing the American Constitution.* New York: Harcourt, 2002.

Beverly, William. *On the Lam: Narratives of Flight in J. Edgar Hoover's America.* Jackson, MS: University Press of Mississippi, 2003.

Brown, Richard Maxwell. *No Duty to Retreat: Violence and Values in American History and Society.* Oxford: Oxford University Press, 1991.

———. "Western Violence: Structure, Value, Myth." *Western Historical Quarterly* 24, no. 1 (1993): 4–20.

Burns, Robert E. *I Am a Fugitive from a Georgia Chain Gang!* 1932. Reprint. Athens, GA: University of Georgia Press, 1997.

Burrough, Bryan. *Public Enemies: America's Greatest Crime Wave and the Birth of the FBI, 1933–34.* New York: The Penguin Press, 2004.

Burton, Bob. *Bail Enforcer: The Advanced Bounty Hunter.* Boulder, CO: Paladin Press, 1990.

Calhoun, Frederick. *The Lawmen: United States Marshals and Their Deputies, 1789–1989.* Washington, DC: Smithsonian Institution Press, 1989.

Carbone, June. "Seeing Through the Emperor's New Clothes: Rediscovery of Basic Principles in Administration of Bail," *Syracuse Law Review*, 34 (1983): 517–74.

Castleman, Harry, and Walter J. Podrazik. *Watching TV: Six Decades of American Television*. Syracuse, NY: Syracuse University Press, 2010.

Clark, Jerry, and Ed Palattella. *A History of Heists: Bank Robbery in America*. Lanham, MD: Rowman & Littlefield, 2015.

De Haas, Elsa. *Antiquities of Bail*. New York: AMS Press, 1966.

Dove, Donna, and Jeffrey M. Maynard. *FBI's Ten Most Wanted Fugitives Program: 50th Anniversary, 1950–2000*. Lisbon, MD: K & D Limited, 2000.

Eysenck, H. J. *Crime and Personality*. London: Routledge & Kegan Paul, 1977.

Fifer, Barbara, and Martin Kidston. *Wanted! Wanted Posters of the Old West*. Helena, MT: Farcountry Press, 2003.

Fish, Stanley. *The Fugitive in Flight*. Philadelphia: University of Pennsylvania Press, 2011.

Fortune, Jan I., ed., with Nell Barrow and Emma Parker. *Fugitives: The Story of Clyde Barrow and Bonnie Parker*. Dallas: The Ranger Press, 1934.

Gentry, Curt. *J. Edgar Hoover: The Man and The Secrets*. New York: W.W. Norton & Co., 1991.

Gerardin, G. Russell, and William J. Helmer, prepared with the assistance of Rick Mattix. *Dillinger: The Untold Story. Anniversary Edition*. Bloomington, IN: Indiana University Press, 2009.

Gard, Wayne. *Frontier Justice*. Norman, OK: University of Oklahoma Press, 1949.

Gorn, Elliot J. *Dillinger's Wild Ride*. Oxford: Oxford University Press, 2009.

Guinn, Jeff. *Go Down Together: The True, Untold Story of Bonnie and Clyde*. New York: Simon & Schuster, 2009.

Harris, Mark A. *Pictures at a Revolution: Five Movies and the Birth of the New Hollywood*. New York: Penguin Press, 2008.

Helmer, William J., with Rick Mattix. *Public Enemies: America's Criminal Past, 1919–1940*. New York: Checkmark Books/Facts on File, 1998.

James, Bill. *Popular Crime: Reflections on the Celebration of Violence*. New York: Scribner, 2011.

Kirchner, L. R. *Robbing Banks: An American History, 1831–1999*. Rockville Centre, NY: Sarpedon, 2000.

Lipsy, Seth. *The Citizen's Constitution: An Annotated Guide*. New York: Basic Books, 2009.

Lotze, Evie, John Clark, D. Alan Henry, and Jolanta Juszkiewicz. *The Pretrial Services Reference Book*. Washington, DC: Pretrial Services Resource Center, 1999.

Lukas, J. Anthony, "On the Lam in America," *New York Times Magazine*, December 13, 1970, 31, 54–56, 59, 62–64, 66–69, 72–74, 77.

Matera, Dary. *FBI's Ten Most Wanted*. New York: HarperTorch: 2003.

———. *John Dillinger*. New York: Carroll & Graf, 2004.

Miles, Thomas J. "An Empirical Analysis of the FBI's Ten Most Wanted." *Journal of Empirical Legal Studies*, 5, no. 2 (2008): 275–308.

———. "Estimating the Effect of *America's Most Wanted*: A Duration Analysis of Wanted Fugitives." *Journal of Law & Economics*, 48, no. 1 (2005): 281–306.

Monk, Linda R. *The Words We Live By: Your Annotated Guide to the Constitution*. New York: Hyperion, 2003.

Newcomb, Horace, ed. *The Encyclopedia of Television*, Second Edition. New York: Fitzroy Dearborn, 2004.

Newton, Michael, and Judy Ann Newton. *The FBI Most Wanted: An Encyclopedia*. New York: Garland Publishing, 1989.

Paulsen, Michael Stokes and Luke Paulsen. *The Constitution: An Introduction*. New York: Basic Books, 2015.

Powers, Richard Gid. *Secrecy and Power: The Life of J. Edgar Hoover*. New York: The Free Press, 1987.

———. *G-Men: Hoover's FBI in American Popular Culture*. Carbondale, IL: Southern Illinois University Press, 1983.

Rakove, Jack N. *Original Meanings: Politics and Ideas in the Making of the Constitution*. New York: Alfred A. Knopf, 1996.

Rosen, Fred. *The Historical Atlas of American Crime*. New York: Checkmark Books, 2005.

Sabljak, Mark, and Martin H. Greenberg. *Most Wanted: A History of the FBI's Ten Most Wanted List*. New York: Bonanza Books, 1990.

Schnacke, Timothy R., Michael R. Jones, and Claire M. B. Brooker. *The History of Bail and Pretrial Release*. Rockville, MD: Pretrial Justice Institute, 2010, https://cdpsdocs.state.co.us/ccjj/Committees/BailSub/Handouts/HistoryofBail-Pre-Trial Release-PJI_2010.pdf.

Settle, William A., Jr. "The James Boys and Missouri Politics." *Missouri Historical Review* 36, no. 4 (1942): 412–29.

———. *Jesse James Was His Name: Or, Fact and Fiction Concerning the Careers of the Notorious James Brothers of Missouri*. Columbia, MO: University of Missouri Press, 1966.

Stiles, T. J. *Jesse James: Last Rebel of the Civil War*. New York: Alfred A. Knopf, 2002.

Sutton, Willie, with Edward Linn. *Where the Money Was*. Reprint. 1976. New York: Broadway Books, 2004.

Swierczynski, Duane. *The Encyclopedia of the FBI's Ten Most Wanted List, 1950 to Present*. New York: Facts on File, 2004.

Toland, John. *The Dillinger Days*. New York: Random House, 1963.

Tracy, Leland. "Favorable Representations of the Fugitive in American Popular Culture: The Story of Bonnie and Clyde," in *Authority and Displacement in the English-Speaking World (Volume II: Exploring American Shores)*, Florence Labaune-Demeule, ed. Newcastle upon Tyne, UK: Cambridge Scholars Publishing, 2015.

Tully, Andrew. *The FBI's Most Famous Cases*. New York: William Morrow, 1965.

Turk, David S. *Forging the Star: The Official Modern History of the United States Marshals Service*. Denton, TX: University of North Texas Press, 2016.

Unterman, Katherine. *Uncle Sam's Policemen: The Pursuit of Fugitives across Borders.* Cambridge, MA: Harvard University Press, 2015.

Yeatmen, Ted P. *Frank and Jesse James: The Story behind the Legend.* New York: Fall River Press, 2000.

Ward, David, with Gene Kassebaum. *Alcatraz: The Gangster Years.* Berkeley, CA: University of California Press, 2009.

INDEX

ABOUT THE AUTHORS

Jerry Clark retired as a special agent with the Federal Bureau of Investigation in 2011 after twenty-seven years in law enforcement, including careers as a special agent with the Drug Enforcement Administration and the Naval Criminal Investigative Service. He received a PhD in public service leadership from Capella University, an MA in forensic psychology from the City University of New York John Jay College of Criminal Justice, and a BA in psychology from Edinboro University of Pennsylvania. Clark is an associate professor of criminal justice at Gannon University in Erie, Pennsylvania, where he owns Fisher Security.

Ed Palattella joined the *Erie Times-News*, in Erie, Pennsylvania, in 1990. He has won a number of awards, including those for his investigative work and coverage of crime. He arrived in Erie after reporting for the *Point Reyes Light* in Marin County, California. Palattella received an MA in journalism from Stanford University and a BA in English literature from Washington University in St. Louis.

Clark and Palattella are the coauthors of *Pizza Bomber: The Untold Story of America's Most Shocking Bank Robbery*, *A History of Heists: Bank Robbery in America*, and *Mania and Marjorie Diehl-Armstrong: Inside the Mind of a Female Serial Killer*. Clark was the lead FBI special agent on the investigation of the Pizza Bomber case, which was FBI Major Case 203.